Marjorie Bligh's HOME

Danielle Wood presents Marjorie Bligh with Housewife Superstar *at the launch of the book, Hobart, 2011.*

Danielle Wood lives in Hobart and teaches at the University of Tasmania. She is the author of *The Alphabet of Light and Dark* (2003; winner of the *Australian* / Vogel and Dobbie awards) and *Rosie Little's Cautionary Tales for Girls* (2006), and the co-editor of *Deep South: Stories from Tasmania* (2012). *Housewife Superstar*, Danielle's biography of Marjorie Bligh, was published by Text in 2011, and will be published in the Netherlands and the US.

EDITED BY
DANIELLE WOOD

TEXT PUBLISHING MELBOURNE AUSTRALIA

textpublishing.com.au

The Text Publishing Company
Swann House
22 William Street
Melbourne Victoria 3000
Australia

First published in 2012 by The Text Publishing Company

Jacket design by W. H. Chong
Page design and layout by W. H. Chong & Imogen Stubbs

National Library of Australia Cataloguing-in-Publication entry:
Author: Wood, Danielle, 1972-
Title: Marjorie Bligh's home : hints on managing everything /
edited by Danielle Wood.
ISBN: 9781922079077 (pbk.)
Subjects: Bligh, Marjorie. Home economics—Handbooks, manuals, etc.
Dewey Number: 640.41

This book is printed on paper certified against the Forest Stewardship Council® Standards. Griffin Press holds FSC chain-of-custody certification SGS-COC-005088. FSC promotes environmentally responsible, socially beneficial and economically viable management of the world's forests.

CONTENTS

FOREWORD

When Danielle Wood wrote my life story in *Housewife Superstar,* I was very pleased. It was superbly written and eagerly bought by people near and far. It only lightly covered my ninety-five years of living, because of course it would take several books to write down the numerous things I have done, especially in recycling, helping others, touring the world and not wasting a thing.

I was born in 1917 in the Midlands of Tasmania. When I was young and went to school I had to garden when I returned home, go for the cows that could be anywhere in the streets, also get the sticks ready to light the fire the next morning. Then, after tea, I knitted or crocheted by candlelight until bedtime. Sundays were spent at Sunday school, church, visiting or walking in the bush.

I left school at fourteen years of age and started work as a cook on a sheep station called Riccarton. It was there that I met my first husband, Cliff Blackwell, whose job was caring for the animals. I received a pound a week wages, and I saved it all and bought a two-storey home in the High Street of Campbell Town. I spent many evenings on that home, painting and papering, before Cliff and I married and moved in. I had two sons I named Gerald and Ross, who incidentally were both born on the twentieth of January, four years apart.

Cliff was very untidy and did not appreciate the lovely home I created. I craved mostly for happiness, freedom and peace of mind, but I always attained them by giving them to someone else. Cliff and I were divorced, and I married Adrian Cooper in the late 1960s, but Adrian and I had only a few years together before he died of a heart attack. He was an outstanding husband in every way. In 1976 I met and married a bus driver called Eric Bligh. He had a house, so sold it, and took me round the world with the money as he loved travelling.

Some of the important things that *Housewife Superstar* missed out are: I was Tasmanian Gardener of the Year in 2001 in the ABC Gardener of the Year competition, and received a golden shovel on a stand. I was on TV and radio as well. In 1989 I was presented with a plaque by the then governor of Tasmania for being the runner-up in the Tasmanian of the Year. I also carried the Olympic Torch in 2000.

HOME is packed with hints and recipes from my many books. I have written a hint book with five thousand hints in it with various sections, but although this book is smaller it contains many of my best ones. My favourite hint is: 'A place for everything and everything is in its place.'

I still do my gardening and cooking, and my favourite pastimes are scrapbooking and writing poetry and quotations, etc. I have made hundreds of scrapbooks and especially enjoy making them for children. I have been making them for over eighty years, so have made gallons of paste with flour and water.

Imagine what I could do if I could do all I can, or God lets me keep living in my own home until I am a hundred. I suppose all I have to do is to accept the impossible, do without the indispensable, bear the intolerable and to be able to smile at anything.

This book is brim-full of hints just like these, and I hope you will enjoy them all. It is like a scrapbook made up of bits of all the books I have written.

Before I go, here is a little poem that I wrote the other day, three days after my ninety-fifth birthday:

PLANS
What's the use of making plans,
As tomorrow is in the Maker's hands,
Better say maybe instead of I will,
Because, by tomorrow, you could be nil.
But that's how it is, the future is dark,
Guess Noah thought the same when inside the ark.
You plan a holiday, or an outing or two,
Then all of a sudden, a tragedy hits you.
But to look into the future I don't want to do,
I would much rather say I haven't a clue,
So enjoy every hour of this very day,
And while the sun shines, go make the hay.

Marjorie Bligh
Devonport, April 2012

" Home is such a cosy word, made up of letters four,
And oh, the satisfaction when your key turns in the door.
The chairs, the table, walls, hearth, these are your own to touch,
No matter if they're shabby, they mean so very much ;
Whether you've a stately home for which some people yearn,
Or whether it's a tiny place with not much room to turn,
Home's a blessed haven, it holds the very core
And the secret of your pleasure, when your key turns in the door.
We search for them as treasures now, and show them off with pride ;
Odds and ends of bygone days, which we once threw aside !"

HOME

It isn't the look of the garden
Nor is it the size of the house
We may be as rich as a monarch
Or as poor as a tiny churchmouse
Our roof may be humble with thatching
Or noble with turret and dome
But only the loving hearts in it
Can turn a house into a home.

* * *

'Home is the kingdom, love is the king'.

* * *

MY IDEA OF HOME

Home's just a corner of the world,
that's sent us to make sweet,
A place for smoothing out the way,
for tired hands and feet.
A little place for tenderness
as well as joy and song,
A little place to cheer and bless,
and help loved folk along.
A place for toil, a place for rest,
a little place for prayer,
A corner where we do our best,
and joys and sorrows share.
A place where everyone can play
his part however small,
But home that is not full of love
is hardly home at all.

* * *

~ *Home* ~

A roof to keep out the rain,
Four walls to keep out the wind,
Floors to keep out the cold –
Yes, but home is more than that:
It is the laugh of a baby,
The song of a mother,
The strength of a father,
Warmth of loving hearts,
Light from happy eyes,
Kindness, loyalty, companionship.
Home is first school,
And first church for young ones,
Where they learn what is right,
What is good and what is kind,
Where they go for comfort
When they are hurt or sick;
Where joy is shared
And sorrow eased.
Where mothers and fathers
Are respected and loved,
Where children are wanted,
Where the simplest food
Is good enough for kings
Because it is earned.
Where money is not so important
As loving – kindness;
Where even the tea kettle
Sing from happiness.
That is home –
God bless it!

Marjorie and Eric survey the scale model of the Batman Bridge, the central feature of the backyard in Madden Street, Devonport.

INTRODUCTION

It all began in 1959, in the northern Tasmanian Midlands. At the Campbell Town agricultural show the undisputed queen of the trestle tables, Mrs Marjorie Blackwell, got wind of whisperings that her amazing success in the domestic categories was the result of cheating. Her prize-winning vegetables, it was alleged, had been grown in another district, not in Marjorie's Campbell Town backyard.

Hurt by these scurrilous rumours, Marjorie determined to suspend her show career and instead plough her energies into writing a book that would share with the public the secrets of her success. *Marjorie Blackwell at Home* hit the bookstands, launching a publishing career that would span three decades and give rise to six wisdom-packed tomes of cooking, home hints, craft, gardening, history and autobiography. Some of the books appeared in multiple and substantially revised editions, and the signature 'at home' book was published under all three of her married names: Marjorie Blackwell, Marjorie Cooper and, most famously, Marjorie Bligh.

Marjorie's self-published books are never lightweight: her autobiography, *Life Is for Living: The Heartaches and Happiness of Marjorie Bligh: With Snippets of Travel, Wisdom and History*, weighs in at more than 250,000 words, and the fourth and final edition of *At Home with Marjorie Bligh* at more than 650 densely packed pages. Through these books, and also through her newspaper column 'Tried and True Hints', Marjorie Bligh has dispensed her forthright and ingenious advice to several generations of homemakers in Tasmania and abroad.

Within the range of her expertise are the arts of cooking, cleaning, gardening, animal husbandry, parenting, romance, beauty, health, poetry, history, knitting, sewing, embroidery, macramé, lace making, basketry, flower arranging, home decorating, parties, travelling and more. Perhaps Barry Humphries, the most famous of Marjorie's fans, goes close to encapsulating the breadth and depth of this living institution when he calls her a 'Renaissance woman'. Even Dame Edna Everage, that icon of domestic goddessery, has never admired anybody as much she admires the multitalented Marjorie Bligh.

—•—

Marjorie's training in being good at everything began early. Born in the rural Tasmania township of Ross in the midst of World War I, she was three years old when her father died, leaving her mother to raise three children on a small government pension. In this household thrift was a necessity.

The garden in which Marjorie and her sisters got their hands dirty, and the animals they laboured to feed and keep, did not supplement shop-bought groceries but provided the basis of every meal. On the kitchen table Marjorie's mother made bread, soap, candles and clothes—and Marjorie paid attention. To keep their hands occupied inside, and to keep themselves in socks and stockings, Marjorie and her sisters spent most evenings at the fireside with their knitting. Each year, each girl had one new dress for church and Sunday school, whereupon their old dress was demoted to daily use. Doctors and expensive remedies were only for cases of serious illness, so the family followed many traditional, home-grown methods for treating minor ailments.

When Marjorie entered the workforce, it was as a domestic in the homesteads of the large sheep-grazing properties of the Midlands. It was here that she refined her cooking and housekeeping skills, and also her understanding of how the other half lived. Soon she was fed up with taking orders: she began to crave the independence that she believed would come with marriage. Marjorie hitched her wagon to that of her first boyfriend, Cliff Blackwell, and got to work on the all-consuming project of setting up her own home in Campbell Town, a town not far from her birthplace.

She had few resources besides her own copious energy, but this she put to good use, taking in boarders and earning extra money by making their meals and doing their laundry. Soon Marjorie was the mother of two boys and facing a mountain of new demands, but she approached these in her usual, capable style. Instead of 'wasting' the time spent breastfeeding, she multitasked by knitting at the same time. Marjorie's boys rarely wore purchased clothes. She knitted all their jumpers, and sewed all their shirts, pants and pyjamas—even sewed their slippers out of rabbit skins.

After about a decade of marriage Marjorie began eyeing off the vacant block next door and sketching plans for a dream home. The result of her dreaming and doodling was Climar, its name a combination of the first three letters of Cliff and the first three letters of Marjorie. Still a landmark on Tasmania's busy north–south Midlands Highway, it was designed in the height of 1950s style and featured a wrought-iron fence studded with the musical notation for Marjorie's sentimental favourite, 'Melody of Love'. Marjorie supervised every last detail of the house, down to the display shelves in the living room (necessary for show trophies and cups), the huge built-in flour and sugar bins in the kitchen, and the silhouette (in black and yellow rubber) on the bathroom floor of the yacht Prince Charles owned as a lad.

—•—

The curving walls of Climar were every bit as beautiful as Marjorie had imagined they would be, but she also knew there was a life beyond them. The local agricultural show was one outlet for her creativity and zeal; the newly founded Campbell Town chapter of the Country Women's Association was another. With her keen curiosity and the view she had from Climar's kitchen window, Marjorie was well placed for a part-time role in the media.

The ABC, as well as each of Tasmania's newspapers, at one time employed Marjorie Bligh as their Midlands stringer. If she wasn't busy preserving apricots and making raspberry jam, mustering her cows or digging potatoes, she was writing up the latest controversy from the local school's Parents and Friends meeting, whooshing up a new dancing frock on her trusty Singer or speeding around the state as a volunteer for St John Ambulance.

The happiness in Marjorie's marriage to Cliff Blackwell was short-lived, but the couple endured their differences and difficulties for twenty-seven years, until 1965, when the partnership dissolved in a series of bizarre and improbable spats. By now Marjorie had another man in her life, the schoolteacher and married father of five Adrian Cooper. After a desperate bid to hold on to Climar through divorce proceedings, Marjorie finally conceded defeat. The home was sold and the profits divided.

Following a series of country school postings, the newly married Coopers relocated to the north-west Tasmanian town of Devonport and bought the Madden Street home where Marjorie still lives today. Marian (first three letters of Marjorie, last three letters of Adrian) was an unprepossessing brick bungalow until Marjorie put her stamp upon the place, transforming the garden into a jungle of food crops and flowering plants, building a scale replica of the Tamar River's Batman Bridge in the backyard, installing a portico in tri-coloured glass, and commissioning a weatherboard pop-top extension that would become a private museum for her handcrafts, scrapbooks, gowns, toby jugs, china, souvenir teaspoons, dolls, toys and memorabilia.

Marjorie and Adrian's marriage was a happy one, though all too brief. Adrian died of a heart attack in the early 1970s, and to alleviate her grief Marjorie again turned her attention to writing. *At Home with Marjorie Cooper* is a modernisation and revision of *Marjorie Blackwell At Home*: among the new inclusions are recipes favoured by her sweetheart (Adrian's Scones, Adrian's Pavlova), as well as an expanded and quite personal poetry section.

Following a rollercoaster romance with a fellow who was good on the dance floor but mercurial in nature, Marjorie met and swiftly married husband number three. Eric Bligh, a widowed bus driver, was perhaps not such a romantic hero as Adrian had been, but he was a solid companion for Marjorie, always willing to model her hand-knits and eager to show her the world. It was during the twenty-two years of her marriage to Eric that Marjorie was at her most productive, turning out two more editions of her 'at home' book, three editions of a book of handy home hints, two editions of a gardening book, an autobiography, a book of craft and a book of local history.

It was also during this time that Marjorie translated her customary thrift and resourcefulness into a passion for repurposing. Scandalised by the quantities of disposable items generated by an increasingly throwaway society, Marjorie embarked on a lone war on landfill, knitting and crocheting thousands of used pantyhose into hats, slippers, shopping bags, table runners, belts and toys; crocheting plastic bags into hats, rugs, bags and coverings for ice-cream tubs and other kinds of plastic containers; fashioning discarded men's ties into aprons and cushion covers; and transforming soft-drink bottles into decorative baskets and toilet-roll holders.

—•—

There is more to Marjorie, of course. Much more. There is her religious conviction, her dedicated Seventh-Day Adventist church-going and the project she set herself to copy by hand every word of the Bible. There is her unwavering opposition to the fluoridation of the water supply, and her commitment to trapping and using rainwater for drinking and for watering her plants. There are the awards and public acknowledgements: gongs in the fields of gardening, community service and active senior citizenry. There are her scrapbooks, hundreds of them, 191 of which are now housed in the Tasmanian Archive and Heritage Office, but the best of which are retained in the museum in Madden Street.

The archive office also holds her daily diary, a masterpiece of discipline and zeal. Though her earliest diaries have been lost, those

Marjorie, Eric and Life Is for Living.

that survive (together with her separate travel journals) account for her activities on every day since 1 January 1964. Her actions bear out her claim that there is nothing she despises more than idleness.

—•—

In *Housewife Superstar: The Very Best of Marjorie Bligh* (2011), I told the story of our heroine's long and eventful life (though not, perhaps, entirely to the great lady's satisfaction), and included a selection of her recipes, tips, homilies, poems and craft patterns. The sheer volume of Marjorie's published output made it a demanding task to select the 'very best' of her offerings, and fortunately we now have the pages of *Marjorie Bligh's HOME: Hints On Managing Everything* in which to discover more of the eclectic magnificence of the woman often described as Tasmania's Mrs Beeton.

In this volume you will find more than five hundred facsimile reproductions from the majority of Marjorie's original works, organised by theme and arranged in true Marjorie scrapbook style. Much of the content has been drawn from her first and I think most beautifully presented book. Held in only a handful of libraries, *Marjorie Blackwell at Home*, with its vintage fonts and layout, is a treasure: a collector's item that is only rarely on the market. Just a thousand copies of this book were printed, and to her regret Marjorie has only one.

In selecting the contents of this book I have attempted to cover the vast range of Marjorie's interests, as well as to give a sense of the historical span of her lifetime. Recipes from her earliest works feature such meats as rabbit, wattlebird and muttonbird, and there is a focus on economising with expensive items such as butter and eggs. In her later works she is frequently concerned with the useful redeployment of waste. In such ways, Marjorie's hints and recipes track the changes in ordinary Australian household consumption over the decades from her childhood to the present day.

I have also tried to capture moments from the spectrum of her work, containing as it does everything from the sensible (*Double Boiler: put marbles in bottom pot and you will know when water is getting low*), to the inventive (*Gown Protected: If you live in the country and walk to parties or dances, protect the bottom of your frock with a rubbish bag. Make 2 leg holes and pull on up to waist. It may look strange, but your frock will keep clean*), to the bizarre (*Car Bogged: If you are bogged and you are near a saw mill, sawdust will get your car out quickly*).

Reading across Marjorie's oeuvre, you cannot help but be impressed by her capacity for taking pains. She considers no small problem or inconvenience to be beneath her careful consideration (*A pinch of Epsom salts once a week stops fish from becoming constipated*; *Christmas Tree Strengthened: Spray with hairspray—if it is an artificial tree*). Not only is she interested in identifying solutions to minor aggravations—she is also keen to find ways to prevent them from developing in the first place (*Mirror Fogging: Mix equal parts of glycerine and methylated spirit together and rub on the tiniest smear, or rub mirror with a cake of dry soap and polish with a dry duster*).

I have not been alone in selecting the finest of Marjorie's offerings.

Over the course of her career Marjorie has collected an impressive retinue of fans, including Barry Humphries and Dame Edna Everage, the scenic designer Brian Thomson, and the author and humorist Kaz Cooke. Marjorie has always been a keen publicist for her books and has worked hard to ensure that people in high places have had access to her knowledge. She took a copy of *At Home with Marjorie Cooper* to Buckingham Palace, where she was able to personally present it to Queen Elizabeth's private secretary. Copies of her works have also been sent to Ronald and Nancy Reagan at the White House, and to successive Australian prime ministers, including Bob Hawke (who wrote a foreword to Marjorie's 1988 bicentennial book, *Tasmania and Beyond*) and Kevin Rudd. Many Tasmanian politicians, journalists and dignitaries have dined at Marjorie's table and been presented with her books.

Throughout *HOME*, some of her better-known admirers have generously shared their favourite Marjorie moments.

—•—

Now in her ninety-sixth year, Marjorie spends her days gardening, keeping up with her correspondence, and enjoying the resurgence of interest in the old-fashioned wisdom she has painstakingly accumulated and documented over the course of her life. She is delighted to see herself quoted and praised on a crop of blogs in which a new generation of young homemakers is teaching itself how to do more with less. What Marjorie has in common with today's frugalistas is a belief that thrift is not about stinginess, but about ethics, commonsense and even style. One of her tips recently recycled by an online 'eco-mama' was the idea of transforming old floral dresses into pillowslips for use in a little girl's bedroom. As with many of Marjorie's tips, the execution costs nothing but imagination and time.

As much as anything, Marjorie enjoys the challenge of being thrifty. To her it would be almost an admission of failure to head off to the pet shop to buy a dog bed (even for a pooch as spoiled as her late poodle, Freda Fi-Fi). Instead, Marjorie would set aside an evening to make a toasty blanket out of felted squares from old jumpers and socks. The money she saved by using butter as a make-up remover could be spent on new nylons, which—when they reached the end of their life—could be recycled into part of a tablecloth. And with the money she saved by making instead of buying a tablecloth she could buy some fruit trees, which would in turn—come harvest time—save her money in the grocery shop.

Less, for Marjorie Bligh, is never, ever more. Her garden can always do with more plants, her mantelpiece with more vases, her couches with more cushions, her walls with more photographs, her kitchen with more shelves, her address book with more friends.

I hope that you will enjoy this book, packed as it is with so many opportunities to savour more, and still more, of Marjorie Bligh's particular brand of genius. Get out those knitting needles, repurpose that milk container, paint that gourd. The challenge has been set, and it is up to us to meet it—thriftily, thoughtfully, wholeheartedly.

Danielle Wood
Hobart, August 2012

BOOKS BY MARJORIE BLIGH

Marjorie Blackwell at Home (1965)

At Home with Marjorie Cooper (second edition, 1973)

At Home with Marjorie Bligh (third edition, 1982; fourth edition, 1998)

Marjorie Bligh's Homely Hints on Everything (1981; second edition, 1988; third edition, 1993)

A–Z of Gardening (1982; second edition, 1990)

Life Is for Living: The Heartaches and Happiness of Marjorie Bligh: With Snippets of Travel, Wisdom and History (1986)

Tasmania and Beyond (1988)

Crafts: Old – New – Recycled (1995)

In Marjorie's kitchen, as in every room of her home, there is a place for everything and everything is in its place.

1. HOMELY COOKING

When Marjorie Bligh listens in to the present-day chatter about eating locally and cooking with in-season produce, she has a little chuckle to herself. She finds it hard to believe that anybody thinks it worth mentioning that it's sensible to make berry puddings in summer, or that it's prudent to preserve the excess apricots from your tree, or that it's wasteful not to eat the offal as well as the prime cuts. For her it's hardly revolutionary to know the producer, or even the name, of the lamb that has become your Sunday roast.

Bookshop shelves may be filling with new manuals on slow cooking and preserving, kitchen gardening and seasonal eating, but it's all old news to Marjorie. In her days as a young housewife, out of necessity she made enough blackberry jam in autumn to last the year. She learned to preserve eggs, so that she'd have some in store when her hens moulted and went off the lay. Wallaby, rabbit, muttonbird and even wattlebird were not rare and expensive delicacies—these meats were near enough to free if you felt like some trapping or shooting.

Over the editions of her cookbooks Marjorie's repertoire expanded and became more multicultural. Complete with a guide to pronunciation came a range of exotic new words, like *gateau (ga-toe)*, *goulash (goo-lash)*, *parfait (par-fay)*, *ragout (ra-goo)*, *ravioli (ra-vee-o-lee)* and *soufflé (soo-flay)*. But while Marjorie accommodated new foods in the pages of her books, she rarely left out any of the old English staples that formed the basis of her childhood diet. Her recipes cover the predictable categories of soups, cooked breakfasts, luncheons, meat-based dinners, cakes, biscuits and puddings—and Marjorie can be surprising in the kitchen too, such as when whipping up a lunch of lettuce fritters.

Marjorie knows as well as anybody who's responsible for putting the daily meals on the table that you can get bored with the same old recipes, week in, week out. And that is why the recipe sections of her books have always been packed with variety. *At Home with Marjorie Cooper* contains eight recipes for pavlova, and eight for chocolate cake. In the fourth and final edition of *At Home with Marjorie Bligh* she includes a staggering forty-six different scone recipes, including one for which she credits the television personality Ray Martin.

A journalist who often ate at Marjorie's 'laden table' observed: 'Her innumerable recipes are not a series of literary exercises, but the proven results of years of trial with very little error.' *Mai oui (may wee)*.

—•—

THE HONOURABLE MICHAEL HODGMAN, AM QC

'My pick of Marjorie Bligh's recipes would have to be her Anzacs. I love a good Anzac. Those, and butternut snaps, are my favourites.

The Honourable Michael Hodgman AM QC *honours his father's memory every Anzac Day.*

'You know, I only really drink beer—Cascade Blue [a lager] is the one I prefer—and the occasional wine. The exception is on Anzac Day. Then, in honour of my father, who was a naval officer in World War II, I have at least one rum and milk. Rum and milk, of course, is also known as Nelson's Blood: a fine naval drink.

'Marjorie Bligh and I have in common that we are proud and patriotic Tasmanians. We would, each of us, say: *God Save the Queen, and God bless Tasmania*.'

ANZACS

Melt ¼ lb. butter and 1 tablespoon golden syrup, add 2 tablespoons boiling water in which has been dissolved a teaspoon of bicarbonate of soda. Sift 1 cup flour with ¼ teaspoon salt, add 1 cup each of coconut, sugar and rolled oats. Mix into a stiff dough with the butter mixture, add a few drops of vanilla. Put into small lumps on a greased tray. Prick and cook in a slow to moderate oven until pale brown. Leave on tray for a minute before lifting off on to a cooler.

—M.B.

MARGARET FULTON, FIRST LADY OF AUSTRALIAN FOOD

'Sometimes the simplest things are the best, and often it is those things that we remember fondly from childhood that we continue to enjoy throughout our lives. I have always loved a good old-fashioned pudding, like a chocolate self-saucing pudding, or a bread and butter pudding—I like a drop of whisky in mine!

For a crowd-pleaser you can't go past a pudding, says beloved Australian foodie Margaret Fulton.

'Making a pudding is so rewarding because it is usually something the whole family enjoys, and something the children look forward to after eating food—like their vegetables—of which they are not so fond. This caramel pudding of Marjorie's, I think, would go down well with any family.'

CARAMEL PUDDING

This is a delightful sponge pudding that is prepared in a jiffy and takes only 30 minutes to cook.

1 ½ cups self raising flour, pinch salt, 1 heaped teaspoon butter, 2 tablespoons boiling water and ½ cup milk.

For the Sauce: 1 cup water, 1 tablespoon butter, 1 tablespoon golden syrup, 3 tablespoons sugar.

Method: Sift flour and salt into a greased basin in which pudding is to steam. Melt the butter in the boiling water, add the milk, and stir into flour into a light dough. Place the sauce ingredients in a saucepan and bring to the boil on the stove. Pour over the dough, but do not stir or mix it in any way. Place lid on steamer and steam for 30 minutes. A delicious sauce forms under the pudding which can be served from the basin.

—M.B.

Breakfast Dishes

POTATO PUFFS

Take 1 cup cold mashed potato and 1 cup S.R. flour. Mix well with 1 egg and a little milk if necessary. Take a desserspoon of minced cold meat moistened with sauce, put it in the centre of rounds of potato pastry, fold over, and pinch edges together. Fry in boiling fat until nicely browned on both sides. Serve very hot.

COIN-SPOT SAUSAGE CAKES

2 fried sausages, 1 cup S.R. flour, ¼ teaspoon salt, 1 egg, ¾ cup milk, 1 teaspoon melted butter, 1 teaspoon grated onion.

Sift flour and salt in a basin. Drop in the egg and mix in the centre of flour. Gradually pour in the milk and mix to a smooth batter. Add melted butter and grated onion. Grease a heavy frying pan. Place 3 or 4 slices of the cooked sausages in groups on pan, cover each group with spoonfuls of the batter mixture and cook slowly until top is bubbly. Turn with a knife and brown on other side. Serve cakes in pairs with grilled bacon between.

KIDNEYS ON TOAST

Chop finely 2 sheep kidneys, add pepper and salt and mix with 1 tablespoon tomato sauce. Melt 1 tablespoon butter in a pan, add kidney mixture and cook gently 20 minutes, stirring occasionally. Stir in 2 well beaten eggs and cook slowly till mixture thickens. Serve hot on buttered toast.

LAMBS FRY

Lambs fry will be hard if you dust it with flour before you fry it in hot fat, so just cut in slices and cook, or dip in egg, then in breadcrumbs, and fry golden brown on both sides.

TASTY WAY TO COOK BACON

Cut the slices fairly thin, soak them in milk, then roll them in S.R. flour that has been seasoned with salt and pepper. Fry in boiling fat and serve with fried eggs.

FLUFFED EGGS

Stiffly beat 4 egg whites with salt and pepper. Pile on to buttered toast. Drop yolks into each hollowed centre. Draw the egg-white over the top. Sprinkle with grated cheese if liked and bake in a moderate oven until egg is set.

* * *

There is no spectacle on earth more appealing, than that of a beautiful woman, in the act of cooking dinner for someone she loves.

* * *

Hints on Cooking

CUP MEASUREMENTS

1 cup flour	4 ounces
1 cup sugar (castor or crystal)	8 ounces
1 cup brown sugar (packed)	6 ounces
1 cup sifted icing sugar	5 ounces
1 cup butter, lard or margarine	8 ounces.
1 cup cornflour	5 ounces
1 cup breadcrumbs	4 ounces
1 cup sultanas or raisins	6 ounces
1 cup currants	5 ounces
1 cup grated cheese	4 ounces

SPOON MEASUREMENTS

2 level tablespoonss flour	1 ounce
1½ level tablespoons sugar	1 ounce
2 level tablespoons cornflour	1 ounce
1 rounded tablespoon butter	2 ounces
1 tablespoon breadcrumbs	½ ounce
2 heaped dessertspoons gelatine	1 ounce
2 level tablespoons cocoa or custard	1 ounce
2 level tablespoons sifted icing sugar	1 ounce
1 tablespoon golden syrup	1½ ounces
1½ tablespoons of rice, barley or split peas	1 ounce
2 level tablespoons sago	1 ounce
2 level tablespoons grated cheese	1 ounce
⅓ cup honey	1 ounce

LIQUID MEASURE

1 pint	20 ounces
4 gills	1 pint
6 tablespoons liquid	1 gill or ¼ pint
2½ cups liquid	1 pint
2 cups liquid	16 ounces

ROASTING TIMES FOR MEAT AND POULTRY

Lamb and Beef—Thick joints : 30 minutes per lb.
Thin joints : 20 minutes per lb.

Pork and Veal : 40 minutes per lb.

Chicken : 30 - 35 minutes per lb.

Duck : 20 - 30 minutes per lb.

Turkey : 20 - 25 minutes per lb. for 8 to 10 lb. bird.
18 - 20 minutes per lb. for 10 to 16 lb. bird.

Tongue (medium-large) : from 4 to 6 hours.

COOKING HINTS IN ALPHABETICAL ORDER

Almonds—will peel more easly if you put them in cold water five minutes after they have been immersed in boiling water.

Apples—as you peel apples, keep them in water to prevent turning brown. Lemon juice in the water keeps them pearly white. Cook in very little water, if they are needed for cakes, etc.

Butter—To make it go further, put into a small saucepan, 2 heaped tablespoons of full cream powdered milk. Add 1 teaspoon powdered gelatine and ½ teaspoon salt. Mix in gradually ½ cup milk, and stir over fire until hot, but not boiling. Cool a little and cut into this ½ lb. of butter. Stir and blend with a wooden spoon and put into a basin. Twice as much butter and more nourishing.

If you haven't any scales, an easy way to cut a ½ lb. of butter if required, is to cut through the pound diagonally and you will be sure of an accurate measure. Another easy way for measuring ½ cup of butter (or ¼ lb.) without scales is to fill a cup half full of water and drop butter in until the cup is full or reaches the top. Drain butter before using.

"Wonder butter" for use at kitchen teas, balls, etc., in sandwiches can be made by putting 1 lb. cut up, soft butter in a bowl and add a teaspoon of salt and gradually add 1 cup hot water and one cup cold water alternately until all used. Beat well with beater when all is absorbed. Goes twice as far.

If uncovered butter has absorbed other food flavours in the refrigerator, cut it into small pieces, cover with fresh milk and leave for an hour. Strain off milk and the butter should be sweet again.

Buy a butter curler and fill up your butter dishes with curls. Takes only a few minutes, but will save up to ¼ lb. of butter a week, as it is easier to spread and saves putting it on bread in big blobs when childrn are around.

Biscuits—when you require pieces of chocolate for your biscuits, do not waste time, chipping pieces off with a knife ; put through a mincer (the coarsest disc).

Bread—Keep the bread tin sweet by using blotting paper. Replace once a week.

A sliced fresh apple or new potato placed in the bread box keeps the bread beautifully fresh.

Broad Beans—Put a bunch of parsley in with broad beans when cooking them, and they will not turn black and the flavour will also be improved.

Cauliflower—Add a good pinch of sugar when cooking to keep white.

Custard—Skin won't form on custard made from custard powder, if you place a damp cloth over it.

Sprinkle 2 tablespoons of coconut on top for a delicious crust and nicely flavoured dessert.

Cakes—Cakes won't stick to the tin if, after greasing, it is dusted with cornflour and castor sugar in equal quantities. It will also have a lovely sugary crust. Some times I use just the cornflour or plain flour, without the sugar. New cake tins should be smeared with lard inside and baked in oven for a while, then washed in usual way when cold. This prevents cakes sticking to the tin as is often the case with new cake tins. If your oven has a tendency to burn the bottom of your cakes, place the cake tin into a size larger which has a layer of salt in the bottom. Salt can be used on the plate of your stove also when cooking jams and pickles, etc., that burn easily. The salt can be used repeatedly afterwards. Foil is also good to line the cake tins with.

When filling cakes for fairs or stalls, add a teaspoon of gelatine to the cream and stand one hour after beating, before adding to cakes. (Mix gelatine in about 1 tablespoon of warm water first and stir until it is dissolved over hot water). It will remain firm and not run down the sides of your sponges when handled or squeezed.

To ice up cakes in half the time and easier, hold cake over frosting upside down and dip into it. Twirl, then turn quickly, right side up, so icing will make a fancy peak. Warm the sugar instead of the butter when making a cake in the winter. The cake turns out better than if you oiled the butter.

A sponge will be lighter if you take out 1 tablespoon of flour and replace it with custard powder

When making a fruit cake, toss the fruit into cornflour. Shake off before adding to the cake—prevents fruit sinking to the bottom. Use a salt shaker to sprinkle toppings such as hundreds and thousands onto iced cakes. Saves waste.

Make a fancy pattern on your iced cake. When the plastic icing is almost set, place a paper doyley on top and press gently down. Lift off carefully.

Cream—To increase cream, whip to the consistency of boiled custard, add a teaspoon of cold water, continue to whip and add more teaspoons of water until the cream has absorbed all it can take without thinning.

Another hint to increase cream for parties, etc., is to dissolve ½ teaspoon gelatine in 2 tablespoons hot water. Whip ¼ pint cream, then add the dissolved gelatine gradually. To make even more, add the stiffly beaten white of an egg. This cream is also lovely for desserts.

Cheese—Keep indefinitely by wrapping it in a cloth soaked in vinegar.

Curry—Too hot? Well, add some tomato sauce, a teaspoon of sugar and juice of ½ a lemon.

Dates—When cutting up dates for a cake, loaf or scones, cut them quickly by tossing them in some of the flour you have measured out for that recipe. The dates won't stick then to the scissors or knife.

Ducks—Add a teaspoon of carb soda to the boiling water when plucking ducks. The feathers will come off more easily after they have soaked for a little while, then plunged into a bucket of cold water, and pluck. (Washing powders act the same). Use for fowls too.

Dried Peas or Beans—should have a pinch of carb. soda boiled with them.

Eggs—Save eggs, also sugar, by using 1 tablespoon golden syrup in 1 cup of warm milk when making a custard. This is equally as good, only not as nutritious. The same amount equalls three eggs if used for a cake.

Cut yolks of eggs into slices with a wet knife then they won't crumble.

Add a dessertspoonful of vinegar to the water if you want a perfectly poached egg.

Evaporated Milk—added to mashed potatoes makes them creamy and saves butter.

Essences—Use an eye dropper to measure essences and colourings for cakes and icings, then you'll be sure of the right amount going into the cake, etc.

Electric Stove—Plates should be kept in good order by greasing them once a week, with suet or salad oil, when they are just warm.

Fish—Add a dessertspoon of vinegar to fat as soon as it begins to boil. This prevents any fat being absorbed into the fish. Add crust of bread to fat to prevent fat splashing.

Scale fish with a spoon instead of a knife and the scales won't fly. To save on egg and breadcrumbs in the winter, cover with flour, dip in milk, then flour again, and fry. Another idea is to mix custard powder to smooth paste with milk, coat fish, then with breadcrumbs, and fry.

Gravy—Make gravy with cornflour instead of flour, if you want a richer, smoother, gravy. Add 2 lumps of sugar to the joint when cooking and your gravy will be nice and brown.

Golden Syrup—To measure easily, dip spoon into boiling water and use quickly. The syrup will fall off spoon without sticking. Another idea is to dip spoon or measuring cup into cold water, then into flour, before pouring in the golden syrup. It should roll off just as easily as above. (1 level tablespoon equalls 1 oz.). Good for treacle, honey, glucose, as well.

Jam Covers—To airtight jam covers and make the jam keep longer, seal with white of egg (not whipped). One white will go a long way.

Lunches—Keep fresh by wrapping them in foil (overnight if busy). Put them in fridge. Wrap anything in foil for safe keeping in fridge—from cakes to vegetables.

Lamb's Fry—will not be tough and flavour will be improved if, after preparing you soak it in a small quantity of milk for 10 minutes before cooking.

Meringues—add ⅛ of a teaspoon of cream of tartar to each egg white for a perfect meringue. Always place on a sheet of foil and they will never stick.

Mustard—for the table will stay moist for weeks if you mix it with vinegar instead of water and add a pinch of salt.

Mint—Preserve mint for winter use by chopping some mint finely, then putting in layers alternately with castor or granulated sugar, starting and ending with sugar. Cover with greaseproof paper before putting in screw top. Spoon it out when needed. Another idea is to add golden syrup to the chopped up mint and put in screw top jar. When it is needed, add vinegar to a small amount of the mixture.

When making fresh mint sauce in the summer, sprinkle leaves with the sugar you will be using, and you'll find the chopping chore much easier and quicker. Cover with equal amounts of vinegar and boiling water to keep the mint green.

Onions—To eat onions raw, make them odourless by standing them in cold water for ½ hour after being peeled. Throw away water, then repeat.

A pinch of sugar added to onions while being fried helps to make them more digestable.

Small onions for pickling will peel more easily if soaked in boiling water for a few minutes. The skin lifts off and there are no tears, either ! Put straight into milk to keep them white, but dry thoroughly on a towel before putting into jars. Fried onions can be cooked in half the time if you put them in the wire basket and lower them into smoking hot fat for a few minutes.

Omelettes—will stay high if you add a teaspoon of cornflour to the eggs just before cooking. Cook first on top of stove then put under griller to cook the top.

Pumpkin—If you have a piece of pumpkin that you do not wish to use for a few days, remove all seeds and soft parts. Then rub some carb. soda well into the cut edges. It will keep until needed. Another idea to keep pumpkin is to cut it into suitable pieces for cooking, removing first the skin and seeds, then pour boiling water over each piece and turn the pieces and repeat. Drain well. The mould on pumpkin is caused by bacteria.

Poultry—if too fat, prick skin all over and the fat will melt out as it cooks.

Pork—will be lovely and crisp if you rub it all over with butter, then rub flour into it thoroughly. Put it in a dry dish at 500 deg. for 10 minutes, then cook at moderate heat for remainder of the time. Don't turn the meat at any time.

Puddings—are better steamed in a billy. The lid fits better and does not let the steam in.

Potatoes—mashed, will be lighter and more easily digested if a teaspoon of baking powder, as well as the butter or milk is added. They will be beautifully light. Add it to the potatoes when making potato pie also. Another welcome change is to add a little raw, finely chopped onion or parsley to the mashed potato.

2 tablespoons of powdered milk added to the potatoes before being mashed makes them white and creamy.

Potato Chips—will be first class if you cut them the size of cigarettes, then put them in a wire basket and lower them into smoking hot peanut oil. Cook two minutes. Lift out basket. Heat oil again. Cook chips another two minutes, then drain on brown paper. (Chef's secret).

Rissoles—If you are short of eggs in the winter and are frying rissoles or cutlets or fish, omit the egg and add 1 dessertspoon vinegar or lemon juice to the rest of the dry ingredients. It is lovely and crisp when cooked. If you are using egg, add ¼ teaspoon of baking powder. It makes the egg thick and foamy and holds more crumbs.

Rolling pin—if it keeps sticking to the dough, lay a piece of plastic or greaseproof paper on dough and try again.

Rhubarb—When cooking rhubarb, save sugar and take away tartness by adding 2 tablespoons of jelly crystals and add less sugar. A couple of tablespoons of sago cooked also with the rhubarb is another way of thickening and making it more appetising.

Steak—or other meat will be tender and delicious if you soak it in vinegar for an hour before cooking. If you have meat on the turn, also use same method before cooking. No one will know the difference.

Salt Shakers—Mix rice with the salt and it will always operate satisfactorily.

Keep salt and pepper mixed together in one large shaker to save time for seasoning.

Soggy Toast—Don't throw it away, cut into squares, brown under the griller till crisp and use as croutons for soup.

Sour Milk—needed for cooking. Add 1 tablespoon of vinegar to 1 cup of milk and warm.

Saucepans—won't burn when you are boiling milk if, firstly, you put some sugar in before pouring in the milk.

Tarts—when making a custard tart use plain flour and baking powder instead of S.R. powder flour. Use warm milk with the eggs and sugar, instead of cold. Custard won't go through pastry in cooking.

Vanilla Slices—when making custard for vanilla slices or trifle, add a jelly crystal as well. It sets firm. Lemon crystals preferred.

Vegetables—Soak a cauliflower in vinegar and water to rid it of grubs.

Add a pinch of bi-carbonate of soda to the water in which you boil your beetroot. It will then keep its colour.

Add a little sugar to old potatoes when boiling. It improves both texture and flavour.

Add a piece of butter to greens when boiling them.

A little vinegar or lemon juice added to the water in which cabbages are cooked will improve the flavour and colour. It also lessens the odour which arises during cooking. It's better to add salt after vegetables are cooked, as ordinary salt neutralises the valuable mineral salts in vegetables.

Freshen wilted vegetables by soaking them for an hour in cold water to which the juice of a lemon has been added.

Most vegetable stains can be removed from the hands by rubbing with a slice of raw potato.

Egg Hints

Hard boiled eggs should not reach boiling point. Cook 15-20 minutes below boiling point, then you'll have firm, delicate, textured eggs. Add a tablespoon of salt to every 6 cups of water. Soak in cold water 1 minute before peeling.

Another method is to first age your egg by leaving it out of the refrigerator for 24 hours where it can breathe. Pierce large end with a thumb tack. This allows more carbon dioxide to seep out. Put egg into a pan of cold water, and bring it slowly to the boil. Turn off heat, leave egg in water with lid on for 15 minutes. Crack shell. Plunge egg into cold water for 20 seconds, then start peeling from the large end, holding it under running water as you peel it and the results will be an aesthetically glorious egg. It will be hard boiled, yolk centred right, perfect for savouries. If you want to keep them awhile, put in closed container in refrigerator and they will keep their fresh yellow and white colouring.

Before slicing hard-boiled eggs, dip the knife in boiling water, then wipe dry (repeat with each slice). Stops crumbling.

Poached eggs will be perfect if you put a spoonful of vinegar into the water. The whites will cling completely to the yolks. Lemon juice acts the same. If you have a large quantity to poach, smear patty pans with oil, drop in eggs, and lower into a baking dish of boiling water. If you only have one to poach, and haven't an appropriate pan, cook it in a scone cutter, or break into a greased soup ladle and carefully lower into water.

To make scrambled eggs go farther, add some cooked rice and a tablespoon or two of evaporated milk, or 1 teaspoon of semolina and a cup of milk and chopped parsely. They will be more stable if you add a little cornflour to the milk.

"Lord give me grace to catch a fish so big that even I
When talking of it afterwards may never need to lie."

Fish Hints

Insides will be cleaned more easily if you rub salt into them, using a toothbrush along the backbone.

Dip in boiling water for a minute, then scale with a spoon, not a knife, and scales won't fly.

Fish that are frozen with scales on are hard to de-scale, so do it with a meat tenderizer mallet (the rough side).

If you have to steam a fish, put in between two plates over a saucepan of boiling water. (When boiling, add lemon juice.)

As soon as the fat comes to the boil when frying, add a dessertspoon of vinegar. This prevents fat being absorbed into fish. A crust of bread prevents splashing ; and cover with foil when cooking, which helps also. Add small quantities at a time to the fat (or oil) when cooking fish, as a large bulk reduces temperature too much.

Add a little salt to the pan before cooking so that the fish will not stick.

Instead of mixing the batter with water, use one part vinegar to three parts water and add ½ teaspoon of bicarbonate of soda, then the fish browns more quickly and won't be greasy.

Rub fish with a cut lemon, then dip in cornflour sifted with a dash of nutmeg.

Add a little sherry or brandy to the egg, before you dip your fish in it, then put into ground rice before frying.

If you are short of eggs, add a tablespoon of salad oil with each egg when preparing egg and breadcrumbs for coating fish. This holds the crumbs well, has no perceptible flavour, and is economical.

Dip filleted fish in flour which has had ginger or curry powder added to it, then fry in margarine. Serve with white sauce flavoured with ginger.

Use plenty of oil when cooking, and don't turn until well cooked on the one side.

Wrap fish in plastic wrap before putting in refrigerator, but do not wash it first, or, sprinkle with salt and wrap in foil and put in the refrigerator.

After cleaning your fish, pour cold tea over hands and the fishy smell will disappear.

"The biggest part of a fish is usually the tale!"

Luncheon Dishes

PORK CHOPS

To give pork chops an extra flavour, simmer in pineapple juice in a hot oven for about 20 minutes. Lamb chops are also tasty cooked this way. They will also be more tender.

TOMATO AND SAUSAGES

4 large tomatoes, 4 ozs. sausage meat, pinch dried herbs, 1 teaspoon grated onion, scrambled egg, plain flour, chopped parsley.

Cut each tomato in half. Mix the herbs, sausage meat and onion together. Shape into four flat cakes the size of tomatoes. Coat with flour and fry in a little hot fat until brown on both sides. Place a cake between the two halves of each tomato. Put into a greased ovenware dish and bake in a moderate oven until the tomatoes are cooked, but still firm. Serve each tomato surrounded by hot scrambled egg. Sprinkle with chopped parsley.

LUNCHEON MOULD

(To use up cold meat)

Combine 1½ cups diced cooked meat, ½ cup chopped cooked ham, ½ cup diced celery, 1 tablespoon chopped shallots and 1 cup cold parsnip, pepper and salt.

Dissolve 1½ tablespoons gelatine in ½ cup hot water, add 1½ cups tomato juice and place a thin layer in wetted mould. Mix remainder of gelatine mixture with meat mixture and carefully fill mould. Chill until firm. Unmould on bed of lettuce. Garnish with parsley and hard boiled eggs.

POTATO PANCAKES

Grate 3 large potatoes and 1 small onion, add 2 eggs, and ½ cup sifted flour with salt and pepper added.

Fry tablespoons in boiling fat. Brown on both sides. Serves family of four.

MOCK CHICKEN ROLL

½ cup milk, 2 cups white breadcrumbs, 2 tablespoons finely minced rabbit, 2 tablespoons finely minced bacon, 1 cup grated carrot, 1 tablespoon finely minced onion, 1 egg, browned breadcrumbs, a few mixed herbs, pepper and salt to taste.

Warm milk, pour over white crumbs, stand for ½ an hour. Fold in the meat, carrot, onion, salt and pepper, and beaten egg. Mix well. Turn mixture into a floured cloth, roll up and tie securely. Place in pan of boiling water and simmer 1½ hours.

CURRY PUFFS

¾ cup S.R. flour, ½ teaspoon each salt and curry powder, 1 egg, ½ cup water, 1 cup minced cooked meat, 1 teaspoon each chopped onion and parsley.

Sauce: 1½ teaspoons flour, ½ teaspoon each curry powder, sugar, lemon juice and chutney, pinch salt, 1 cup water.

Sift together flour, salt and curry powder. Mix in the egg yolk, water, and then the egg white beaten stiffly. Add the meat, onion and parsley. Drop by the teaspoonfuls into deep hot oil or fat and cook 3 to 5 minutes. Serve hot with the sauce.

Sauce: Blend together flour, curry powder, sugar, lemon juice, chutney and salt. Add the water, stir over low heat until boiling and cooks 3 minutes.

SAVOURY POTATO BALLS

Four boiled potatoes, 1 chopped medium onion, 1 dessertspoon chopped mint, pepper, 3 tablespoons mayonnaise, extra chopped mint.

Mash potatoes, add onion, mint, pepper and mayonnaise and mix thoroughly until smooth. Mould into small balls and sprinkle with extra mint. Serve chilled with fish or meat.

PIQUANT CASSEROLE

1½ lbs. of topside steak (minced), 1 large carrot, 1 potato, 1 onion, 1 stick celery, pinch grated lemon rind, 1 tablespoon sweet fruit chutney, 1½ cups of stock or water, 1 teaspoon salt, pepper, 1 skinned chopped tomato, 1 teaspoon Worcestershire sauce, 1 cup shelled peas.

Put meat in saucepan with diced carrot, finely chopped, peeled potato, chopped onion and celery, lemon rind, chutney, and stock or water. Cook slowly until meat changes colour. Season with salt and pepper, add chopped tomato and Worcestershire sauce. Turn all into an ovenware dish, cover, and cook 30 to 40 minutes in moderate oven. Add peas and continue until peas and meat are tender.

LETTUCE FRITTERS

These are delicious and are excellent for that Saturday night tea, or any, for that matter. Makes a nice meal for a family of four.

1 heart of a lettuce, 1 onion, 1 egg, fat, S.R. flour, pepper and salt.

Shred lettuce finely, add grated onion, beaten egg, salt and pepper to taste. Mix well. Add enough S.R. flour to make a good stiff batter. Drop by tablespoon into hot fat and cook on both sides until well browned. Serve at once.

LAMB AND BROAD BEAN CASSEROLE

Cut 2 lbs. of breast of lamb into 1 inch cubes, roll lightly in seasoned flour. Fry in hot bacon fat, until brown. Turn into a casserole, add 1 cup of boiling water, 1 teaspoon salt and ¾ teaspoon pepper. Cover and simmer about 1½ hours. Add 2 cups tinned or fresh tomatoes, and 2 cups fresh broad beans. Return to oven and cook for 35 minutes. Serve on toast with potato balls.

Potato Balls :

Sift 4 ozs. S.R. flour with ½ teaspoon salt. Rub in 1 oz. butter, then 4 ozs. cooked mashed potatoes and some chopped parsley. Mix in 1 gill milk and turn on to a floured board. Knead into flattish balls and fry in hot fat for ½ hour, turning often. Drain on kitchen paper.

BACON PUDDING WITH MUSTARD SAUCE

3 slices bacon, 1 onion, 2 cups S.R. flour, 1 tablespoon sage, pepper and salt, 3 tablespoons shredded suet, water to mix.

Mustard sauce : 1 tablespoon cornflour, 2 teaspoons sugar, 1 tablespoon vinegar, ½ teaspoon mustard, pinch salt, 1 cup milk.

Chop bacon and onion, add S.R. flour, sage, pepper and salt and suet. Mix with water to a good consistency. Place in a greased pudding basin and steam 3 hours. Serve with the sauce.

Mustard Sauce : Mix all ingredients to a smooth paste with the milk. Cook, stirring constantly until boiling point is reached.

CHEESE AND BACON LOAF WITH MUSHROOM SAUCE

1 lb. hamburger steak, ½ cup grated cheese, 1 small onion, finely chopped, salt, 2 bacon rashers.
Mushroom Sauce: 1 tablespoon flour, 1 tablespoon butter, ½ cup milk, small can mushrooms.

MUSHROOMS

½ lb. S.R. flour, ¼ lb. butter, ¼ lb. sugar, 1 medium egg, ½ teaspoon essence.

Rub butter into flour, add sugar, then beat in egg and essence. (If butter is very soft, use a small egg). Roll out very thin, cut into rounds and bake in greased patty tins for 10 to 15 minutes in a hot oven. Roll some stems to use for the mushroom stalks and cook. When cold, put a teaspoon raspberry jam in each, then a tablespoon of cream and sprinkle over cream some grated chocolate or cocoa. Push in stems.

PICCALILLI

Any vegetable such as small onions, shallots, little green tomatoes, butter beans, cauliflower, marrow and cucumber, etc.

To every quart of vinegar allow 1 oz. mustard, 1 oz. tumeric powder, 2 ozs. castor sugar, 1 teaspoon mixed whole spices and 1 teaspoon cornflour. Peel onions and shallots, string beans, stalk tomatoes, remove leaves from the cauliflower and wash well. Peel marrow and remove seeds. Peel the cucumber. Cut all vegetables into small pieces and put them into a bowl. Sprinkle with salt (about a dessertspoon to a quart of vegetables) and leave for 24 hours. Mix the tumeric with the vinegar. Put them in a preserving pan. Add the sugar, mustard, then the spices tied in a muslin bag. Put in the vegetables and boil all gently for 10 minutes. Mix the cornflour with a little vinegar to make a thin paste. Let the veges cool a little. Take out the spices, stir in the cornflour and boil for 4 minutes, stirring all the time. Turn into dry warm bottles and seal securely when cold.

"A third of what we eat keeps us alive — the other two-thirds keeps the doctor alive."

Potato Hints

New potatoes will cook in much less time and be nice and floury if a teaspoon of vinegar is added to the water when putting them on to boil. They are easier to scrape if soaked in salt water first.

If potatoes are old, add sugar to water to improve texture and flavour. Put a few drops of lemon juice in water and they will boil white.

If you haven't much time to cook your potatoes, grate them, add a tablespoon of milk, a teaspoon of butter and stir until cooked. Beat well and serve.

If you are going to be busy, peel more than you want and put in a bowl of cold water containing vinegar or milk and place in refrigerator for further use.

When they are scarce, add cooked rice, chopped mint, parsely or onion, to the mashed potato to "stretch" it.

Instead of putting butter into potatoes before you mash them, add some mayonnaise for a different flavour ; or,

Add a dash of curry powder, left over dip, or grated cheese.

Add some powdered milk, too, with a teaspoon of baking powder. Beat well and eat immediately.

If you want nice crusty baked potatoes, boil them for 5 minutes first, then coat them with seasoned flour and bake as usual.

If you like potatoes baked in their jackets, scrub them, dry thoroughly, prick with a fork (or push a skewer right through them ; that ensures them cooking quicker), brush with oil and bake on foil for 1½ hours in a hot oven. Cut a cross on top, squeeze open and top with butter, or with cream cheese mixed with chopped chives. Do *not* wrap in foil or they will be steamed, not baked.

If potatoes are watery when cooked, add some bought potato flakes, or some powdered milk, and whip gently.

The secret of well-browned and crisp roast potatoes — old or new — is to wipe them dry after peeling, then sprinkle with salt, or flour, then place in hot fat beside the roast.

To make a potato salad easily, dice the potato before you cook it. Place in a fry basket and cook in water until soft. Drain, add butter, parsley, and seasonings.

A left-over baked potato can be re-baked if you dip it in water and bake it at 350° for 20 minutes.

A potato topping for a shepherd's pie can be enhanced by the addition of ½ cup grated cheese, 1 teaspoon chopped mint and parsley, and a dash of cayenne pepper.

Add a few pinches of cream of tartar to mashed potatoes to make them soft, white and fluffy.

After you dish up mashed potatoes on the plates, try squeezing a little lemon juice over them.

For heating up cold cooked potatoes, cut potatoes into slices, tip into a frypan that has melted butter or oil in it, add some chives and a clove of garlic and turn with an egg slice until brown, or, dip slices of potato into seasoned flour and fry in hot oil. Serve with bacon.

Potato Salad Dressing

Mix 1 can condensed milk with 1 cup white vinegar, 2 tablespoons chopped mint and 2 teaspoons dry mustard. Pour over peeled, cubed, steamed potatoes and add if liked, 1 cup of peas, tin drained corn, sliced radishes and 3 hard boiled chopped eggs.

MOCK CHICKEN POTATO PIE

1 large or 2 small rabbits, salt, ½ lb. bacon rashers, 1 chopped onion, 1 cup diced cooked potato, 1 cup diced cooked carrot, 2 tablespoons chopped parsley, 1 clove garlic, 1 tablespoon crushed almonds, salt, pepper, 1 packet creme of chicken soup, water, 4 hard boiled eggs, sliced in halves, potato pastry, green peas, pumpkin.

Cook rabbits until tender with bacon. Cut meat into cubes, cut up bacon. Mix together in deep pie dish, the rabbit, bacon, onion, potato, carrot, chopped parsley, crushed garlic, and almonds. Add salt and pepper. Prepare the soup, using only 3 cups of water, and add. Arrange hard boiled eggs on top of mixture. Make potato crust thus : mix 2 cups cold mashed potatoes with 1 cup flour, sifted with ½ teaspoon baking powder, ½ teaspoon salt ¼ teaspoon cayenne pepper. Add sufficient milk to make a dough. Roll out, dot with dessertspoonful butter, fold in 3, roll again. Repeat 3 times, using about 2 ozs. butter in all. Put the crust on the pie and cook in moderate oven one hour. Serve hot with green peas and pumpkin.

Oyster (mock)

Cooked mashed brains, seasoned with salt and pepper and a little lemon juice. Mix into a rich, thick, white sauce and you'll have a mock filling for oyster patties.

Ways with Rhubarb

RHUBARB AMBER with MACAROON TOPPING

Children love and prefer this to plain stewed rhubarb.

1 quart of rhubarb cut into 1 inch lengths, stewed with 4 ozs. sugar and very little water. Add 4 ozs. cake crumbs and the yolks of 2 eggs. Grease a pie dish, put in the mixture and bake 20 minutes in a moderate oven. Whisk the 2 egg whites stiffly, add 2 ozs. sugar. Beat again, then add 2 tablespoons coconut, and spread roughly over the pudding. Cook in a very slow oven for an hour and serve.

RHUBARB CRISP

4 cups diced rhubarb, ¼ cup sugar, ¼ cup flour, ⅓ cup butter, ⅓ cup sugar.

Mix rhubarb and ¼ cup sugar and place in a greased pie dish. Mix flour, sugar (⅓ cup) and rub in the ⅓ cup of butter until like crumbs. Sprinkle topping over fruit and bake 35 minutes in moderate oven. Serve hot.

RHUBARB JELLY

Make a pint of lemon jelly. Stew 1 pint of cut up rhubarb with 2 ozs. sugar and very little water until soft. Stir into the jelly and pour into a wetted mould. Serve with cream when set. The jelly seems to lessen the sourness of the rhubarb.

MOULDED RHUBARB CREAM

1½ cups milk, 1½ tablespons cornflour, 1 tablespoon sugar, ½ teaspoon grated lemon rind, 2 eggs, 2 cups cooked rhubarb (drained of syrup) pinch salt.

Cooking in Foil

Not only does cooking in foil save power, but it keeps all the juices and steam in the meat, etc. It will even make the toughest meat tender, but do not use it for pork. If you want to cook crumbed cutlets, grease the foil first then wrap around the chop, cutting a ½ inch air vent in the foil to allow steam to escape and keep the chop crisp. Remember too, that when cooking with foil, allow more time to cook, as foil cooking takes longer. If you want your roast or poultry to have a crusty finish on the outside, remove foil ½ an hour before serving. Always put the shiny side towards the food. It is the reflected heat from this which helps tenderise the meat. Do not use fat, just place foil wrapped meat in the dry baking dish. Veal needs brushing over with butter first, as that has no natural fat, or wrap a piece of bacon around it first. Poultry needs the bacon too, as does the veal, before wrapping in the foil. Don't forget that fish is delicious cooked in foil too. Cook 20 to 30 minutes as you do the meat. Baked potatoes can be baked in same dish if you put the fat around the foil covered joint and allow it to get very hot before putting in the potatoes, but I advise cooking them in a separate dish. As for saving fuel, 3 or 4 vegetables can be cooked in the one pot by wrapping each in foil and putting in a saucepan with 2 or 3 inches of water in it. Bags for the vegetables are made quite easily, by cutting a piece about 17 x 7 inches for, say, to hold enough for two. Fold the piece in half lengthwise then fold the sides together, thus forming a bag. Place in vegetables, sprinkle with salted water, then screw the top together. To save power again when you are cooking cutlets, place them in foil in a scone tray in the top part of your oven, vegetables in middle or bottom and the pudding bottom or middle. All will cook in the one cooking time. Foil is not expensive as it can be used over and over again. Wash carefully in warm water and dry carefully with a towel. If you have to keep your husband's tea hot (like I have to for hours on end), place a piece larger than the plate over the dinner on the plate and press foil under, before placing in the oven. Keeps tea from drying out. For barbecues, wrap foods in foil and cook on coals without fear of burning. Grease foil before wrapping to prevent food sticking. Meringues will not stick if you cook them on foil.

Meat Dishes

HINTS ...

The quickest way to make patties or even sized rissoles is to roll the meat, etc., into a long sausage and then slice it into cakes. Very little extra shaping is needed.

A nice preserve to eat with cold lamb is made as follows: Dissolve a packet of lemon jelly crystals in hot vinegar instead of water. Stir in 2 tablespoons of freshly chopped mint. Blend well and fill into small jars for use when required.

The rind of roast pork will always be crisp and brown if coated with the following mixture before cooking: A tablespoon of vinegar, ¼ cup brown sugar and a pinch of ground cloves, blended well together.

When making rissoles add 1 teaspoon of baking powder to 1 lb. of minced steak. The baking powder makes them rise and keeps them light.

WATTLE BIRDS

Brush each bird over with warmed butter after plucking them. (Do not clean birds in any other way; their insides are left intact). Tie a thin slice of fat bacon over each breast. Put in a fry pan (electric) on a wire grid and cook slowly for 5 or 6 hours. Take off wire grid after 3 to 4 hours, and cook in the fat that has dripped off them. Baste often. Serve on buttered toast.

* * *

Those that make the best use of their time have none to spare

DELICIOUS PIGEON PIE

2 or 3 pigeons, ½ lb. rump steak, 3 eggs, 1 oz. butter, seasoning, pastry, parsley and breadcrumbs.

Fill pigeons with stuffing made of the breadcrumbs, parsley, pepper and salt.

Place half the steak in a pie dish, place the birds on the steak, then the remainder of the steak and pour around it one cup of water. Place another pie dish on top and simmer for one hour. After that time, remove pie dish, arrange the 3 hard boiled eggs cut in quarters around the pigeons, cover with pastry and cook another hour. Serve hot with green peas and mashed potatoes. To make potatoes fluffy when mashing, add a dessertspoon of butter and ½ teaspoon baking powder and whip thoroughly, but serve immediately.

MUTTON BIRD DISH

6 mutton birds, 6 ozs. breadcrumbs, 2 medium onions, 1 small apple, little parsley, pepper and salt.

Soak birds in washing soda for ½ hour, wash well, cover with cold water, boil 20 minutes. Strain, cover with cold water again, boil 15 minutes, then strain. Prepare seasoning, place one sixth into each bird, double over, and press together. Tie around with string in a couple of places and place on a wire grid-iron, or cake cooler in a meat dish and place in moderate oven about ½ hour. The fat will drip into the dish and the birds will be lovely and brown. Turn over during the cooking process. Serve hot or cold.

BRAIN PIE

Soak 3 or 4 sets of brains in salted water for 1 hour. Drain and skin. Put in pot and bring to the boil, then drain and chop lightly. Butter a pie dish, cover bottom thickly with bread crumbs. Add a layer of brains, pepper, salt and herbs. Repeat till filled, finishing with crumbs. Beat 2 eggs with 1 cup of milk. Pour over contents of dish and dot with butter. Bake 20 minutes in a hot oven.

What a wonderful world this would be if all other folks were just like you, and what a calamity if they were all like your neighbours.

* * *

MINT JELLY

2 cupsful mint leaves, 1 pint water, ½oz. gelatine, 6ozs. sugar.

Choose young mint; remove leaves from stalks and wash. Put leaves into a jug and pour the boiling water over them. Cover closely and leave until cold, stirring occasionally. Strain the water into a saucepan, bring to boil and stir in gelatine, which has been softened by soaking in cold water. Add sugar, and bring to boil, boiling 2 minutes. Turn into small heated jars, and cover as for jam. Store in a dry place. Serve in cubes with lamb, or put on top of prepared grapefruit halves for a cocktail.

RADISH FLOWERS

Split radishes (after scraping lightly) into 4, to nearly the bottom. Drop into cold water until they curl. These make pretty decoration for salads.

FRENCH FRIED ONIONS

Peel 4 large onions, wash and dry, then cut into ¼-inch slices. Separate these into rings. Dip into milk, and then into S.R. flour seasoned with salt and pepper and paprika. About ½ cup milk and ½ cup S.R. flour is needed for 4 onions. Fry in boiling-fuming fat or oil until golden brown then drain on paper and serve.

CORN FRITTERS

Sift a small cup of flour with 1 level teaspoonsful baking powder, 1 level teaspoonful salt, and pepper to taste. Add 1 cup of cold minced meat and 1 cup of sweet corn. Mix together with 1 beaten egg and a little milk if necessary. Drop tablespoonful in boiling oil or fat and cook both sides until golden brown.

GLAZED CARROTS

Boil young carrots until tender but not soft. Brush whole with melted butter, roll in brown sugar and place on greased oven slide, cook in moderate oven until sugar has melted. Serve hot with grilled meat.

POTATO PANCAKES

Mash 2 cups of potatoes with 1 egg and a little milk. Add enough S.R. flour to make mixture dry enough to form into shapes. Cut into circles and fry in boiling fat.

CHINESE CABBAGE

Shred desired quantity of cabbage, one medium onion, sliced finely, a little celery if available, 1 pkt. chicken noodle soup, rice (1 cup), water.

Mix vegetables, soup and water. Bring to boil. Add the rice and boil until cooked (not over cooked) about 20 to 25 minutes. Serve with meat and mashed potatoes.

TOMATO, ONION AND APPLE MEDLEY

4 large tomatoes, 2 cooking apples, 2 onions, salt and pepper to taste, ½ cup dry breadcrumbs, and dessertspoon butter.

Butter sides of pie dish. Fill with alternate layers of thinly sliced tomato, apple and onion, seasoning each layer in turn. Cover with the crumbs, dot with the butter and bake 1 hour in a slow oven. Tomato Pie is made same way, only leave out the apple.

PARSNIP BALLS

Mash hot cooked parsnip with butter, milk or cream, pepper and salt and a beaten egg. Let cool. Shape into balls, dip in beaten egg (or milk) and then toss in breadcrumbs. Fry in deep boiling fat until golden brown.

Relish

TOMATO RELISH

(Prize Recipe)

Scald 4 lbs. ripe, firm tomatoes, peel and cut up roughly. Skin and slice finely 3 large onions. Put both in preserving pan with $1\frac{1}{4}$ pints of vinegar and 1 lb. sugar, 2 tablespoons salt, 1 dessertspoon of both mustard and curry powder. Boil for half an hour. Blend 1 heaped tablespoon flour with $\frac{1}{4}$ pint of vinegar, well (no lumps) and stir into relish. Simmer 3 or 4 minutes. Bottle and seal when cold.

TOMATO RELISH

1 lb. ripe tomatoes, 1 lb. onions, $\frac{1}{2}$ dessertspoon salt, 1 cup sugar, 1 cup vinegar, 1 dessertspoon mustard, 1 dessertspoon curry powder.

Slice tomatoes and onions finely. Place in large saucepan and add all other ingredients. Boil with lid off for 20-30 minutes. Thicken with 1 teaspoon cornflour blended with 1 tablespoon vinegar. Cool and bottle. Seal when cold.

Chutneys and Pickles

HINTS—

- When making chutneys, all ingredients should be minced or chopped finely.
- It is always better to overcook the fruit and vegetables before sugar is added, rather than undercook them. The flavours will then blend better and the result will be more mellow.
- Long, slow cooking is best for chutney.
- Store in small jars if possible, so that it can be used quickly once the jar is opened.
- Make jars completely airtight, so the vinegar will not evaporate and the chutney go dry.
- Plastic or polythene is a good covering, or corks covered with greasproof paper.
- Do not use metal tops (they go rusty) ; or paper with paste, as it is porous.
- Chutneys are best kept a couple of months before use.
- Always use an enamel pan for cooking.

CAULIFLOWER PICKLES

2 cauliflowers, 2 ozs. mustard, $\frac{3}{4}$ cup sugar, 3 pints vinegar, 2 lbs. onions, 2 large tablespoons flour, 1 teaspoon tumeric, 2 handsful salt.

Break cauliflower into small pieces. Cut up onions and cover with salt. Let stand overnight. Next day bring to boil, and boil gently until tender. Strain off brine. Place vinegar and sugar in a saucepan on stove, and when boiling add mustard, flour, and tumeric mixed to a smooth paste. Boil for 2 minutes, stirring all the time. Then add cauliflower, and make very hot. Bottle. Seal when cold.

ONION SAVOURY

4 large onions, 2 tablespoons cold minced meat or bacon, 2 tablespoons breadcrumbs, 1oz. grated cheese, pepper and salt.

Boil onions until cooked. Remove centres and mix with meat, crumbs and seasoning. Stuff onions. Sprinkle with cheese. Fry in deep boiling fat.

JELLIED BEETROOT

3 teaspoons gelatine, 3 tablespoons hot water, cold water, 3 - 4 medium-sized beetroots, 6 cloves, pinch of spice, 1 tablespoon sugar, ¼ cup lemon juice, salt and pepper.

Peel raw beetroots thinly ; cut into slices. Place in saucepan with water to cover (just cover). Add cloves, and pinch of spice. Cook until tender. Leave to cool. Remove beetroot and strain liquor ; add to it the sugar, lemon juice and make up to ½ pint with cold water. Dissolve gelatine in hot water and add to liquor. Arrange beetroot slices in mould and carefully add the mixture when thickening.

ONION ROLLS

Peel and mince 3 onions. Fry in butter until pale brown and cooked. Add 2 cups breadcrumbs, salt, cayenne and herbs if liked. Bind with beaten egg and form into small rolls. Cut rind from bacon, wrap each roll in a slice and secure with a tooth pick. Place on greased slide in hot oven and cook until bacon is clear. Serve hot with gravy.

PARSNIP FRITTERS

1 cup seasoned mashed cooked parsnip. Add yolk of 1 egg, then the stiffly beaten white. Drop spoonfuls into boiling oil or fat and cook until golden brown. Serve with parsley on hot dish.

P.S.—1 cup soft breadcrumbs can also be added.

BEETROOT RELISH MOULD

Boil beetroot and slice thinly. Mix 2 tablespoons of gelatine with ½ cup boiling water ; when dissolved add 2 cups vinegar and pour over red beet. Wet a mould line with sliced boiled egg, pour in the beetroot and stand aside to set. (Makes a little beetroot go a long way).

ORANGE, APPLE AND ONION SALAD

2 red skinned apples, 2 white onions, 2 oranges, shredded uncooked cabbage, mayonnaise, celery curls, lemon juice.

Wash and dry apples and oranges, peel onions. Cut into slices, using stainless knife. Remove cores from apple slices, drench with lemon juice to prevent discoloration. Arrange alternate overlapping slices of apple, onion, and orange on serving platter. Toss shredded cabbage lightly with mayonnaise heap in centre of platter. Garnish with celery curls. Serve with any sliced cold meat, but particularly good with poultry.

WINTER SALAD

2 tablespoons condensed milk, ½ teaspoon sugar, pinch salt, pinch cayenne, ½ teaspoonful made mustard, 3 dessertspoons vinegar, ½ gill cream or milk, 2 eating apples, 1 head celery, curled celery, chopped nuts.

Place condensed milk in a basin with sugar, salt and mustard and cayenne. Add vinegar gradually, stirring well. Then add cream slowly, and mix well. Peel apples, wash and dry celery, cut all into dice, mix together and pour salad dressing over. Serve in a salad bowl, garnished with curled celery and chopped nuts.

He who takes, but does not give may last for years, but does not live.

* * *

POTATO SALAD

2 lbs. new potatoes, 1 tablespoon butter, 1 tablespoon vinegar, 1 tablespoon chopped parsley, 1 small finely chopped onion.

Boil potatoes until tender. Peel, and cut into ¼-inch slices. Melt the butter into the vinegar. Pour this over the potatoe slices in a billy or saucepan with a tight fitting lid. Add the parsley and the onion. Shake the billy until the ingredients coat the potato slices well, but be sure that potato is still hot when you are doing it.

NEW WAY TO COOK BEETROOT . . .

Cooked in this way, the beetroot does not go mouldy, but keeps for ages in the fridge.

Peel the amount of beetroot you need and then cut into slices. Put into the saucepan with 2 parts vinegar to 1 part water, add salt and pepper to taste and some sugar. Cook until tender, and turn into serving dish. You will find it has not lost any of its flavour or colour, and is delicious.

BETTY'S WAY OF COOKING CABBAGE

Shred heart of a cabbage, like you would for a lettuce salad. Put a little vegetable oil or dripping into a saucepan and melt, then add salt to taste. Put in the cabbage and stir well. Add a little water and steam until cabbage is tender. Add a tablespoon of sugar 5 to 10 minutes before serving, stirring well. Do not drain. About ½ cup water is sufficient for a small cabbage.

CABBAGE CUNNING

Wash and shred cabbage, chop 2 white onions finely, 2 tomatoes coarsley and put all in a saucepan. Season to taste. Add a tablespoon of butter and a little stock and simmer for half an hour.

BUTTERED CARROTS

Boil young carrots until tender in a little water. Add 1 teaspoonful sugar, salt and pepper to taste and a little chopped parsley. Beat up an egg and add. Stir until the mixture coats the spoon (about a minute). Can be served on toast.

*"If you could sell your experience for what it cost,
you wouldn't need the age pension."*

Onion Tips

Render them odourless by standing in cold water with 1 teaspoon sugar added, for 5 minutes ; pour off water and repeat, or chill in refrigerator. The odour leaves them in the frige and doesn't taint the other food, but leave skins on. Keep some always there for use.

To peel small onions the easy way, place them in a mixing basin, cover with boiling water, and let stand for 5 minutes to loosen skins. Drain, and run cold water over them. Trim tops, bottoms and skins will slip off ; or,

Slice thinly and cover with boiling water. Cover and stand an hour. Drain. (Lessens the bite.)

When you are cutting slices from onions, after cutting onion in half, lay cut side down on board to slice it.

Slice onions *before* peeling. It is easier to slip peeling off each slice.

Before frying onions dip the slices into evaporated milk, then into flour, with a teaspoon of sugar, to get crisp onions.

Before baking onions, insert tooth picks into them and this prevent the centres protruding ; or, don't cut off root. This is easily removed after cooking.

For pickling, put straight into milk to keep white after peeling. After a few hours, dry and pack into jars. Put on brine.

For savoury cases, simmer small white onions in tomato puree, dash of sugar and a few sultanas, until soft, Fill into tiny cases and serve hot.

Add a little honey to the butter in which you saute onions for an out-of-the-ordinary dish. Add onions when mixture begins to sizzle.

Soak onion rings in beetroot juice for an hour or so before decorating a salad.

Remove smell of onions from hands by rubbing with dry mustard, salt, or milk.

KANGAROO MEAT LOAF

2 lb. kangaroo meat, 1lb. stewing steak, ¼ lb. bacon, ¼ lb. suet, 2 medium onions, 1 large apple, 1 large potato, salt, pepper, seasonings, ½ cup plain flour, 1 egg.

Mince kangaroo and steak together, then mince again with bacon, suet, onions, apple and potato. Add salt, pepper and seasonings. Mix in flour and egg to bind. Place in a greased basin and steam for 2 hours. Serve hot with vegetables or cold with salad.

Gravy Hints

Put 2 teaspoons sugar and one of vinegar in the baking tin with the joint, or a bit of instant coffee for a rich brown gravy. Make with cornflour for a smoother gravy. Keep a clove of garlic in a jar with cornflour or flour and use it for making your gravy. For beef, add some red wine and crushed garlic.

Or, you might like to try ½ cup of orange juice instead of water, especially if you are having mutton.

To make gravy for a special treat, add some canned mushrooms; or, finely chop an onion. Fry in margarine with a sprinkling of flour until brown. Add a glass of port wine, 1 tablespoon of soy sauce and a dash of Worcestershire sauce, then thicken with flour and water. You can add a dash of curry too, if you like.

IN THE SOUP

I guessed my pepper, my soup was too hot ;
I guessed my water, it dried in the pot ;
I guessed my salt, and what do you think –
For the rest of the day we did nothing but drink.
I guessed my sugar, my sauce was too sweet,
And then by guessing, I spoilt my treat.
But now I guess nothing,
For cooking by guesses
Will ruin all skill, and produce nothing but messes.

SOUP WITH A TASTY RABBIT DISH TO FOLLOW

Joint a young rabbit and simmer 1 hour in slightly salted water. (2 hours for an old rabbit). Make a stiff pancake mixture and dip boiled pieces of rabbit in it. Have some fat boiling and fry the coated pieces until brown. Remove ; drain on kitchen paper and serve hot. Tastes like chicken. Grate a few vegetables and add to the stock with a tablespoon of pearl barley and macaroni and cook until done. This is a nourishing meal served with vegetables and the soup is cooked by the time the rabbit is fried.

COOKING TERMS

a la King — Food served in rich cream sauce sometimes flavoured with sherry.

Appetizer — Small portion of food or beverage served before or as the first course of a meal.

Aspic — A jelly made from meat stock that has been boiled down sufficiently to become firm when cold ; also stock (fish, vegetable, fruit, or tomato juice) which has been thickened with gelatine.

Au Gratin (or-grar-tan) — Food creamed or moistened with other ingredients (eggs, milk or stock) covered with bread crumbs and butter or cheese and baked or grilled until the top is brown.

Bard — To tie thin slices of fat bacon over a bird's breast. This method is usually employed before roasting a dry bird.

Baste — To moisten roasting meat or other food while baking with juices from the pan or with additional liquid.

Batter — A blended mixture of flour, liquid and other ingredients.

Bisque (Bisk) — A thick cream soup usually made from fish ; also a rich frozen dessert.

Bechamel (Beshamel) — A rich white foundation sauce.

Blanch — To cover first with boiling water and then with cold, often for the purpose of removing skin (almonds) or to whiten.

Blanquette (Blahnket) — A white fricassee or stew, made with white meat (veal, chicken, rabbit) and white sauce.

Borsch (Bortsch) — Russian soup with beets.

Bouillon (Boo-yawn) — Clear soup made from lean beef.

Bouquet Garni (Booka-gar-ny) — Herbs (usually parsley, thyme and bay leaves) tied together and used for flavouring.

Braise — To cook meat by searing, then simmering in a covered dish in a small amount of liquid, either in an oven or over direct heat.

Broil — To cook by exposing food directly to the heat.

Cafe au Lait (Kafay-o-lay) — Coffee with hot milk.

Canape (can-a-pay) — An appetizer made of a small piece of bread spread with well-seasoned food.

Capon (Ca-pon) — A de-sexed male chicken, usually large, with tender meat.

Caramel — Burnt sugar syrup used for colouring and flavouring ; also a candy.

Chantilly (shahnte-yi) — A dish containing whipped or plain cream.

Charlotte (sharlotte) — A sweet made in a mould lined with cake, bread or biscuits and filled with cream or fruit mixture.

Condiments — Food seasonings such as salt, pepper, vinegar, herbs and spices ; relishes are frequently called condiments.

Consomme (consom-ma) — A highly seasoned clear soup made from one or a combination of meats and vegetables.

Coq Au Vin (cock-ovan) — Pieces of chicken cooked in rich wine sauce.

Coq Au Vin (cock-ovan) — Pieces of chicken cooked in rich wine sauce.
Croquettes (craw-kets) — A mixture of chopped or ground cooked food, cereals, cheese, meat, etc., bound together by eggs or a thick sauce, shaped, then dipped into egg and crumbs, and fried.
Croutes (Kroots) — Fancy pieces of fried bread used as a base for savouries.
Croutons (Kroo-tawns) — Small pieces of fried bread used as a base for mouthful savouries. Served also with soup (usually diced) or for garnishing.
Cube — To cut into squares.
Cutlet — A small piece of meat cut from the leg or rib, a piece of boned fish or a croquette mixture made into the shape of a cutlet.
Demitasse (de-metasse) — Small cup of after-dinner coffee.
Devilled — Highly-seasoned food.
Dice — Cut into small cubes.
Dredge — To coat with flour or sugar.
Entree (on-tray) — The main dish of an informal meal or a sub-ordinate dish served between main courses.
Fillet — Cuts of boneless or boned meat or fish.
Flake — To break up into small pieces with a utensil.
Frappe (fra-pay) — Sweetened fruit juice frozen until of a mushy consistency.
Fricassee — A stew or to stew meats, poultry, etc., in stock or sauce.
Garnish — To decorate one food with another, usually something bright or savoury.
Gateau (ga-toe) — A cake usually round and flat and richly decorated.
Glaze — To coat with a thin sugar syrup that has been cooked to the crack stage or with thin aspic or diluted fruit jelly.
Goulash (goo-lash) — A Hungarian thick meat stew.
Hollandaise — A sauce made of eggs and butter served hot or cold, with vegetables or fish.
Hominy — A food made from ground maize.
Hors D'Oeuvres (or-derve) — Piquant or crisp foods served as appetizers, such as canapes, fish, olives, celery, sausages, etc.
Julienne — Food cut into narrow lengthwise strips.
Kirsch (kersh) — A cherry cordial.
Macedoine (mac-id-wahn) — A mixture of various fruits or vegetables, cut in small pieces. Salad of various fruits set in jelly.
Marinade — An oil and acid mixture, such as French dressing, in which food is allowed to stand to gain flavour or tenderness.
Marinate — To soak in French dressing, vinegar, lemon juice, sour cream, etc.
Masque — To cover completely with a sauce, jelly, or mayonnaise.
Mignons — Small pieces of fillet of beef served as an entree.

Mocha — A flavouring made with coffee infusion to which chocolate may be added.
Mousse — A mixture of sweetened whipped cream and other ingredients frozen without stirring or combinations of cream, fruit, meat, vegetables, etc., thickened with gelatine.
Mulligatawny — A soup flavoured with curry.
Pare — To cut off the peel of potatoes, apples, etc.
Parfait (par-fay) — A frozen dessert consisting of beaten egg whites or yolks cooked with hot syrup and combined with whipped cream, or a mixture of ice cream, fruit and whipped cream.
Pasteurize — To kill bacteria by using a high degree of heat.
Pate de Foie Gras (Pat-ay de fwah grah) — Goose liver paste.
Piquant (Pee-kant) — Sharply flavoured ; applied generally to a sauce.
Pot Liquor — Water in which vegetables are cooked.
Puree (pure-ay) — To press fruit or vegetables through a sieve ; also a soup made with food put through a sieve and thinned with cream or stock.
Ragout (Ra-goo) — Being French ; a de luxe concoction, but literally a thick, well seasoned stew.
Ramekins — Individual baking dishes.
Render — To free fat from connective tissue by heating slowly until fat melts and can be drained off.
Roe — Eggs of fish.
Saute (so-tay) — To toss foods lightly in a little shortening in a frying pan.
Scallop — To bake food in an oven-proof dish in layers with sauce and crumbs.
Score — To make light cuts in a surface, usually in lines.
Sear — To brown the surface of meat by the quick application of intense heat, usually in a hot pan or in a hot oven.
Shortening — Any kind of fat suitable for baking.
Simmer — To cook in liquid that is kept just below the boiling point.
Sliver — To cut or shred into lengths.
Souffle (soo-flay) — A light baked dish made with a basis of eggs and cream sauce.
Souse — Method of pickling fish in vinegar and spice before serving.
Steep — To cover with boiling liquid and permit to stand.
Sterilize — To kill bacteria by a high degree of heat.
Stock — The liquid resulting from cooking meat, fish or vegetables.
Tammy cloth — A thick cloth for straining soups and sauces.
Timbale (tanbah-l) — A baked mixture made with a white sauce base to which meat, fish or vegetables may be added.
Timbale Case — A fried batter used as a shell for creamed food.
Truss — To tie a fowl or other meat so that it will hold its shape.
Vol-au-vent (vol-o-vahn) — A large case or puff paste in which creamed game or white meat, or fish, etc., is served.

"The greater the difficulty the greater the glory"

Jam, Marmalades and Jellies

HINTS ON JAM

- The flavour of jam will be greatly improved if, about 10 minutes before it is cooked, 2 level teaspoons salt are added to every 4 lbs. fruit.
- Do not add sugar to jam whilst it is boiling or it will go sugary. Pull it off onto side of the stove and stir in the sugar (heated for preference) until it dissolves ; or, add very gradually so that it dissolves quickly.
- Raspberry jam must be light and bright, so boil quickly and **only** for a few minutes.
- When a Show schedule states three varieties of jam, remember that the judges prefer three distinct colours, .g., peach, greengage and cherry.
- A competitor gains more points for jams that are harder to make.
- Fruit should be a little underipe for jam-making. Some fruits are rich in pectin such as black and red currants, gooseberries, raspberries, quinces, lemons and cooking apples.
- Fruit and vegetables which are poor in pectin content include strawberries, blackberries, pears, nectarines, cherries, rhubarb, and marrows.
- To test for pectin content, simmer the fruit with the water until it is soft, then put 1 teaspoon of the juice into a cup. Add 3 teaspoons of methylated spirits, shake gently and leave for a minute. If a firm clot forms, the pectin content will be good ; if the test shows that the fruit is too low in pectin, add other fruit which are rich in pectin, or a home made extract as follows . . .

    Use sour cooking apples (like Sturmer) or crab apples, or even parts of windfalls will do. Wash and cut up 3 lbs. (do not peel or core). Cover with 1½ pints of water and stew gently for ½ hour, until well pulped. Strain through a jelly bag, replace pulp in pan, add more water to make a mash then repeat the stewing and straining. Mix the extracts and sterilise to keep it, if not for use immediately.

- Use lemon juice (or ½ teaspoon of citric or tartaric acid equals juice of 1 lemon) if extra acid is needed with fruits such as blackberries, cherries and marrow.
- Pectin extract can be made from gooseberries, red currants, etc., using the same method as for apple extract. With these two, use slightly less water.
- Fruit off the japonica bush will set your low-in-pectin fruit jam. Cut up three very finely and add to jam.
- Berry fruits should not be gathered wet — wait at least 36 hours after rain has fallen. Jam will ferment if fruit it wet.
- If there is no way to avoid using wet fruit, boil longer before adding sugar, to allow any water to escape from fruit. Allow also 10 minutes longer cooking time after sugar has been added.
- A little butter added to berry jams saves skimming and helps set it. Use factory butter.
- Two or three minutes after bottling jam, remove the skin to allow all steam to escape. This will prevent jam from moulding or not setting.

O that men's ears should be, to council deaf but not to flattery.

*　　　*　　　*

15

Cakes

HINTS ON CAKE MAKING

If your cake has a sticky surface, you have used too much sugar. Always weigh ingredients. Don't guess. Follow the instructions carefully for best results.

If the cake has a cracked top, the oven has been too hot, or a little too much flour used in making.

A holey texture can be caused by not using enough butter or shortening, and yet another reason is not to over-mix once the flour is added.

If your cake is too coarse, you have used too much baking powder or sugar.

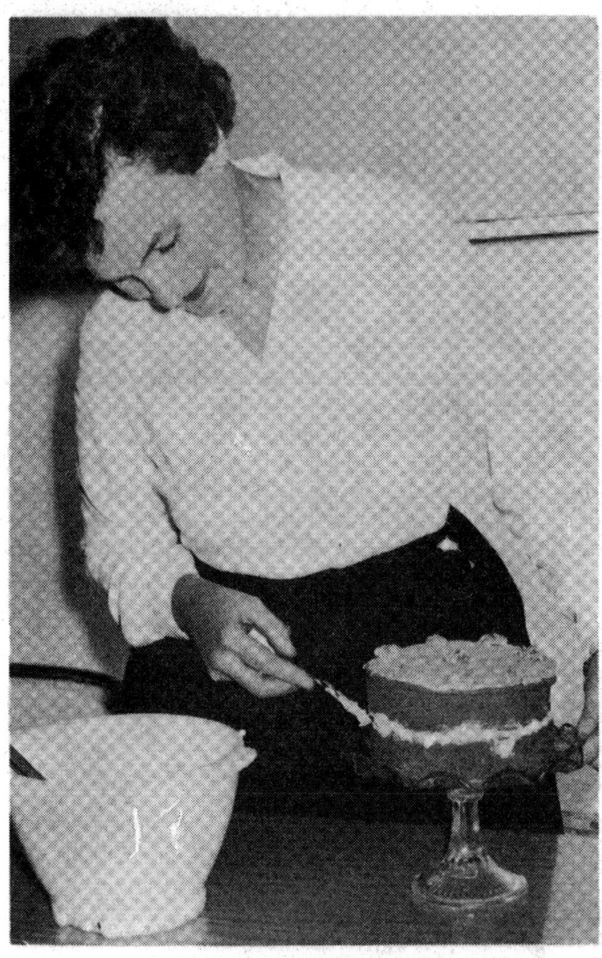

Filling a Blowaway spice sponge.

*　　　*　　　*

He labours in vain who tries to please everybody

Always cream the butter and sugar thoroughly as well (not to the oily stage though) as this is another reason. Too slow an oven and insufficient liquid are other reasons also.

If your cake rose, then fell, too much baking powder (or risings) were used; or the oven was too slow, or probably you took it from the oven before it was cooked.

For sandwich cakes use tins 3 inches high, if you want your cakes high.

Place your cake in centre of oven shelf, so as to ensure even rising. Always sift the flours and rising 2 or 3 times. Do this on a piece of grease-proof paper as it adheres to newspaper and brown paper.

Mix cocoa with warm water, for a chocolate cake. Not so dry when its cooked. A dessertspoon of raspberry or plum jam makes it also nice and moist. For an orange cake, grated rind, creamed with the butter and sugar, makes a nicer cake than using orange juice.

HOW TO KEEP YOUR CHRISTMAS CAKE MOIST UNTIL CHRISTMAS

- Wrap it right away, straight from the oven in a dry tea towel (tin and all) and several layers of brown paper.
- Leave until next day. Remove from the tin by standing the tin in a larger one of hot water (to melt the paper from the tin).
- Wash the cake tin and dry thoroughly and put the cake back, pressing the paper that extended above the rim over the top of cake.
- Wrap the whole of the tin and cake in greaseproof paper and then in brown paper. Insert in a plastic bag and tie the top.
- Better still, if you have one of the lovely air tight plastic containers that are available now.

RICH BOILED CHRISTMAS CAKE

1 lb. butter, 1 cup water, 1 lb. currants, 1 lb. sultanas, 1 packet mixed fruit, 2 cups sugar, 5 eggs, 1 egg cup brandy, 4 cups flour, pinch salt, 1 teaspoon carb. soda, ½ teaspoon allspice.

Put butter, water, fruit and sugar into saucepan and bring to the boil. Remove from heat and let cool. Put into a bowl, add eggs (well beaten) and the brandy. Add sifted dry ingredients. Bake in moderately slow oven 4 hours.

MOIST CHRISTMAS CAKE

This is a lovely moist cake and keeps well.

½ lb. butter, ½ lb. sugar, 1 teaspoon caramel, 1 orange, 1 lemon, 6 eggs (medium) 1 gill brandy or sherry, 10 ozs. flour, pinch of salt, 1 teaspoon mixed spice, ½ lb. sultanas, ½ lb. currants, ½ lb. raisins, ¼ lb. citron peel, 4 ozs. peanuts (cut up small), 2 ozs. dates or figs (chopped), 2 ozs. crystalised cherries (cut in half).

Grease a round or square tin, about 9 inches across. Line it also with greaseproof paper coming up the sides well above the tin. Cream butter and sugar, add caramel, orange and lemon juice and grated rind, adding a tablespoon of the sifted flour with salt and spice to stop curdling. Add the brandy the same way, then one by one the 6 eggs, adding some flour with each egg. Add fruit and nuts, then remaining flour. Bake 2 to 3 hours in a moderate oven.

CHRISTMAS PLAIN CAKE

1 lb. flour, ½ teaspoon salt, ½ teaspoon soda, 1 teaspoon cream of tartar, ½ lb. butter, ¾ lb. sugar, 4 eggs, ½ pint milk, 12 drops essence of lemon, ½ oz. icing sugar.

CINNAMON COFFEE TEACAKE

½ lb. plain flour, 3 teaspoons baking powder, ½ teaspoon salt, ¼ lb. castor sugar, ¼ lb. butter, 1 egg, 6 tablespoons milk.

Crumble Topping : 3 tablespoons flour, 1 dessertspoon cinnamon, 3 tablespoons sugar, 1 oz. butter.

Prepare Topping first : Sift flour and cinnamon, add sugar, rub in butter. Sift flour, baking powder and salt for cake. Add butter, cut into small pieces. Add sugar, beaten egg and milk and beat all for 1 minute. Put into a greased sandwich tin, about 3 inches high. Sprinkle over the topping and bake in a moderate oven approx. ¾ hour. Turn out very carefully on to a tea towel placed on the cake cooler to preserve crumble top, then carefully invert onto another cake cooler. Cut and serve freshly made.

TEACAKE

Cream 1 tablespoon butter with 1 small cup castor sugar, add egg, then ½ cup milk. Lastly, 1½ cups S.R. flour. Put into 2 greased sandwich tins. Cook 20 minutes in a moderate oven. While still warm spread top of cake with softened butter and sprinkle with a mixture of 2 teaspoons sugar and ½ teaspoons cinnamon. Eat immediately.

QUICK-MIX COFFEE CAKE

1½ cups S.R. flour, ½ teaspoon baking powder, pinch salt, 1½ tablespoons instant coffee powder, ½ cup castor sugar, 4 oz. softened butter, 2 eggs, 1/3 cup milk.

Sift dry ingredients into small basin of electric mixer, add remaining ingredients. Beat on medium speed 3 minutes, or beat with wooden spoon until smooth. Spread mixture into well-greased 7 x 11 in. lamington tin. Bake in mod. oven 25 to 30 mins. Top with Coffee Glaze Icing; sprinkle with chopped walnuts, if desired.

LAMINGTONS

Prize Recipe

Cream ½ lb. butter with 7 ozs. sugar and 3 drops essence of lemon, add 5 large eggs (two at a time), beat a little only. Sift 1lb. flour with 2 level teaspoons cream of tartar and 1 level teaspoon soda. Add half to egg mixture. Beat well. Add 1 cup milk and remainder of flour alternately, finishing with the milk. Put mixture into greased lamington tin well floured out. Bake in moderate oven 45 minutes. When cold, cut into squares, ice with chocolate icing and dip in coconut. A carving fork doesn't break the lamingtons as much as a table fork when you prod it into them before dipping in the icing.

Chocolate Icing :

Dissolve 1 dessertspoon butter in 2 tablespoons boiling water, stir in ½ lb. icing sugar and 1 level dessertspoon cocoa sifted together. Place over a low stove until just warm, stir well but do not boil. To ice the lamingtons, keep icing warm by standing the pot in a basin of hot water, otherwise the icing will become too stiff.

COLD PORRIDGE SCONES

These scones, unlike others, are eatable and keep fresh for several days after baking. They have a nutty, different taste to others and are very nourishing, besides using up left-over porridge. Cream 2 tablespoons sugar with 1 tablespoon butter until light and fluffy. Add 1 egg, then 1 cup cold porridge (rolled oats). Fold in 2 cups S.R. flour, sifted with ½ teaspoon salt. Knead a little, press out with hands and cut into rounds. Bake on a greased slide in a hot oven for 10 to 15 minutes. A handful of sultanas can also be added for a change.

PRIZE CHEESE SCONES No. 1

½ lb. self raising flour sifted with ½ teaspoon salt and a pinch of cayenne. Rub in 1 oz. butter and 2 ozs. grated cheese. Mix all into a soft dough with 8 tablespoons milk and knead into shape lightly. Cut into rounds, glaze with milk and bake on a warm floured tray for 10 minutes in a hot oven.

CHEESE SCONES No. 2

Sift 8 ozs. flour, 2 teaspoons cream of tartar, 1 teaspoon carb. soda, pinch salt, pinch cayenne. Rub in 1 tablespoon butter. Add 2 ozs. grated cheese, and 1½ gills water and mix all into a soft dough with a knife. Turn on to a floured board, roll lightly half an inch thick, cut into rounds and place on a floured oven slide, brushing over with milk or egg. Cook in a hot oven 7 to 10 minutes. A beautiful scone, lovely flavour, and texture like bread.

"DIFFERENT" SCONES

2½ cups S.R. flour, 2 tablespoons icing sugar, pinch salt, 2 tablespoons or 1 oz. butter melted, 1 cup milk,

Sift flour, sugar and salt, twice. Mix in the liquids. Knead a little, then roll out 3 times. Cut into scones with knife and bake 10 to 15 minutes in hot oven.

GEM SCONES

Sift 1½ cups of S.R. flour with a pinch of salt. Cream 1 tablespoon butter with 2 tablespoons of sugar. Add 1 egg. Add ½ cup of evaporated milk with ½ cup of water. Half fill greased gem irons. Cook 10 minutes in moderate oven.

Ray Martin's scones

Mix 4 cups self raising flour with equal parts cream and water until of scone consistency. Cook 12 minutes at 220°C.

Cake, (gone wrong)

1. Cake Burnt

Grate off the charred pieces. Better than cutting. Prevent by putting a layer of salt into a larger tin then lower your cake (with mixture) into this larger one to stop the bottom burning.

2. Cake Cracked

Too much flour, mixture too dry, or too hot an oven.

3. Cake Crumbly

Too much butter or liquid, too little flour, and insufficient cooking.

4. Cake "Domed or Peaked"

Temperature too high.

5. Cake Dry

You used too much flour, and too little butter. If it is a fruit cake, sprinkle liberally with brandy, or whatever spirit you added to ingredient when mixing, and wrap in foil until required.

6. Cake Sticky

Too much sugar used and baked too slowly.

7. Cake Sunk in Middle

Opened oven too soon. Use it by cutting out centre, crumble, then blend with an egg. Steam for ½ an hour, and eat as a pudding. Split the rest, fill with cream, ice top, and use as a ring cake.

8. Cake with Bad Colour and Unpleasant Odour

Too much rising agent.

SAND CAKE

This is one of my favourite cakes. Don't ice, I think it spoils it.

½ lb. butter, 6 ozs. castor sugar, 3 eggs, 4 ozs. each of flour and arrowroot, ½ teaspoon salt, grated rind of 1 lemon.

Cream butter and sugar, add eggs one at a time, beat well. Fold in sifted flours and salt, and mix well for 10 minutes (by hand) 5 minutes (electric). Add rind of lemon. Place in a greased and floured square tin (about 7 inches square) and bake in moderate oven for one hour.

MARJORIE'S CAKE

A very delicious and unusual cake and one of my favourites.

Cake mixture : 2 eggs, 1 small cup sugar, ½ cup butter, 1 small cup milk, 1 cup S.R. flour.

Pastry mixture : 1½ cups S.R. flour, ½ cup butter, ¼ cup milk.

Rub the butter into the flour, until there are no lumps. Add milk and mix to a soft dough. Roll out and line a square cake tin 7 in. x 7in. Spread with raspberry or plum jam, then sprinkle with 1 cup of currants. Make sponge by putting all ingredients in a bowl (butter melted) and beat vigorously for 3 minutes. Pour into pastry case over currants, etc. Bake in moderate oven 1 hour. Ice when cold with plain icing.

Icing Hints

To be sure you are using pure icing sugar, dissolve some in water, and it will remain clear. If it is cloudy it is a mixture.

Try adding a tablespoon of custard powder to icing sugar when mixing with butter and boiling water. It makes a lovely topping, as well as a filling.

If you are short of icing, add powdered milk to the icing sugar and mix as usual.

When icing a cake that tends to crumble, try spreading it first with melted butter.

When icing a Christmas cake, before putting on the almond paste, etc., pour more brandy on top of the cake.

After icing a cake with plastic icing, press a fancy paper d'oyley on to the icing when almost set. Gently lift off, and you will have an attractive pattern on the cake.

The bottom of a cake is flatter to ice than the top. The "rounded" top will sink into the cream when it becomes the middle piece (of sponge cakes).

A teaspoon of rum added to icing will add a nice flavour for a topping on gingerbread.

To ice cup cakes quickly, hold them upside down over the frosting, then dip them into it, twirl, then turn quickly, right side up, so icing will make a fancy peak.

A good icing is made with 200g of icing sugar and juice of a lemon, then enough milk to make it smooth.

An easy icing for small cakes is by spreading tops with jam, then dip in coconut.

For a change, add 2 teaspoons of jelly crystals to the icing sugar.

When mixing icing for a sponge cake, mix with warmed fruit jam instead of water to give it a lovely tang.

To ice a large cake and coat sides evenly, do the sides first, not the top, then place the nuts, coconut, or whatever you are using, on greaseproof paper ; next, take the cake in your hands by the top and bottom, and roll gently in the decoration. Now, ice the top.

Add coconut to icing to stop it going hard.

FAIRY FLOSS SPONGE

This is simple to make, cheap and light as a feather.

2 large eggs, 1 tablespoon each of custard powder, cornflour, and plain flour, $\frac{1}{2}$ cup sugar, 1 teaspoon cream of tartar, $\frac{1}{2}$ teaspoon soda.

Beat eggs well, add sugar and beat until frothy. Fold in sifted flours and rinsings. Cook 10 minutes in moderate oven in 2 greased sandwich tins. Ice and fill with cream or raspberry jam.

P I K E L E T S

(Prize recipe)

1 cup S.R. flour, ¼ teaspoon salt, 1 egg, ½ cup milk, 1 heaped tablespoon sugar, butter.

Sift flour and salt. Beat egg, add milk. Add sugar to flour. Make a well in centre, and pour in egg and milk. Stir well with a fork or wooden spoon. Stand for ¾ of an hour. Grease a Menu-Master if you have one, or top of stove (electric), or just a hot fry pan, and when moderately hot, drop dessertspoons on, and cook until bubbles appear. Turn over (and brown the other side) with a knife. Makes a dozen. Do not stir after the mixture has stood for the ¾ of an hour, otherwise they will go flat.

MY RECIPE FOR HOT CROSS BUNS

1 lb. plain flour, 1 teaspoon salt, 2 teaspoons spice, 1 teaspoon cinnamon, 2 ozs. butter, 2 ozs. sugar, 4 ozs. sultanas, 1 egg, 1 oz. compressed yeast, 1 teaspoon each flour and sugar, ½ pint lukewarm milk.

Crumble yeast into basin, mix in the 1 teaspoon each flour and sugar. Stir in the lukewarm milk, firstly mixing it into a paste with a little of the milk, so it won't be lumpy. Add the rest and stand in a warm place for ¼ of an hour. Add the beaten egg. Sift the flour, salt, spice and cinnamon. Rub in the butter, add sugar and sultanas. Mix to a soft dough with the egg mixture. Cover basin with clean tea towel and stand in warm place about ¾ of an hour, or until well risen. Turn onto lightly floured board and knead until smooth. Cut into 16 pieces, knead each separately into a round and mark a deep cross on each with back of knike. Place on a greased tray close together, set aside to rise again for ¼ of an hour. Can be cooked in a greased baking dish. Bake in a hot oven 15 to 20 minutes. Turn onto a cake cooler and brush tops with the following glaze : 1 tablespoon gelatine, 1 tablespoon sugar, dissolved in 1 tablespoon hot water.

P.S.—Do not use egg from refrigerator because the sudden cold may kill the yeast and prevent any further rising. Too much heat is also detrimental ; also, do not knead the dough on a cold-topped table or marble slab.

S A W A B I S C U I T S

I won a trip to Melbourne in 1958 and whilst I was there holidaying, I watched cooking demonstrations at Myers. The lady was using a Sawa biscuit forcer that acts like a miniature jack. It jacked the biscuits out so beautifully with no old-fashioned pushing against the waist, that I bought myself one. With it, you got the recipe free, of the biscuits she was demonstrating. It is a beautiful recipe, makes over 100 biscuits of all sorts of shapes that goes with the forcer. You can buy extra cutters if you require them. They taste and look nicer than shop-bought. Here is the recipe that I have named . . . SAWA BISCUITS

½ lb. butter, 1 egg, 4 ozs. icing sugar, 14 ozs. self-raising flour.

Method : Cream butter and icing sugar, add egg, then S.R. flour. Put in the forcer any shape cutter, force onto a greased tray and bake in a fairly hot oven till a light brown. Join with butter icing, and ice the top as desired.

THE PERFECT PAVLOVA (or Classic Meringue)

Named for a famous ballerina, the Pavlova can be temperamental at times. Here are a few tips that will help you make a perfect Pavlova.

Bowls and beaters must be scrupulously clean; the slightest trace of water or grease will prevent whites whisking stiffly. Carefully remove any trace of broken yolk, small piece of egg-shell, etc., before beating. Prepare oven tray before beating egg-whites, which will collapse if not used immediately. If you are not using quilted aluminium foil, brush oven tray with oil; other fats will solidify as meringue cools and makes it difficult to remove it from tray. Use eggs that are a few days old. If you use fresh eggs, the whites are thin and do not beat up to great volume. They should be at room temperature before beating. Add a pinch of cream of tartar or a few drops of acid (lemon juice or vinegar) to egg-whites; this strengthens the protein in the whites, giving a stronger structure and more volume. Egg-whites must be really stiff before you add sugar (in methods where whites are beaten first), otherwise the meringue will not be firm enough to support the sugar and mixture will not hold a firm peak. Beat whites until bubbly, add cream of tartar, and beat again until whites are stiff (if cream of tartar is in recipe). In some recipes castor sugar is used for quick dissolving; for others, granulated sugar gives a firmer result. Add sugar, a dessertspoon at a time, and beat after each addition until sugar is completely dissolved. Make sure that all sugar is dissolved, otherwise the undissolved sugar will melt during cooking and give a 'weepy' sticky Pavlova.

Where sugar is added gradually, make sure each addition of sugar is dissolved before any more sugar is added, otherwise the weight of undissolved sugar will break down egg-white aeration and mixture will collapse. When sugar is dissolved, the foam will be satin-smooth and glossy. To test if sugar is dissolved rub a little of mixture between two fingers. Lift beaters from basin; the white that adheres to them should stand in stiff peaks. If peaks bend over, continue beating. Cornflour prevents sugar 'weeping' and helps dry out Pavlova; the more cornflour used, the drier will be the Pavlova. The combination of vinegar and lemon juice helps to form the marshmallowy centre; also whitens the Pavlova. Use cool oven (unless stated otherwise) to just dry out, not cook, and leave in oven until cold.

TIPS FOR TOPPING MADE WITH MERINGUE

For meringue toppings, use slightly less sugar than for a meringue which has to set firm; about 1½ oz. per egg-white is sufficient, because toppings must cook more quickly. Spread or pipe meringue topping round edge of pie and work toward centre; make sure meringue touches pastry round edge, thus sealing the filling. This prevents meringue shrinking, softening, or weeping during cooking. Be sure to use a fairly cool oven to cook meringue toppings. If oven is too hot, meringue will brown on top but remain uncooked underneath and, as pie cools, meringue may collapse. Spread topping evenly over pie, avoiding too many high peaks, because these will burn before the remainder of topping cooks.

CHOCOLATE RIPPLE CAKE

½ lb. chocolate ripple biscuits, 1 teaspoon castor sugar, ¾ teaspoon gelatine, ½ pint cream, vanilla essence, chopped nuts.

Add sugar, gelatine and a little vanilla essence to cream and whip until very stiff. Join chocolate ripple biscuits together with generous spread of cream. Cover all over with cream and sprinkle with chopped walnuts. Allow to stand 6 hours in the refrigerator before cutting. When cutting, cut diagonally, and you will get a striped effect, cutting across 2 or 3 biscuits, otherwise you would just cut in between them.

16

Summer Puddings

TOPPING FOR STEWED FRUIT

A wonderful topping for stewed or canned fruits can be had by putting 2 teaspoons gelatine into a small cup of fruit liquid from canned fruit and dissolving over hot water. Beat 3 egg whites stiff and beat in 2 level tablespoons icing or castor sugar and ½ cup evaporated milk. Keep beating, gradually adding the cooled gelatine mixture. Keep beating until it holds its shape. Quickly spread over the fruit and sprinkle with walnuts. Delicious.

BLACKBERRY VELVET

1 lb. blackberries, ½ pint water, 4 ozs. castor sugar, juice of 1 lemon, 3 ozs. cornflour, little whipped cream, finger wafer biscuits.

Melt sugar in the water, add blackberries and cook over gentle heat until tender. Put through a sieve. Measure pulp and, if necessary, add water to make two pints. Blend cornflour with a little of the blackberry puree. Stir into remainder, then pour into pan. Stir over gentle heat until mixture thickens and comes to the boil. Stir in lemon juice. Add a little more sugar if necessary. Pour into a mould or moulds that have been rinsed with cold water. Decorate with whipped cream and serve with wafer biscuits.

BRANDY SNAPS

Melt 3 ozs. butter, 3 ozs. golden syrup and 3½ ozs. castor sugar. Sift 3½ ozs. flour, pinch salt and 1 teaspoon ground ginger, add the grated rind of one lemon and the butter mixture. Drop in small lumps on a tray, leaving plenty of room for spreading. Bake 10 minutes in moderate oven. While still hot, roll into a lily shape around the handle of a greased wooden spoon. Push smaller ends through the square holes of a cake cooler to get cold.

17

Winter Puddings

GOLDEN ROLY POLY

Rub ½ cup margarine into 2 cups self raising flour which has been sifted with a pinch of salt. Mix to a firm dough with water and roll out thinly to an oblong. Spread with sliced apples (2 medium apples are sufficient) and sprinkle with sultanas and sugar. Roll up firmly, securing edges and bake ¼ of an hour in a moderate oven in a well greased pie dish. Mix 1 cup golden syrup with 1 tablespoon lemon juice, warm slowly, pour over roll and bake slowly in a very moderate oven for a further ½ hour, basting frequently with the syrup mixture. See that it cooks slowly as the syrup tends to burn if the oven is too hot. Result is a delicious golden brown roll to be served with cream.

* * *

Aim at what is highest and you will secure what is between.

GOLDEN SHOWER MARMALADE

Take 12 nicely coloured oranges, wash and grate rind, using none of the white skin. Put in 2½ pints of water and let stand all night. Cut up oranges and 6 lemons finely and put into preserving pan. Add 3 pints water and cook gently 1 hour. Pour into a jelly bag and leave all night. Next day, put juice onto boil and add the grated orange rind and water it was soaked in. When boiling add 6 lbs. sugar (previously heated in oven) and boil quickly till it jells. Stir when cold, then bottle.

FIG JAM

3 lbs. figs, ½ lb. preserved ginger, 2 lemons, 3 lbs. sugar.

Place figs in pan with a little water, add ginger and juice of lemons and skin of 1 lemon, and boil until figs are tender. Add the sugar and boil until setting. (About 30 minutes). Remove lemon skin, and bottle.

A triumphant Marjorie grasps the W. T. Findlay Cup for best exhibitor in the 1959 Campbell Town Show. In the hours before this photograph was taken Marjorie overcame an attempt—by those disgruntled at her amazing success—to deny her the right to have the cup presented by the then governor of Tasmania, Sir Stanley Burbury.

2. SHOWING OFF

Off Marjorie would go to the Campbell Town show each June, laden with cakes, biscuits, slices, bread, preserves, sauces, chutneys, pickles, clarified dripping, jams, cordials, confectionery, home-laid eggs, home-made soap, home-grown vegetables, sewing, knitting, embroidery, patchwork, photography, pot plants, rock gardens and more. And home she would come, her baskets overflowing with blue ribbons, and usually with the W. T. Findlay cup for best exhibitor firmly in her grasp.

Marjorie would be so excited by her victories that she would immediately begin planning her campaign for the following year, and such passionate commitment paid off. Over a decade she followed a steady upwards trajectory: in 1951, she won twenty-six prizes and the cup; in 1955, forty-four prizes and the cup; in 1956, forty-five prizes and the cup; in 1957, sixty-two prizes and the cup; and in 1958, no fewer than seventy-eight prizes and the cup.

By 1959 Marjorie had become aware of rumours that her

spectacular success could not have been honestly achieved. Hurt by both the innuendo and some ugly scenes, Marjorie decided to write a book revealing her trade secrets.

If you've ever wanted to know the correct way to assemble a rainbow cake fit for the show table, or how to prevent a holey texture in your Swiss roll; or debated whether four-hole buttons ought to be stitched on in criss-cross fashion, or not; or puzzled over how to ensure your lamingtons do not go soggy; or wondered what is the width of a proper French seam; or wished you knew how to stop your scones from leaning over when they rise in the oven—well, Marjorie is only too happy to set you straight.

—•—

MERLE PARRISH, SHOW COOK

Since her sudden rise to *Masterchef* fame and the publication of her cookbook, *Merle's Kitchen*, eighty-year-old baking sensation Merle Parrish has been in constant demand—as has her signature peach blossom cake.

Like Marjorie, show cook and Masterchef *regular Merle Parrish has a cupboard full of blue ribbons. Many of them are for her signature peach blossom cake. Photo by Steve Brown Photography, courtesy of Random House Australia.*

Merle, who has lived all her life in Cudal, in central western New South Wales, got a taste for competitive baking at the age of seven when she entered a batch of Anzacs in her local show, and has been entering shows ever since. She says she loses as often as she wins, but she doesn't mind so long as she's fairly beaten. Of course, she prefers the thrill of bringing home yet another blue ribbon to give to her daughter, who is working them all into a commemorative quilt.

Merle's prize-winning cakes have almost always been created in a small and modest 1950s-style kitchen, where a foldaway card table provides extra space for mixing bowls, cake tins and ingredients. Her husband of fifty-seven years, Clyde, was both her biggest fan and her chief dishwasher.

Merle's top pick from Marjorie's repertoire is the Sponge Cake Prize, made with no rising agent. 'The secret of my peach blossom cake is to have the egg whites really stiff, and I imagine this cake of Marjorie's would be much the same,' Merle says. 'I can't wait for a chance to try it out.'

Sponge Cake Prize
(No rising)

This is my husband's favourite cake – a cake that I have never been beaten with, in competitive work.

4 eggs, 1 level cup sugar, pinch salt, 1 rounded cup plain flour, 1 teaspoon lemon juice.

Grease a square tin, then dust out with plain flour or icing sugar. Separate yolks from the whites of the eggs. Beat yolks and sugar together until creamy (about 3 minutes with an electric beater). Beat whites a little before adding the salt, then will till a stiff froth. Now add both together, and beat about 10 minutes. It should be thick and creamy. Fold in the plain flour (sifted), then the lemon juice. Bake 1 hour in a very moderate oven to cook it well. If the oven is too hot, the sponge will rise in the centre and crack, or if, on the other hand, the oven is too slow, the cake will be sticky underneath and on top.

—*M.B.*

Custard For a Show

Remember that yolks of eggs make a finer-grained custard than whole eggs. Cook custard slowly, set in a pan of water for perfection.

Flowers Crystallised

These are lovely for decorating cakes, etc. Put 1 cup sugar, ½ cup water and 1 dessertspoon glucose into a saucepan and stir until boiling. Boil till soft ball stage is reached, then cool to lukewarm. Colour syrup to match flowers. Paint flowers all over with syrup. Let dry. Repeat, then coat with matching sugar. Let dry, and set on waxed paper. Another method is —

Beat one egg white with one tablespoon cold water until well mixed. With a tiny brush, coat each flower lightly with the liquid egg white (not froth). Hold flower over castor sugar and spoon over the sugar, until flower is well covered. Place on a wire tray and put aside to dry in a cool place. When thoroughly dry, store in an airtight tin. Violets, freesias, roses, daisies, fern and ivy, all look good crystallized.

"Most of the things worth doing in the world had been declared impossible before they were done."

ROSE COMPETITIONS

In rose competitions an exhibition rose means one with no less than 35 petals; a decorative rose is smaller and looser; full bloom—the judge must be able to see the centre, it must be deep through, and circular. A container of 6 (or more or less) must never have different blooms in the one vase. A container of miniatures must have foliage with them.

Hints for Show Entrants

When sewing on a 4-hole button, never criss-cross. Work each hole separate to form a square, then blanket stitch the bars on the wrong side. Sew press studs on in the same way. Hooks and eyes should be button-holed or blanket stitched. Do not use press studs for children's dainty frocks.

When making a tailored blouse, the button-holes should be worked horizontally, and a French bar each end (that is loops and blanket stitch). The button-hole stitch is then used double with thread around needle from eye end, firstly working a running stitch around edge of hole for strength. For any other type of blouse, the button-holes are vertical.

Button-holes that have a bar one end, and rounded the other, are done by using firstly, only one thread. The bar is four over and over stitches; then blanket stitch the bar on the right side, turn to wrong side and blanket stitch too. The rounded end must not be blanket stitched—just plain—and only use nine stitches on the round. The rest of the button-hole is blanket stitched

When stitching a calico top to a thick skirt, sew the usual way, but press upwards towards bodice (both seams) then overcast or loop stitch together for neatness. Turn flat seams under in woollen materials or button-hole the seams, or loop stitch them.

A French seam must only be 3/8 of an inch when finished and when held up to the light the seam must be FULL of material. This is only for fine materials. Run and fell—seen only on boys' blouses—is done by turning under ¼-inch and then do the flat seam. When finished it must be 3/8 of an inch wide only.

When doing satin stitch on scalloped d'oyleys, etc. (or rounded flowers) the stitch must be perfectly straight for show work; that is, straight up and down, not following the curve. For the scalloped edges of your d'oyley, first run a thread around the curve at bottom, for perfection afterwards. The fineness or thickness of the material governs your thread.

If you are crocheting around a d'oyley, do two d.c. into each hole instead of one to cover up the ghastly cut edge. Crochet around d'oyleys must not be mercerised and must be same colour as the linen and fairly stiff—not floppy. Crochet around a d'oyley must be ½-inch wide.

* * *

There is no substitute for talent.

* * *

I am always ready to learn, although I do not always like being taught.

Envy is a kind of praise

*   *   *

To prevent **holes** in the cakes, do not beat hard towards the end, so that most of the air can escape before turning into the tin.

The white spots on a Madeira cake can be almost prevented if you cream a few drops of lemon essence with the butter and sugar. Do not allow the mixture to stand, once you start to mix it. It will not rise as good if you do. If **over-cooked,** there will be brown streaks through it. The cause of a cake rising in the centre and cracking is that the oven was too hot when you put the mixture in.

Cakes—Chocolate : Grease tins very carefully. Let cake settle in tin 5 to 10 minutes before turning out. This prevents breaking. Do not "fork" the icing after you have smoothed it over the cake. Use a butter icing always and colour it sparingly

Gingerbread—see Chocolate Cake.

Lamingtons : Use a butter cake foundation. Always leave a day or so before cutting into a 1½-inch square, or the same depth as the cake, so it will be a perfect square. Icing should be well flavoured and coloured nicely. It should be thick enough, so as cake won't go soggy. My recipe for lamington icing that I use at Show time (and I'm seldom beaten with Lamingtons) is made from the following ingredients : ½ lb. icing sugar, 1 level dessertspoon cocoa, 1 dessertspoon butter, 2 tablespoons boiling water. Dissolve butter in boiling water. Stir in icing sugar and place on stove until just warm, stirring all the time. Use quickly whilst warm. An easy way to cover with coconut is to place each as you ice them, in a paper bag of coconut and shake well.

Sandwich or Sponge Cakes : Grease **and flour** tins carefully. Eggs and sugar **must** be beaten until sugar dissolves. The texture is determined by this. Sugar grains will melt in the hot oven and leave pin holes in cake if not beaten sufficiently; also the top of the cake will be greasy. You will know when the mixture is sufficiently beaten because the mixture will be thick and creamy with large air bubbles rising in the mixture which immediately break. When you begin beating a sponge, do not leave it at all, until it is in the oven. It starts to rise the moment you start beating. Do not use a knife when turning out of tins. Gently shake. Place right side up on cooler so the surface is not marked. Do **not** place on paper or towel or the surface will go moist. Only use a **small** amount of raspberry jam. The **top** jam in a bottle is preferable, as it is firmer. Do not ice. Dust with icing sugar and fill with jam sparingly.

Shortbread : Must be light in colour when cooked, so cook very slowly. Always mould by hand — never cut. Pinch edges and prick with fork.

Small Cakes : If a collection is required, do not use **same** mixture, but coloured **differently.** Use **separate** mixtures. Use pale icings and do not use paper containers. Put names of cakes beside each one. Try to use different shaped tins for each variety.

10

Hints for Show Cooks

(Given me by Show Judges)

Biscuits : Cook slowly, even temperature. Use butter if possible and always castor sugar, as it gives a finer texture because it dissolves more easily. Mixture should be stiff if making a short biscuit.

Cakes—Large fruit : A ½lb. mixture, cooked in an 8-inch tin, is sufficient size to enter in a plain or fruit cake for show purposes. Cut up the fruit (raisins and sultanas, etc.) to improve the texture. Fruit cakes should be shiny on top, rise evenly without cracking, so be sure that they are cooked slowly. To get an even surface, level cake with hand, cut through several times with a knife and sprinkle with cold water. Place a sheet of brown paper over top before putting in the oven, or cook the cake inside a baking dish with lid firmly on. Never put the scrapings of the bowl in the cake tin (for show purposes) as there will be a light streak through cake when cut. Long, slow cooking will ensure the fruit will not burn. When lining the cake tin with grease-proof paper, see paper comes up about 2 to 3 inches above top of tin, **and** put the paper in first for the sides, then the round piece for bottom last. If you place that in carefully, it will hold the sides up and so your cake will come out the shape of the tin instead of bits of cake between the paper and tin, as often seen. Decorations should be done by hand. Do not use silver leaves, cachous or bought decorations.

Cakes—Large, Plain : To ensure that the mixture, when cooked, will be nice and smooth, do not let the mixture **curdle,** when adding the eggs one by one to butter and sugar. To prevent this, just beat the eggs a little after each addition, and then quickly add about ¼ of the flour, and if there are risings in the ingredients, sift that with the flour, too, then beat well. You will know when the cake is cooked because it will leave the sides of the tin. (So will sponges and sandwiches). Mix quickly and lightly.

* * *

Love your enemy, it'll drive him crazy.

Envy poisons joy. How true !

SECTION 28—

HINTS FOR SHOW COOKS

IT NEVER FAILS!

With that competition entry
So methodically you bake,
Weighing, creaming, sifting, folding,
Yet . . . it's just another cake.
But the one for next day's lunches,
Made in just three minutes flat,
Slapped up, hurled in the oven,
Is a cake to marvel at!

SULTANA CAKE

Fruit must be evenly distributed. Do not add lemon peel. Do not overbeat as this causes mixture to become too light to support the fruit.

CHOCOLATE CAKE

Grease tins very carefully. Blend cocoa with a little hot water, for better colour and flavour. Cool before adding. Let cake settle in tin 5-10 minutes before turning out. This prevents breaking. Do not 'fork' the icing after you smooth it over cake. Use a butter icing and colour it sparingly.

GINGERBREAD

Even baking—no burnt patches, top smooth—no burst or bubbly centre. Texture moist, fine and velvety—no harsh crumb or taste of soda. Rich mellow flavour—entirely free from harshness of too much ginger. No streaks in mixture.

ORANGE CAKE

See Chocolate Cake. Never put orange juice into an orange cake or sandwich (in many cases it makes the cake heavy). Use the grated rind of 1 orange for them, but first sprinkle with salt and let stand 1½ hours. Drain off any juice before adding to cake, preferably at the last. Outer surface must be an even, golden brown. Texture is most important—must be fine, even and well flavoured with orange.

RAINBOW CAKE

Always put the chocolate next to base, then pink, with white on top. Do not have cake too high, as it spoils the appearance (about 4 in.). Cook layers in all same size tins, with same amounts of mixture so layers will be even. Use cochineal sparingly as it bakes darker. Join with raspberry jam and ice top with white butter icing.

SPONGE CAKE

Baked in one tin. No rising. Fine texture and rather dry.

SPONGE SANDWICH

No butter. Two layers—identical in thickness. No wrinkles on top. No overhang—caused by too small tins. Must not be sticky. Dust top with icing sugar, but use no filling. Grease and flour tins carefully. Eggs and sugar must be beaten until sugar dissolves, so use castor sugar as it dissolves quicker. The texture is determined by this. Sugar grains will melt in the oven and leave pin holes in cake if not beaten sufficiently, also the top of the cake will be greasy. You will know when the mixture is sufficiently beaten because it will be thick and creamy with large air bubbles rising in the mixture, which immediately break. Sift flour at least three times. Do not leave a sponge once you start beating it. It starts to rise the moment you start beating. Do not scrape out bowls; this will show when it is cut. Leave in tins a few minutes before turning out. Do not use a knife when turning out of tins. Gently shake. Place right side up on cooler so surface is not marked. Do not place on paper.

VICTORIA SANDWICH

A sponge mixture with melted butter (1 tablespoon, see above). It should have a finer texture than the sponge sandwich. Fill with jam, top of the jar is the firmest.

SWISS ROLL

Use a large Swiss roll tin so mixture will not be too high. Roll tightly, but keeping to three rolls only. Cut off side edges first to prevent roll breaking. (Some judges rule out cut edges, some don't.) Texture should be fine and moist. Grease sides of tin only, but put brown paper in the bottom. When cooked, turn out on to a thin damp cloth that has been wrung out tightly. Brush paper quickly with cold water and a pastry brush. Peel. Spread with raspberry jam using the end of silver spoon. Leave in cloth a few seconds (warm jam will ensure a more even spread). Dust lightly with icing sugar.

SHORTBREAD

Should be about 1/2 inch thick. Dainty pieces—neatly cut and uniform in size. Even, pale golden throughout. Texture fine and crisp—rich buttery taste—no essence. Too slow cooking results in a loose surface.

SMALL CAKES

If a stated number of varieties are called for, distinct varieties must be shown, and not the same mixture. They must be iced in different colours, or same mixture flavoured differently. They should be moist and fine textured. Use pale icings. Different shaped tins for each variety helps. Put names of cakes beside each one.

SEWING HINTS, ETC., FOR SHOW PURPOSES

- Back stitch your knitted sleeves into the jumpers, and splice wool, do not take it to the edge. Always herringbone the sides of jumpers on ribbed bands only —not oversew, and press garments with a dry cloth, not damp.
- Remember blanket stitch is single action and buttonhole, double.
- Trinity stitch that is recommended by Show judges on the first row in crocheting around a doyley, is two d.c. in every hole. It covers up the ghastly cut edge.
- Crochet around doyleys must not be mercerised and must be same colour as the linen and fairly stiff, not floppy. Crochet around a doyley must be ½ inch wide. Do 2 d.c. in each hole instead of 1, to ensure there are no holes or gaps. Do not use gaudy colors, pastels preferred.
- Pinking seams must not be used if you are entering the article in a show, except in Taffetas.
- Don't use press studs for smocked frocks or any dainty children's frocks if entering them for show purposes.
- Turn flat seams under in woollen materials or button hole the seams, or loop stitch them.
- A French seam must only be ⅜ of an inch when finished and when held up to the light the seam must be **full** of material. This is only in fine materials.
- Run and fell—seen only on boys' blouses—is done by turning under ¼ inch and then do the flat seam. For show, it must be ⅜ of an inch wide when finished.
- When stitching a calico top to a thick skirt, sew the usual way, but press upwards towards bodice (both seams) then overcast or loop stitch together for neatness.
- When doing satin stitch on scalloped doyles, etc., or rounded flowers, the stitch must be perfectly straight for show work ; that is, straight up and down, not following the curve. For the scalloped edges of your doyley, first run a thread round curve at bottom for perfection afterwards. P.S., Fineness or thickness of the material governs your thread.
- When sewing on a 4-hole button, never criss-cross. Work each hole separate to form a square, then on the wrong side blanket stitch the bars.
- For a shank used in costumes, etc., put a nail across top, then work as usual. Finish with a bar.
- Press studs should be sewn on the same as the buttons. Hooks and eyes should be buttonholed blanket stitched.
- When you make a tailored blouse, the buttonholes should be worked horizontal, and a french bar each end (that is loops and blanket stitch). The buttonhole stitch is then used double with thread around needle from eye end, firstly working a running stitch around edge of hole for strength. For any other type of blouse, the button holes are vertical.
- Buttonholes that have a bar one end, and rounded the other, are done by using : firstly, only one thread. The bar is four, over and over stitches, then blanket stitch the bar on the right side, then turn to the wrong and blanket stitch that too. The rounded end must not be blanket stitched, just plain, and only use nine stitches on the round. The rest of the buttonhole is blanket stitched.

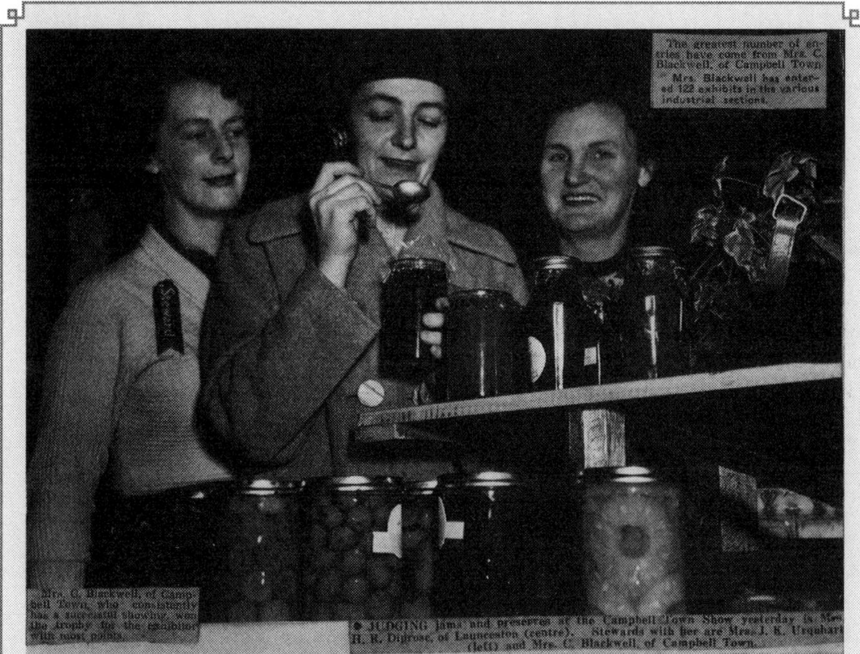

Being a stewardess at a competitive show is a little like being a bridesmaid, where the judge is the bride. 'Stewardesses,' Marjorie writes, 'can greatly assist the judge by presenting the items to her in a steady stream and removing them speedily.'

When I didn't take entries to those meetings I was the judge. It took four scrap books to paste all my 1300 prize winning tickets in, but they are tidier in these than loose boxes. The worst thing I can remember that has happened to me when preparing for a show, was way back in 1964, on the 8th June, at Campbell Town, when the door fell off my Belling stove at "Climar" just after I had put a sponge cake in the oven. Luckily, my neighbour, Mrs. Marjorie Bye, was there helping me label my entries, so she squatted on the floor and held the door in place with her back – a cushion in between. The sponge received a second prize, mainly because the stove had an inner door of glass as well. That oven was the only one I've seen with an enamel lid to close down when the elements cooled, so that you could use it for a table or whatever, when not using it as a stove. It was a perfect cooker – the cakes came out the same shade of brown all over.

Another thing that happened once, was the night before a show, I had all my entries ready and labelled sitting on the dining table. I went into the room for a last look before I went to bed, and a big piece was gone from a sandwich cake. It had been taken by my cat, so I set to and made another, but it was just as well the cat stayed out of the way.

"Without labour, nothing prospers."

CREAM PUFFS

Crisp and well dried out inside. Golden brown and even. Not too light. At least one left unfilled.

BISCUITS

Cook slowly, even temperature. Use butter if possible and always castor sugar, as it gives a finer texture because it dissolves more easily. Mixture should be stiff if making a short biscuit. A good flavour is essential. Where different varieties are called for, definite flavours and mixings should be used—not just different shapes. Shape and size must be dainty and, whatever varieties are used, they should be uniform in size. See trays are spotless.

SCONES

Cut with medium-size cutter from dough ½-inch thick. Have scones about 1½-2 inches across. Don't use a tumbler or anything that has a closed end. Scones must be evenly brown, level on top with smooth sides. Glaze with milk to ensure an even brown top and to remove surplus flour. Grease tray; do not flour it. Knead dough lightly so as to have an even outer surface and a fine texture. Scones will run to one side if mixture is too moist, or you lean on the cutter. Cook in hot oven 10 minutes. Always choose evenly sized scones for a collection on the plate. A show scone should be elastic to the touch. Fruit scones should be cooked in a moderately hot oven so as not to burn the fruit.

NUT LOAF

Even golden colour all over. Top should be flat. No hole in centre or wet patch. Portions of nuts clearly visible—not minced. Crumb fine and moist.

PASTRY (Shortcrust)

Even biscuit colour; crumb should be short, not leathery or tough. Must have a hot oven for first 10 minutes.

PASTRY (Puff or Flaky)

Pale brown in colour. Layers should be very light and continuous. Pastry should melt in the mouth and not be harsh and dry. For sausage rolls use puff, rough puff, or flaky pastry. They must be small and dainty and a rich golden brown all over. Have meat very hot before placing on pastry then the pastry won't be soggy underneath when cooked. For jam tarts the pastry must be cut with a fluted cutter, be golden brown throughout, and with glazed tops. Put jam in them before baking, and do not use too much jam. Put a pinch of flour on top of jam to absorb moisture.

PUDDINGS (Boiled or Steamed)

Shape, texture, colour, type of mixture, flavour and general appearance are all important judging factors. Fruit must be clean and well prepared. Judges prefer fruit to be cut to uniform size. For the boiled pudding it must have a dry surface with few cloth marks (to obtain this, pleat cloth, instead of just bunching it all up around pudding). Use plain, dry cloth, placed in colander for good shape. No coarse suet should be visible when pudding is cut; no sodden core of under-cooking, or seepage of water. Colour should be dark, without streaky patches; fruit evenly cut; flavour rich and mellow. For the steamed pudding in a basin, put mixture to within 2 inches of top. Cover securely with 2 layers of paper, greased on both sides. Have water to come up half way up the basin. Lid of steamer or saucepan should fit securely and removed as seldom as possible. When cooked, stand for a few minutes, then turn out on to a hot plate.

* * *

Money is a good servant, but a bad master.

JAMS AND CONSERVES

Points are allotted for flavour, colour, consistency and general neatness (seals, labels, uniform jars, etc.). When making jam or conserve from a bright coloured fruit the cooking should be done as rapidly as possible to retain the bright colour and natural colour of the fruit. With quince, apple or pear conserve, a slow boiling is desired so that the fruit will change colour with the cooking. All bottles should be clean, and jam should be allowed to cool a few degrees before putting into the jars, as this will give a more even distribution of fruit or jelly. Do not put water on fruit and leave overnight, as a lot of the pectin will be lost. Cut up the fruit if liked. If fruit is low in pectin, use 2-3 large seeds of japonica (especially good for peaches). Wipe and cut up finely and add to jam. Pectin can also be made from apples slightly less than full grown (while pips are still white). Cut up apples (roughly), put in saucepan (with pips, too) and add water until it is ¾-inch below top of fruit. Boil until soft. Put into a jelly bag and let drip for 48 hours. It can be sterilised if you have too much. In the steriliser, bring water quickly to boil, and boil until contents have reached boiling point too. Pectin is at its best in freshly picked fruit, so make jam as soon as you pick the fruit. For best results use a 'little under-ripe' fruit. If fruit is wet when picked, or over-ripe, it will not set as well.

JELLIES

Overcooking will make jellies too stiff. To slow boiling will have same effect. Too much sugar or overcooking before adding sugar makes jellies sugary on top. If not sufficiently cooked, it will be too thin. Marks are awarded for flavour, clearness, consistency, colour and general neatness, and there should be no sign of crystallisation. Jelly should cut easily, breaking with distinct cleavage, and the angles retaining their shape. Containers should not be too large, and the covers should fit tightly.

PRESERVING

Do not use over-ripe fruit, as they should retain as much as possible their original shape, colour and flavour (quinces an exception). Pack tightly. Do not overcook, as the least time in the preserving outfit, the better the bottled fruit will look. It should be plump and firm, yet tender. Make sure that good exhibits are not spoiled by lids in poor order. Let fruit stand ½ hour after packing, so fruit will settle down and make room for more. Keep it from going brown whilst you are packing by dropping each piece in a basin of water with a pinch of salt. When placing in bottles, put water in after each layer. Preserve in water only for show work. Keeps a better colour. After peeling pears, rub off cutting marks with emery paper until smooth. Do not put two fruits in one bottle (unless it says so), and three distinct colours catch the judge's eye better than three of one colour.

VEGETABLES

Do not put two vegetables in one bottle, unless it says so. If schedule states 3 bottles of vegetables, 3 varieties, you would have 4 varieties if you included two in one bottle, so you would be disqualified. Judges like three distinct colours; for example, carrots, sweetcorn and Brussel sprouts; not sweetcorn, parsnips and turnips. Fancy shapes for carrots, etc., can be made with biscuit cutters. Add sugar to tomatoes when preserving to preserve colour (1 level teaspoon to 7 lb. of tomatoes and 1½ level teaspoons of salt).

PICKLES

The fresh, crisp texture of the vegetables is important with pickles, and the pieces should not be too large. Pickled onions are more attractive done with white vinegar.

SAUCES AND CHUTNEY

Flavour, consistency, colour and neatness are what the judges look for, and over-salting should be avoided. Bottles should be corked and sealed with wax.

* * *

Love never loses sight of loveliness.

SECTION 29

SHOW COOKING HINTS

"The pleasure we derive from doing favours is partly in the feeling it gives us that we are not altogether worthless."

If you are called upon to judge a show exhibit for the first time, the following ideas will be of help:

Adopt a professional attitude. Become familiar with conditions and requirements for exhibitors and judges.

Check schedules and ensure that foods have been prepared accordingly. For example, if schedule states a cake is to be un-iced, it should be disqualified if it has been iced. If schedule calls for four varieties of biscuits, there should be four separate mixtures, each different in appearance, flavour and texture.

However, judges' attitudes should be flexible and they should make allowances if schedules are ambiguous.

Cutting Cakes: Judges must be allowed to cut cakes (except decorated cakes) preferably in half to compare texture and baking and to taste.

Cakes should be cut with the utmost care. A knife with a curved, scalloped-like edge will help in smooth cutting.

Do not cut cakes with a firm, downward pressure. Use a gentle, sawing motion; allow this sawing action to do the cutting. Cut surfaces are then disturbed as little as possible and offer much better opportunity for appraisal of texture.

Decorated cakes: Some exhibits, for icing purposes only, should not be cut. These can be marked "Not to be Cut". On others, a judge can test consistency of fondant with the point of a sharp knife (do this where mark won't show).

A judge can also pierce an exhibit if necessary, to check whether the cake has been used as a base, as specified in the schedule. (This also should be as inconspicuous as possible.)

Stewardesses play an important part in the smooth running of judging; they can greatly assist the judge by presenting the items to her in a steady stream and removing them speedily as possible after the judge has considered them. (As the stewardesses receive the entries, they should ensure they are correctly marked according to the schedule.)

Judges should have complete privacy for consideration of entries.

Stewardesses should be the only ones allowed to approach the judges, or enter the judging area or room, while judging is in progress.

"I am only one, but I am someone; I cannot do it all, but I can do something."

23

Prizes I have Won in Shows and Competitions

"Aim at what is highest and you will secure what is between."

MY first success at winning at a show goes back to when I was nine years of age. I received a second prize with a hand-written piece of poetry at a Kempton Show. I was an excellent writer in those days and my teacher, Mr. Alex Stewart, certainly gave me a lot of encouragement by sending my work to different shows around Tasmania. The next year I did even better as I received a first prize at Kingborough with the writing of " God save our gracious King ", a second at Ulverstone, and at Beaconsfield with Transcription Books. The following year it was a first at Lilydale, St. Mary's and Longford shows, and a second at Glamorgan, with writings and drawings. I continued on like that – firsts and seconds – until I left school, with the biggest thrill being second prize in England with a painting of Fuchsias. I have all the award tickets in sequence in scrapbooks, as I dislike having loose tickets, photos, clippings, etc., lying around.

As I mentioned in another chapter, the first prize I won when I was an adult was when I was working at " Riccarton " for Mr. and Mrs. Crosby Lyne, and that was for a pound of butter. Two years later in 1939, just after I was married, I entered a cake and received a first prize, so I kept that in mind while I raised my sons. Then in 1948, I entered quite a few articles of different natures and brought home 13 awards. In 1951, I received 26 prizes and a silver cup donated by Mrs. W. Findlay, so that really spurred me on. I was so excited I started right away to make things for the show the following year. I was well stocked by the next June, and this paid off as I came home with 36 prizes and again, the cup.

I was quite satisfied then, so did not enter the next year, but people told me they missed my entries, and the benches were bare. They kept at me until I gave in and entered again in 1955 when I won 44 prizes and the cup once more. In 1956, I won 55, and the cup ; also 9 awards at the State Exhibition, 62 prizes and another cup in 1957, 78 prizes and the cup in 1958, and 72 and the cup in 1959.

I'll never forget that show in 1959. The cup was not on the shelf – only the perpetual one which was kept for twelve months. I was very annoyed, and so were others – who also said if it was good enough for the winners of the horse events and prize sheep to receive their cups from the then Governor, Sir Stanley Burbury, it should be good enough for winners of home crafts. So I was spurred on to have that happen, but when I went to get the cup, it still wasn't there, only the perpetual one, and worse still, that was locked behind the wire netting enclosure in front of exhibits, and on the top shelf. Then a kind reporter who was very tall, put his hand over the top of the wire netting and retrieved it for me and the presentation took place (as you will see on page 456 of the 3rd edition of "At Home with Marjorie Bligh ").

Among the dignitaries to have supped at Marjorie's table, and sat upon her throw rug (crocheted from used pantyhose), is the late Jim Bacon, a former premier of Tasmania.

3. HAVING A 'DO'

Polish up the silver serving spoons, break out the crystal, fill the punchbowl with your best parsnip wine, and invite your friends and neighbours in for a spot of dancing.

Do everything you can think of with hardboiled eggs: colour them with cochineal, stuff them, devil them, make them into little boats with toothpicks and a white paper sail.

Crystallise your mint leaves; lay out bunches of frosted grapes.

Turn an orange into a sputnik with toothpick-skewered cocktail onions; wrap vermouth-soaked prunes in bacon.

Arrange a ring of pineapple, half a banana and a glace cherry in the fashion of a lit candlestick for an unforgettable party table statement.

Top crackers with mini-carrots made out of a squidge of Kraft cheese; cut your radishes into accordions.

The calendar is full of excuses. Whether it's Valentine's Day, Easter Sunday, Mother's Day, Christmas, a birthday or an anniversary, there's always a reason to load up the table with nibbles and savouries and sweets—and no one knows how to do it better than Marjorie Bligh.

—•—

BARRY HUMPHRIES, COMEDY MEGASTAR

'Both Edna and I are great fans of Marjorie Bligh. The things that woman made! And from such unexpected constituents!

'Back in 1976, when Edna penned her advice manual *Dame Edna's Coffee Table Book: A Guide to Gracious Living and the Finer Things of Life by One of the First Ladies of World Theatre*, she naturally turned to Marjorie Bligh for inspiration, especially in the culinary department.

'Edna, always fond of putting on a bit of a "do", was especially taken with Marjorie's party table favourite, Candlesticks. However, when Edna whips up this little number, she puts her own stamp on it and includes a little dribble of mayonnaise on the banana, representing melted wax.'

Dame Edna Everage, seen here outside Ednaville *(a reconstruction of her 1950s Moonee Ponds home), is a colossal fan of Marjorie's, and refers to her party recipes whenever she's hosting a soiree. Photo courtesy of the Arts Centre Melbourne.*

Candlesticks :

Open a tin of preserved pineapple. Put slices on a bread and butter plate. Peel bananas, cut about 2 inches off one end. Push a banana into the centre of the pineapple slice (through the hole). Place on to a plate. Place a crystallised cherry on top of banana to represent flame. Peel an orange with orange peeler. Take about 3 inches of peel. Push one end in with the banana, the other end under the slice of pineapple to represent handle.

Fill small moulds with red jelly. When set, turn out onto small plates. Peel small bananas, cut 2 inches off one end and split the other. Place a blanched almond coloured with cochineal inside the split to represent flame. Scoop a round hole in the middle of the jelly. Insert banana. If not firm, melt the scooped out piece and pour around to make it firm. Decorate base of jelly with whipped cream. Different coloured jelly candlesticks look most attractive on the table.

—M.B.

{SEE LAST COLOUR PLATE FOR AN EXAMPLE}

When the drink is in, the wit is out!

* * *

PARTY FOODS (ADULTS)

Here are some hints, recipes, drinks, etc., to help you make your party a super-duper occasion!

HINTS

* Cut some white or brown bread into finger lengths. Fry each in boiling fat, after being dipped quickly in cold milk. Drain on brown paper. Spread with mayonnaise and top with a sardine.

* * *

* Frosted grapes make an attractive party dish. Wash and dry well, then dip in whipped egg-white, toss in castor sugar, and dry on a rack.

* * *

* Cut some celery into 4-inch lengths. Fill the centre with creamed cheese or mayonnaise and top with cocktail onions.

* * *

* Imitation carrots look very realistic and a savoury expert friend (the late Mrs. Knowles) gave me this recipe: Take 1 teaspoon butter and 1 teaspoon Kraft cheese. Colour with cochineal. Shape in to a miniature carrot and put a tiny sprig of parsley in the crown. Place each one on a buttered savoury biscuit.

* * *

* Cut Belgium sausage into slices (thinly). Insert a small coloured onion in centre of each slice and roll up. Push a small coloured onion on to a tooth-pick, then through the roll of sausage, then finish with another differently coloured onion. Place on plate.

* * *

* If you want coloured eggs for your savoury eggs or salad, boil them in the water that you have left over from your redbeet. What a colourful salad you will have.

* * *

* Cut a pineapple in half lengthwise and scoop out pineapple and cut into squares. Put back in pineapple case and top with cream.

* * *

* Spread square wafer biscuits (that are bought with cream betweens) with butter, then shredded cheese. Bàke in a slow oven until pale brown. Eat when cold.

* * *

*Grill a piece of bacon that has been wrapped around a prune and held by a tooth-pick.

* * *

* Don't forget to make sausage rolls when you make the pastry for the patty pan cases; also asparagus rolls in the last few hours. Cut the buttered bread very thin before cutting off the crusts, then roll around a piece of asparagus.

* * *

* To avoid confusing glasses at your next party, and also reduce washing up, label glasses with guests' names or initials. Cut them from coloured paper and secure with clear sticky tape, or glue (the one that renders itself useless when wet).

* * *

* Another suggestion for the party table: Take oranges and cover with tooth-picks. Make some cream cheese, mix with chopped parsley into a paste. Form into balls, and push one on each tooth-pick. Soak some prunes in gin or sherry, then make a jelly with the gin or sherry and half water and gelatine. Dip the prunes that have been put on a tooth pick into the jelly and when almost set, take out and stick into an orange.

Beer Parties

Having a beer party? Here are some savouries and ideas just right for a super-duper party.

- **Hard boil some eggs. Cut them lengthwise and take out yolks and fill with mayonnaise. Top with a toothpick through a tiny sail made of white paper. Garnish with grated carrot.**

★ Hard boil some eggs. Cut in halves. Take out yolks. Colour the white halves with vegetable colouring or cochineal by adding drops to water, then immersing them in it till right shade. Fill with mayonnaise and top each with a coloured onion. Set each on a lettuce leaf on a square of buttered brown bread.

Cut some white or brown bread into finger lengths. Fry each in boiling fat, after being dipped quickly in cold milk. Drain on brown paper. Spread with mayonnaise and top with a sardine.

PATTY CASES FOR SAVOURIES

Cut some thin rounds of bread. Cut off crusts and cut round with a cutter. Spread both sides with melted butter. Place and push into position in patty tins and bake a golden brown. Fill with mayonnaise at the last minute and top with grated carrot. Be careful as cases break easily.

SARDINE PIQUANTE

1 tin sardines, 1 chopped hard-boiled egg, ½ teaspoon finely chopped onion, salt and pepper to taste, 1 dessertspoon mayonnaise, 1 dessertspoon lemon juice, parsley sprigs, 3 lemons to be used as cases.

Cut lemon in halves lengthwise; remove pulp and cut edges in peaks with scissors. Cut a thin slice from the bottom of each to enable them to stand evenly.

Drain sardines, mix with egg, onion, juice and mayonnaise and season with pepper and salt. Fill into lemon shells. Garnish with parsley sprigs. Serve with salad accessories.

Frosted grapes make an attractive party dish. Wash and dry well, then dip in whipped egg white, toss in castor sugar, and dry on a rack.

CASES FOR DIFFERENT FILLINGS:

Make some pastry and cut rounds to fit patty pans. Prick well and bake in hot oven. These can be made and stored in an air-tight tin a week before the party. On the night of the party fill cases with crayfish (curried) or just cut up crayfish in thick white sauce with chopped parsley added. The recipe for Salmon Savoury mixture (next page) is also nice warmed up in these cases, and yet again so is a whitebait savoury. Just add a tin of whitebait to 1 cup white sauce, season with pepper and salt and add a cup of boiled green peas.

STUFFED EGGS

Hard boil eggs. Shell them and cut in halves. Scoop out yolks. Mash these in a basin with sauce, minced onion, curry powder, mashed sardines, grated cheese, salt and pepper, or you can use them singly if you wish, or pickles instead of sauce. Moisten with salad-dressing and worcestershire sauce (or just one of them) and a teaspoon or more of melted butter, according to quantity used. Cut a slice off bottom of egg white. Place on a dish, pile mixture into cases and garnish each with a small sprig of parsley.

Have the cocktail saveloys ready in a pot for warming up.

Don't forget to make sausage rolls when you make the pastry for the patty pan cases; also asparagus rolls in the last few hours. Cut the buttered bread very thin before cutting off the crusts, then roll around a piece of asparagus.

CRYSTALLISED MINT LEAVES

Crystallised Mint Leaves are good garnishes for fruit cocktails or iced drinks, or even frozen desserts. Here's what you do : Wash, dry and remove the leaves from the stems. Brush both sides with beaten egg-white and dip in sugar. Spread on greaseproof paper, and put on a cake rack. Leave in a warm place, or dry very slowly in the oven, repeating the process, if necessary, until leaves are thoroughly coated with sugar.

Prune Kick

Soak for a couple of months in vermouth (dry).

PARSNIP WINE

Peel and slice thinly, and then weigh, 10 lbs. parsnip. Boil in 2 gallons of water till thoroughly cooked. Strain and force out all water through a fine sieve. Add liquid to 6 lbs. sugar and boil ¾ of an hour. Pour into a vessel to cool, then add a slice of toast, thinly spread with yeast. Leave 10 days, stirring each day, then strain liquid into a cask. Leave tightly corked until fermentation ceases, then make air tight. Bottle in 6 months.

RHUBARB PUNCH

1 lb. rhubarb, 1 cup water, 1 teaspoon cinnamon, 1¼ cups sugar, ½ cup lemon juice, 1 cup pineapple juice, 1 quart water.

Wash rhubarb and cut in pieces, add cinnamon and 1 cup water and cook for 10 minutes. Strain and add sugar. Chill and add remaining ingredients. Serve with cracked ice. This should make 2 quarts.

Tea (mint) Sparkling (for a party)

9 cups of strong tea, 4½ cups soda water, 1½ cups castor sugar, 2 cups lemon juice, mint, ice. Make tea in usual way, allowing 4 teaspoons tea to 6 cups boiling water. Infuse, then strain. Add sugar, stand until cool. Stir in lemon juice, add soda and serve in tall glass jug with blocks of ice. Put springs of mint on rim of glass and on jug. A few berries, green grapes or slices of orange or lemon may be added to each jug.

Party Glasses

Party glasses for children can be made attractive by first dipping the rims into cold water or lemon juice, then into hundreds and thousands, or castor sugar. Write their names, on them, too, with nail polish.

If making ice cubes to add to drinks for their parties, add coloured cordials to the water.

Radish Accordions

Cut long radishes not quite through in 10 or 12 narrow slices. Chill in ice water, so slices will fan out, accordion style.

Place Cards

Write guests' names on both sides of place cards. Guests can find their places easily, and see who is sitting opposite.

"What I read I forget, what I see I remember, what I do I understand."

"He who eats till he is sick must fast till he is well."

Place Cards

For children's party, try piping their names with icing onto plain biscuits.

Minties

Heat a tablespoon butter, 2 rounded tablespoons sugar, 3 tablespoons golden syrup, until dissolved. Remove from heat, add ½ teaspoon peppermint essence and 1½ cups full cream powdered milk. Beat well. Roll pieces between hands into sausage-like rolls. Twist like barley sugar, cut into lengths. Allow to set.

ROLLED SANDWICHES

Rolled sandwiches are easy to make and look and taste better than ordinary flat triangle sandwiches. Below are suggested fillings for the rolled sandwiches.

Rolled : Cut the crusts from the bread, slice thinly and spread each slice with warmed butter. Spread on filling and roll up with the spread side inside. Place the rolls side by side on a table napkin. Fold firmly round and leave in a cold place until required. The butter will harden and hold the rolls together.

Fillings for rolled or any sandwiches. If for children, spread the filling onto rounds of bread (2 together) and cut out with star cutter or any fancy shape you might have.

- Peanut butter and sweet orange jam on alternate slices, or egg with chopped parsley.
- Mixed chicken moistened with a little parsley sauce.
- Cream cheese with crushed pineapple.
- Vegetable extract spread with lettuce (chopped finely) and walnuts.
- Chopped raisins and cream cheese.
- Sugared banana.
- Thin tomato slices, carefully drained, combined with any shredded cold meat or fish.
- Marmite spread sandwiches, then complete with thin slices of cucumber and salt and pepper to taste.
- Whitebait well drained and mashed, adding lemon juice and pepper to complete.
- Grated cheese and finely chopped celery, moistened with a little mayonnaise.
- Thick white sauce, mixed with flaked, cooked fish flavoured with lemon juice, and a little finely chopped parsley.
- Cheese and finely crushed pineapple.
- Finely minced meat, moistened with tomato juice or sauce.
- Raw carrots and salted peanuts ground together and moistened with salad dressing is very nice as well as being healthful.
- Hard-boiled egg, mixed with a little finely-chopped parsley or mint.
- Marmite and chopped celery.
- Grated apple and chopped celery with mayonnaise.
- Minced cold boiled ham, pork or chicken, moistened with mayonnaise and flavoured with mustard pickle.
- ½ cup honey warmed slightly and beaten with a tablespoon peanut butter. Nicer on brown bread sandwiches.
- Slices of hard-boiled eggs placed on lettuce leaves on white or brown buttered bread, seasoned with salt and pepper.
- Dates, raisins, or crystallised fruits, chopped finely and flavoured with orange juice.

- Honey spread on the buttered bread, then sprinkle with chopped nuts.
- Cream cheese and finely chopped onion.
- Vegemite and slices of banana.
- Golden syrup spread on buttered bread then sprinkle with walnuts.
- Grated cheese and finely chopped celery. Mix together with salt, small pinch cayenne and 2 tablespoons cream or melted butter.
- 2 ozs. liver wurst mixed with 1 oz. grated cheese and 1 small finely chopped hard-boiled egg. Season with pepper and salt. Mix with a tablespoon salad dressing.
- Slices of cheese, lettuce and chutney.
- Spread bread with butter then vegemite, grated apple and Kraft cheese.
- Shredded cabbage, cheese and mayonnaise.
- Cheese, and orange marmalade.
- Peanut butter, grated carrot combined with cheese.
- Grilled bacon and vegemite.
- Sardines mashed with lemon juice and grated cheese.
- Sliced ham and mustard with sliced cheese.
- Chopped dates, peanut butter, sliced cooked meat and vegemite.
- Combine 2 hard-boiled eggs, 1 teaspoon Worcestershire sauce, pinch curry powder and cheese spread.
- Fish paste with chopped lettuce and finely chopped celery.
- Jam or jelly, grated cheese and sultanas.

★ **A novel idea to hold the sweets for the party table is to make a "Bird's Nest" from meringue mixture. Dry out slowly in warm oven. Fill with sweets and if you can, have a couple of china birds sitting on the edge. These are procurable in city and some country stores, so are cotton wool ones that are very life-like.**

* * *

A great favourite of mine, "Where there's a will, there's a way."

Snail Eating

Put a dozen brown snails into a box or bucket with a couple of lettuce leaves. Replace when eaten. A couple of days on this diet ensures that the snails have eaten only healthful food. Now starve them for another 2 days, cleaning out their box regularly. Then, fill a saucepan with water, add a tablespoon salt and a pinch of herbs. Bring to boil. When water has reached 100° C drop snails in. Cook 15 minutes, then eat.

SECTION 35—

PARTY FOODS, HINTS AND GAMES (CHILDREN'S)

IDEAS FOR CHILDREN'S BIRTHDAY CAKES

● For a novel top to your child's birthday cake, ice in usual way, then place an animal-shaped biscuit cutter on centre and sprinkle in 100's and 1000's. Pipe around cutter with another coloured icing, then remove cutter carefully.

● When making the birthday cake for a tiny, use alphabet mararoni. Dye the letters (that you require to spell child's name, etc.) in a saucer with food colouring. Let dry. Easy, cheap, effective and edible.

RECORD CAKE

Make an ordinary sandwich cake, not too deep. Ice with chocolate icing—all but a circle in centre of cake. On a piece of white circular cardboard draw some music notes and HAPPY BIRTHDAY. Lay it carefully on cake where you haven't iced. Mark grooves of record with a fork.

CLOCK CAKE

Again make a sandwich cake. Ice all over with white icing. Lay a saucepan lid on top of cake then cover the sides with chocolate sprinkles. Remove lid. Cut numerals, watch-hands from licorice; put in place on cake, one hand on XII and the other on the childs age.

HUMPTY DUMPTY

Make a cake in a loaf tin, ice with chocolate icing, stand cake on a board sprinkled with green coconut. Mark into brick shapes with a match box case. (Make sure you remove the phosphorus sides first.) Dip match box in cocoa so it does not stick to icing. Blow contents from a fresh egg, rinse out, paint on features, put in position on cake and add pipe cleaners for legs with coloured sweets for boots, bow tie and hat. A circular jube with a short length of licorice pushed into it makes a good hat. They also make good flowers to adorn sides.

MAYPOLE CAKE

Make a round cake, ice, decorate edge of top with coloured flat lollies. Cover a skewer with aluminium foil; push it down the centre of top, secure lengths of ribbon to top of skewer and into hands of tiny dolls standing around cake base. The cake can stand on a board covered with icing and sprinkled with green coconut.

UTILITY TRUCK

Make two loaf cakes. Cut one up to use as cabin. Place on top of the uncut one and ice all over. With a different coloured icing, ice two oblong biscuits and press on to cabin for doors. Outline a window with silver cachous and use one as door handle. Round chocolate biscuits make good wheels, and use jubes for lights.

FLOWERPOT

Make a cake in a pudding basin. Cover with icing, and whilst still wet cover sides with popcorn. Sprinkle top with cocoa to represent earth, and push flowers into top made from jubes and toothpicks. Stand in a dessert dish.

FARMYARD CAKE

Make a round cake, ice top and sides. Sprinkle green coconut on top, and press chocolate biscuit sticks around the side to represent a fence. Leave an opening for a gate and buy animals and gate at a variety store and decorate top.

BUTTERFLY CAKE

Make a large slab cake or two smaller ones. Cut out butterfly wings on paper first, then lay on cake and cut around paper with a sharp knife. Ice all over with pale yellow icing, then, with melted chocolate in a plastic bag with one corner out, pipe lines of chocolate down length of wings about 1 inch apart. Using a knife, and working from centre of wing, draw knife across chocolate one way, then come back the other way, working on an angle. This must be done quickly before chocolate sets. Use pipe cleaners, curled, for feelers.

Games at the Party

TREASURE HUNT

Plant peanuts in various places in a backyard, paddock, or lawn, or even in the lounge room (if an adult keeps her eye on the children). This is a good game for when the children arrive; it helps them to mix and get to know each other, and it will help the party to get off to a good start. Hide the peanuts along the fences, under hedges, stones—just anywhere. For the one who collects the most, give a small prize. You will know if they have all been found or not by just counting the peanuts.

HAPPY BIRTHDAY (for the Tinies)

All children sit around in a circle. One child is blindfolded and sits in the centre and points to a child, who says, 'Happy Birthday'. The blindfolded child must guess the name of the child who spoke. He is allowed three guesses, and if he fails he must point to someone else. If, of course, he guesses who has spoken, that child goes into the centre and is blindfolded and turned around three times by an adult before allowed to sit down and point to one in the circle and repeat 'Happy Birthday'.

MATCHBOX RELAY

Two teams face each other in rows. The first person in each row places the cover part of an ordinary matchbox over his or her nose. At a given signal he must transfer it to the next player's nose without touching it with his hands. If the box falls to the ground he can replace it on his own nose and start again. The team which manages to get its match box on to the last player's nose is the winner. Sweets could be given to each of the winning team.

WHEELBARROW RACE

One competitor in each pair becomes the wheelbarrow and must run on his hands while his partner propels him by the ankles. The wheelbarrows are lined up, and at a given signal, begin to race towards a finishing line about 30 yards away. Give a prize to the winner.

MUSICAL BALLOONS

This is another version of musical chairs, but this game can be played in a much smaller space. Music and a balloon is all that is needed. Players stand in a circle and blow the balloon to each other. The balloon must be held in cupped hands. When the music stops the player caught with the balloon is out.

PING-PONG RACE

Divide the children into two teams. Give each leader a ping-pong ball and a teaspoon. The leader from each team carries the teaspoon with the ball placed in it, to the end of the room and back, then hands it to the next in line, and so on, until one team is finished first. If the player drops the ball he or she must return 'home' and start again. The ball is very light, so it is best to walk slowly and gently. A good idea for a prize for the winning team is a packet of sweets.

NOSEY PARKER

Have a number of small lawn bags made. Put coffee, pepper, cinnamon, spice, ginger, tea, etc., in them. Number each bag 1 to 12, or how many you have. Give players pencil and papers and let them write down what they think is in each bag after they have smelt them. Rice, sago, tea, pearl barley, etc., could also be used in bags another time, and let the players feel this time, instead of smelling. The one who gets the most right, of course, is the winner.

The best place to find a helping hand is at the end of your own arm.

* * *

25

Children's Party Cakes, Games and Hints

POPCORN PARTY CAKE

6 ozs. butter, 6 ozs. sugar, 1 teaspoon grated orange rind, 3 eggs, 3 cups S.R. flour, about ¾ cup milk.

Cream butter and sugar with the orange rind. Add eggs one at a time, beating well. Sift flour and salt and add alternately with milk to make a fairly soft mixture. Place in a well greased square tin and bake in moderate oven for 45 minutes. When cold cover with icing.

Icing: 2 tablespoons butter, 12 ozs. icing sugar, milk, green colouring, popcorns. Cream butter with as much of the icing sugar as it will take. Soften with a little milk, and add remaining sugar. Color pale green. Cover the top and sides with the icing, using a knife dipped in hot water to give a smooth surface. Cover the sides only with popcorns and write the child's name in popcorns on the top.

P.S.—A Dolly Varden cake idea suitable for a young girl's party is to be found in Icings. Make the cake itself from the madeira cake recipe.

WITCHES' HATS

Make a batch of round biscuits (about 3 inches in diameter). When cold ice with different coloured icings. Before icing sets stick small sized ice cream cones on the biscuits. Sprinkle "brims" with hundreds and thousands. Cones may be filled with set jelly or whipped cream first.

A TRAIN BIRTHDAY CAKE

Boys love a "Special" birthday cake and this as a centre-piece, was a great favourite with my two sons when they were small. Their cake was always a top secret until the very moment the party was on. As their birthdays both fell on the 20th January, the one cake (until they were in their teens) did the two boys.

The engine of the cake I made from Madeira cake recipe in a nut loaf tin, iced with chocolate icing. Ice the funnel also in chocolate icing. This can be made from a large cotton reel, or from the cardboard inside the large spools of cotton bought at any chain store. Cotton wool acts as smoke. The tender, trucks, guard's van, etc., can be made from one square of plain cake, cut into oblong pieces. Ice each a different shade. Plain, round biscuits iced, will make the wheels and put on the train with tooth picks. Join sections together with 2 tooth picks. The boy's name can be iced on the front of the engine if desired. "Logs" may be stacked on one carriage by cutting some tiny lengths of raspberry canes (dried) or other wood—washed, of course. Tyres off a dinky toy (washed) can be piled on another to make it more realistic. Cover a piece of plywood with tissue paper and put the "train" cake in the centre of your table.

DOLLY VARDON CAKE

To make a Dolly Varden cake, cook the cake first in a basin. When cold, cover with almond paste, then plastic, a small doll sawn in two sits on top of the cake, then make an apron and top of dress from the plastic icing coloured blue, also a bonnet; decorate around hem of dress, apron and bonnet with flowers made from water-lily paste. These icings can be found in Section 26.

MERRY-GO ROUND CAKE

Make two cakes in two 8-inch cake tins (not sandwich tins). When cooked and cold (preferably next day) trim top of one cake to a dome shape for top of merry-go-round, level top of second cake to make a flat surface. Cover both cakes with fondant icing.

Fondant Icing : Sift 2 lbs. icing sugar into a basin, make a well in the centre and drop in two unbeaten egg-whites, 2 tablespoons melted glucose and ½ teaspoon vanilla. Work icing-sugar in from the sides until a smooth paste is formed. Turn onto a board dusted with icing sugar. Knead until sufficient icing sugar is absorbed for mixture to hold its shape on the hand. Add dabs of colouring (blue or green) and knead until evenly coloured. Divide into two. Roll each portion ¼-inch thick. Brush both cakes with egg-white, place icing on cakes and mould over with hands dusted with icing sugar. Trim edges, stand cakes overnight.

To Decorate : Cut out a coloured picture of a circus and paste it around an empty condensed milk tin. Place the tin in the centre of the flat-topped cake. Carefully stand dome-topped cake on top. Cut three candy sticks to required length and arrange around edge of cake, resting on the lower cake, and with the top cake resting lightly on top of the sticks. Arrange tiny toy horses around bottom layer of cake. Decorate top and sides of upper cake and sides only of lower cake with rossettes from icing bag. Birthday candles may be pressed into icing on top of the "merry-go-round".

Trees in Tubs :

Buy some ice cream cones. Make some jellies and when at the setting stage, pour into cones. Stand cones upwards in a cake cooler to set. Pour made jelly into small moulds also to set, and for serving in. (Peanut butter jars are excellent). Get some fairly long tooth picks or clean sticks, push one end in the cones of jelly. Have some jelly almost set, dip cones in it, covering all. Dip into hundreds and thousands and put away to set once again. When set, push stick down into "tub" of jelly. Will look like miniature trees.

TINIES CAKE DECORATION
(Cheap)

When making the birthday cake for a tiny, use alphabet Macaroni, now on the market. Dye the letters that you require to spell child's name, etc., in a saucer with food colouring. Let dry. Easy, effective and edible.

"FUNNY FACE" CAKE

Sponge Mixture :

4 eggs, $\frac{3}{4}$ cup flour, 1 teaspoon cream of tartar, 1 oz. butter, $\frac{3}{4}$ cup sugar, 1 tablespoons cornflour, $\frac{1}{2}$ teaspoon soda, 1 tablespoon milk.

Separate whites from yolks. Beat whites until stiff. Beat in yolks till light and creamy, then add sugar. Beat for $\frac{1}{4}$ of an hour. Sift in flour, cornflour and cream of tartar which has been sifted three times with pinch of salt. Fold into eggs very lightly. Melt butter in boiling milk. Add soda and stir into mixture. Add flavouring. Pour into 2 well greased and floured sandwich tins. Bake 20 minutes in hot oven. When cold put together with cream. Ice top with white or pale pink icing. Place 2 crystallised cherries on cake for eyes. Push a silver cachou into centre. Smaller pieces add to cake for nose and 2 lolly red jubes (half moon shape) place together for mouth. Cut two eye brows from another jube and place in position and your Face Cake will be ready for eating.

HONOLULU FROST

1 shredded pineapple, $\frac{3}{4}$ cup sugar, 2 cups water, $\frac{1}{3}$ cup lemon juice, $\frac{1}{2}$ cup orange juice, 2 bottles ginger ale, crushed ice.

Boil pineapple with sugar and water for 10 minutes. More sugar can be added if pineapple is not sweet and ripe. Add lemon and orange juices, chill. Just before serving, dilute with chilled ginger ale, and add crushed ice.

BOSTON CREAM

Boil 1 lb. sugar and a quart of water for half an hour then strain through muslin. Leave until cold, then add 1 oz. tartaric acid, crushed evenly, and 6 drops of lemon essence. Beat whites of 2 eggs to a stiff froth and stir altogether until dissolved. Pour into bottles. This cream will keep for 2 to 3 months. When using, add water and a pinch of carb. soda to make it fizz.

MOTHER'S DAY POSY CAKE

12 ozs. flour, 1 teaspoon cream of tartar, $\frac{1}{2}$ teaspoon carb. soda, pinch salt, 3 eggs, 4 ozs. crystallised cherries, 4 ozs. walnuts, 8 ozs. castor sugar, 8 ozs. butter, 1 gill milk, essence.

Cream butter and sugar, add eggs, one at a time beating in well, add 3 table-spoon of sifted flour with last egg to prevent curdling. Add milk gradually, then essence. Mix well. Mix in lightly half the flour, then lastly, flour that is remaining, cherries and walnuts, all at once. Place in a round, well greased tin and bake in moderate oven for $1\frac{1}{2}$ hours. When quite cold, ice with the following icing : 2 cups sifted icing sugar, 1 dessertspoon melted butter, 3 dessertspoons hot water, $\frac{1}{2}$ teaspoon vanilla, green colouring. Place sifted icing sugar in small saucepan. Add melted butter and hot water. Mix to a smooth paste. Add vanilla and green colouring. Warm over low heat to pouring consistency. Cover cake smoothly with a flexible knife dipped in hot water. Allow to set. Cut the centre from a gold or silver doyley. Place on top of cake, press down lightly. Decorate with small artificial flowers shaped into a posy (stalks cut short) by placing it in centre of doyley. Make a bunched bow with ribbon and complete decoration by fastening to cake with straight pin.

EASTER EGG SWEETS

2 cups sugar, 1½ cups water, 1 tablespoon gelatine, 1 egg-white.

Boil sugar and one cup of the water for 3 minutes. Meanwhile, put the gelatine into the other ½ cup of water and soak. When soaked, add to syrup and whip until slightly cool. Add stiffly beaten egg-white and some vanilla essence. Continue beating until thick. Pour into egg cups or gemscone tray to set. When set, stick two together and roll in coconut.

JELLY EASTER EGGS

Carefully make a hole in top of some empty egg-shells. Make some coloured jellies, using a little less water than usual. When cool, fill each shell with jelly. Stand in an egg carton to set. Carefully chip off shell when set, toss in coloured coconut and pile on a dish.

One must be poor to know the luxury of giving.

* * *

There is no substitute for talent.

* * *

Politeness costs nothing and gains everything.

* * *

Everything in the world is good for something.

* * *

Don't judge a day by its weather.

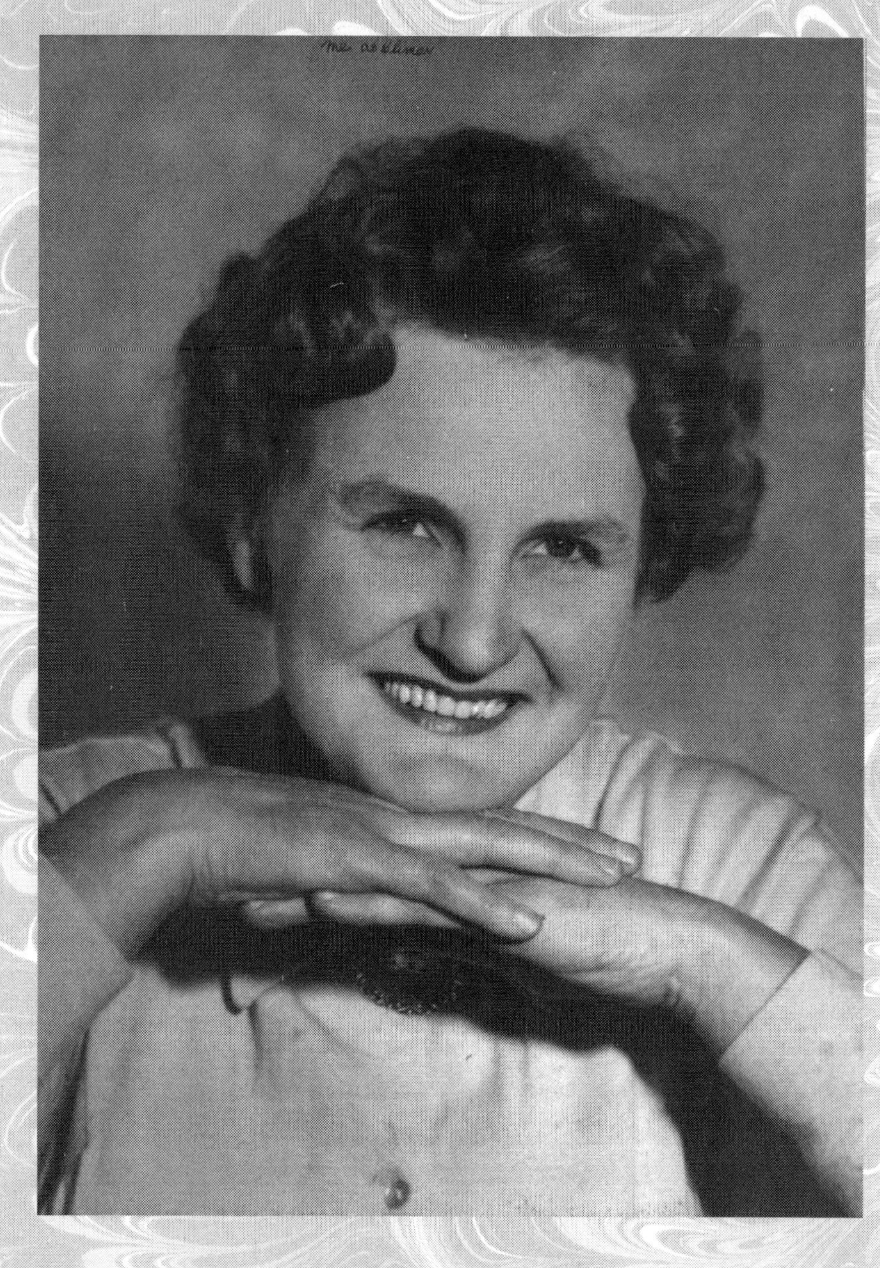

One of Marjorie's favourite pictures of herself, taken at her Campbell Town home, Climar, in the 1950s.

4. HEALTH & TEMPER

Like many who encounter Marjorie's old-style health tips and remedies, the Tasmanian gay rights activist and Marjorie Bligh aficionado Rodney Croome raised a sceptical eyebrow at her tip for keeping her boys safe from whooping cough by placing slices of garlic inside their socks. But one of his friends brought that eyebrow back into line, saying: 'Rodney, you do realise that chemists charge heaps for little bags of herbs that are meant to keep you healthy by being put in your socks?'

He didn't—but he checked, and his friend was right. These days you can even buy 'therapy socks', their fabric impregnated with health-giving herbs and oils. While some of Marjorie's health tips are outmoded, one newspaper columnist of today agrees, some of her tips from earlier days are 'prescient', such as eating gelatine (protein) to take the edge off your appetite, or using a fruit enzyme—in Marjorie's tip, tomato pulp—to brighten up dull or oily skin.

Though Marjorie has advised her readers on everything from

biliousness to bruises, chicken pox to chilblains, hangover cures to whooping cough, sunburn to splinters, it's probably best to take any of her medical advice with a liberal pinch of salt.

—•—

DR BOB BROWN, ENVIRONMENTALIST

'Marjorie not only offers a wonderful tip on how to use a pipe cleaner to protect the labels on bottles, she also makes lemon juice an essential ingredient for dealing with a hangover. Lemon juice just on its own will help.

One-time GP Bob Brown knows there's a treasure trove of old-fashioned remedies in the pages of Marjorie Bligh's books. And he's used to taking advice from women called Marjorie: it was his mother's name, too.

'As a doctor in London in 1970, I came across the simple mouth-cleaning wizardry of lemon juice, not least for old folk with thinning jaws, loose dentures or sore gums which made tooth brushing out of the question. A quick swish with a teaspoon of lemon juice does wonders. Your mouth is suddenly clean and fresh again (though don't try this too much, or too often, as lemon juice is acidic and can do more than shine your enamel).

'That done, you can once again really enjoy a slice of Marjorie's husband's favourite sponge cake, in which lemon juice is the ingredient of success!'

Bottles (medicine)

To catch drips and keep label clean, twist a pipe cleaner around neck of bottle.

'Hangover' Cure

Half teaspoon Worcestershire sauce, pinch salt, squeeze lemon juice and one egg. Put all in glass (don't beat egg), close your eyes and down it in one gulp! Or, use a mixture of ascorbic acid (Vitamin C) and fructose (apple juice). Lemons can be used for the same purpose without any added vitamin supplementation.

—*M.B.*

* * *

Who lives medically, lives miserably.

* * *

Health Hints

- **Sunburn** will be reduced when gardening or playing sport if you rub your face, neck and arms with equal parts of water and vinegar.
- **Warts :** Try applying a mixture of kerosene, lemon juice and castor oil, 3 times a day for a week.
- **Clean combs and brushes** easily, by adding 1 tablespoon of ammonia to a quart of water and soaking them in it for 10 minutes.
- **A tube of shaving cream** is easier to carry and handle when travelling from place to place, instead of a cake of soap.
- **To prevent blistered heels** when going without stockings, rub your damp heel with a cake of laundry soap.
- **For rough hands** rub all over with dripping, then rub a teaspoon of sugar well over the dripping also. Massage back and front for a few minutes, then wash off with soap and hot water.
- **Sore throat and coughs** can be relieved by mixing equal parts of honey, olive oil, glycerine and lemon juice. Take every half hour.
- **Sore gums and toothache** can be eased by carbonate soda. Put some under the plate for sore gums, or on cottonwool and push into hole of tooth and leave, for toothache. Rinse mouth with carb. soda diluted in water is also good.
- **Cough cures :** A handful of sage boiled with a little water, then pour onto the juice of three lemons, and 1 cup of honey is excellent. Take in teaspoons.
- **Cough mixture for your child :** Beat the white of one large egg, add 1 tablespoon of honey, 1 teaspoon olive oil, and the juice of a lemon. Keep in a warm place and shake well before giving one teaspoon when cough is troublesome. (1 teaspoon honey and 1 teaspoon lemon juice mixed is also good).
- **Pimple cure :** 3 tablespoons treacle, 2 teaspoons sulphur mixed together. Take 1 teaspoon after each meal.
- **Easy way to take castor oil :** Squeeze the juice of an orange into a glass, add the castor oil, and stir in a little bi-carbonate soda. Drink while frothing.
- **Mosquito or spider bites** can be rubbed with vinegar to alleviate.
- **If your finger nails** are brittle, drink a teaspoon of gelatine dissolved in hot water every morning, and rub castor oil well into the cuticles every night. Nails will grow long and strong.
- **A teaspoon of carb. soda** to a cup of cold water acts as an effective underarm deodorant. Dry thoroughly, then dust with talc powder.

Biliousness

The juice of a lemon, ½ teaspoon bicarbonate of soda mixed with two tablespoons of warm water.

Bruising

Pain on elbows or knees can be relieved by making a paste of vinegar and oatmeal and spreading it thickly on bruise and keep on overnight (or for at least an hour or two), or apply a bandage dipped in cold water to which has been added methylated spirit — 1 tablespoon to 1½ cups water. Renew every few hours. A rag soaked in vinegar is also good.

Chicken Pox

Bathe in water to which some bicarbonate of soda has been added.

Chilblain Liniment

Beat an egg, add 1½ cups vinegar, 1 tablespoon of mineral turpentine, 15g (½ oz.) methylated spirit, 15g (½oz.) camphor. Bottle, and shake for 10 minutes. Keep tightly corked. Apply to affected parts but not if skin is broken.

Start treating your fingers and toes before the cold weather sets in. Make up a solution of equal parts of lemon juice, glycerine and Eau de Cologne. Blend well and rub this into your toes and fingers at least twice a day.

Chilblains

An old wives' remedy — soak them in water in which unpeeled potatoes have been boiled. Other hints are — to mix equal parts of milk and turpentine and apply frequently to the affected parts, but not if they are broken. Or, mix together a white of egg, a tablespoon each of eucalyptus, kerosene and turpentine and apply. Take vitamin C and K.

Or you can try whiting mixed to a paste, or, ½ teaspoon of bicarbonate of soda mixed to a paste with a teaspoon of vinegar. Another method is to rub the affected parts with a cut onion. Do not remove skin of onion. Repeat until cured.

Honey as a compress soothes.

To relieve the irritation and inflammation of chilblains on the feet, paint with tincture of iodine, but never when the feet are damp, e.g., after a shower or bath. Repeat until they disappear.

"The living need charity more than the dead."

Circulation

A pinch of cayenne pepper taken every day helps circulation.

Colds

Eat onions and garlic and it prevents colds. If you feel a cold coming on, dissolve one teaspoon bicarbonate soda in a teacup of warm water and drink every four hours. Pineapple, tinned or fresh, contains all the properties which enable you to resist colds. Black currant syrup is also good for a cold. To every cup of fruit, put ½ cup each of sugar and water. Boil 15 minutes, then strain. Whilst boiling, mash fruit as much as possible. Lemon juice is also good.

Try this in place of the usual aspirin and hot lemon drink routine for colds.

Cut into an orange (not right through) to form a lid.

Place a dessertspoon of honey inside and bake until orange is heated.

It is marvellous at bedtime.

Friar's Balsam is also good, when you feel a cold coming on, or have blocked nostrils. Put some in boiling water. Place a towel over your head and inhale vapour. Friar's Balsam is an alcoholic solution of benzoin, styrax, tolu balsam and aloes. It is also good for wounds and ulcers. Keep a cut up onion (raw) near your bed so fumes are inhaled during sleep.

Cold Sores

Dab with eau de Cologne or perfume, when you first notice one, or, put on some plain yoghurt if it is already there.

Cough Mixture

Mix together 2 teaspoons each of olive oil, glycerine and honey with 4 teaspoons of orange juice. Shake before using. (For babies, ½ teaspoon four-hourly) or,

Equal quantities of rum and olive oil mixed together. A dessertspoon every two hours is correct dose.

Cough Stopper

My mother stopped our coughing at night, by roasting an onion before an open fire (leave skin on), turning it often. Then, with two forks, the centre was pulled out, topped with homemade butter and served.

"A cold is both positive and negative ; sometimes the Eyes have it and sometimes the Nose."

Dandruff

Can be cured by washing hair in following :—Boil some lemon leaves in 3 cups of water. Simmer until 1½ cups liquid is left. Strain into a dish of warm water, then wash your hair. Do once a week, until hair is free of dandruff, or mix equal parts of cider vinegar and water and apply to scalp between shampoos.

Dandruff Deterrent

Boil a couple of sprigs of rosemary in 5 cups of water, strain, and after washing and rinsing your hair, give a final rinse with the rosemary water.

Dandruff or Dry Hair

Mix equal parts of lemon juice and olive together and rub into scalp and leave overnight.

Dandruff Tonic

Mix half a litre each of bay rum and rain water, plus one teaspoon of salt. Shake before using each night.

Deodorant Cream

Mix 2 teaspoons of bicarbonate of soda with 2 teaspoons of petroleum jelly, and 2 teaspoons of talcum powder. Melt over low heat, and stir till a smooth cream forms.

Diarrhea Cure

If a plain junket tablet is taken as a tablet (crushed) with a little water to wash it down, it will be effective. A plain unsweetened junket made with half the quantity of milk advised can be eaten at the next meal ; or,

Dilute a teaspoon of vinegar in some water and drink it, or eat grated apple ; or, drink hot water off cooked carrots at meal times.

Separate the white from the yolk of a newly laid egg. Beat until stiff, then add a cup of cold water. Leave for an hour to give the white time to dissolve. Drink a small cup at a time. Add a pinch of salt or dash of lemon juice to improve taste if you like, or,

Boil some lemonade, cool and drink.

In India they take nutmeg for diarrhea. Mother gave us bananas to eat.

This is Bishop Nixon's cure: mix equal parts of laudanum peppermint and Sal Volatile (Sal means salt). Take ¼ to ½ teaspooon in ½ cup of water.

When Diarrhea Strikes: Guidlines in Treating Children

Do not stop feeding: Fluids should be given. Tea, rice water, barley water, and soups are beneficial. Have drinking water available. Keep giving breast milk to nursing babies. Meals should be given as soon as the child can eat. Small but frequent meals, however, are best. Easily digested, energy-rich foods such as cooked cereals and bananas are good.

Feet Tired

Put ½ cup Epsom salts in 2 litres warm water. Soak feet 15 minutes, dry and rub with Eau de Cologne, or, dissolve a cake of camphor in about a cup of methylated spirit and rub on feet night and morning.

Finger (hit by hammer)

Put immediately in some vinegar. Leave till pain ceases.

Fish Bone in Throat

If in throat beyond reach swallow at once the white of an egg, and it will generally carry down the offending bone ; or,

Cut a lemon in half and suck the juice very slowly. This will soften the bone and give relief until a doctor is available.

"There are more fish taken out of a stream than ever were put in it."

Fits (and Convulsions)

Do not attempt to restrain fits. Place victim on floor away from furniture ; if possible put rolled handkerchief between teeth to prevent biting of tongue. If a fever is present, apply cold compresses to face and neck. Turn head on side to allow saliva to drain. Loosen tight clothing at neck, chest and waist. Keep warm, call doctor. See also convulsions.

Freckle Lotion

Equal parts honey, lemon juice and Eau de Cologne.

Garlic

Reduces cholesterol levels in the blood-stream and is excellent for the circulatory system. Garlic rubbed on ringworm, three times daily will heal in a little over a week, and it takes three weeks to heal when treated with tolnaftate solution.

Garlic (for infection)

Putting slices in your socks is an ancient way of protecting against infection..

Garlic Ointment

Cut desired amount of garlic into slices and bruise well. Put into a jar with clarified lard to cover and stand in pan of boiling water for 2 hours. Stir well, but do not strain.

Gout

Celery can ease gout, because it is highly alkaline and a remarkably powerful solvent of three harmful acids — oxalic, uric and butyric. When present in crystal forms in the body those acids cause most rheumatic and gout complaints. Celery is also good for nerve disorders. Cherries are also good for gout. Also, drink a glass twice a day of the following: Macerate 100g (4 oz.) onion (chopped) in 6 cups of white wine for 48 hours. Add a tablespoon of honey.

Face Mask

Halt the formation of excess oil on the skin, if only by cleaning the skin deeper than soap and water can reach. Try mixing a teaspoon or so of brewer's yeast with enough plain yoghurt or milk to make a loose, thin mixture. Pat this thoroughly into all the oily areas of the face. Allow to dry and remain on face 15 minutes. Rinse with warm, then cool, water. Blot dry ; or,

Wear a fruit mask made of soft pulpy fruit, to correct a variety of complexion ills. A fresh ripe pear is a helpful mask for an acne condition. Watermelon offers instant stimulation and many in America claim it can remove fine-line wrinkles.

"When the drink is in, the wit is out!"

Headache

Firstly find out the cause ; meanwhile relieve it with one of these remedies :— Drink a cup of black coffee (without sugar or milk) to which has been added the juice of half a lemon. Seldom fails. Or, drink a hot, sugarless, cup of black tea, flavoured with 2 whole cloves.

"Chip on shoulder — too much wood in head."

Headache (Migraine)

Take one teaspoon of honey dissolved in a small glass of warm water every morning. A hint tried by a friend and proved good ; or, lie down with a cloth wrung out in vinegar on your forehead. Keep a bottle in the refrigerator for this purpose, as the colder it is the better it "works". Sliced onion works the same.

In the British Medical Journal, 1988, it mentioned that the herb Feverfew (Chrysanthemum parthenium) was affective in treating migraine headache and arthritic inflammations. More than a century ago, the mother of Sir William Bowyer suffered for years with migraine headaches. Doctors couldn't help her, but a servant crumbled dried Feverfew leaves in her foods and soon the headaches disappeared.

Feverfew is a wonderful herb. See what I have written about it in the 2nd edition of the "Marjorie Bligh's A—Z book on gardening", as it is not only cures a headache.

Influenza Remedy

Here is an old-fashioned 'flu remedy: Cover a layer of finely chopped white onions with a layer of brown sugar. Continue this until a basin is full. Let stand an hour, then sip the juice—2 or 3 teaspoons every 2 hours. Keep basin covered in a warm place.

Splinters

Tape a slice of onion to the skin and the splinter can be easily removed the following day, or, apply kerosene, or,

Hold a piece of ice against the affected area to numb it first, especially good for a child.

To take a deep splinter out, mix equal parts of castor oil and boracic acid to a paste. Put it on lint and wrap up the part. In the morning it will be near the surface. Repeat if very deep (or mix flour with castor oil). To remove from under your nail soak a cloth in peroxide and tie the soaked cloth around that finger (pour a little peroxide under nail first). You should be able to remove splinter in a few hours, or, (mother's recipe) —

Draw it to the surface by making a poultice of crushed soap and sugar mixed together. Apply to wound overnight.

Stinging Nettle Relief

Rub part with rosemary, mint, sage leaves, or dock leaves.

"It's one thing to itch for something, and another thing to scratch for it."

Stomach (feels woozy)

Combine 1 teaspoon bicarbonate of soda, squeeze of lemon juice in a glass of warm water.

Sunburn

Sunburn can be relieved by bathing the face in this mixture :— Cut a cucumber into slices. Stand in a tumbler of milk. Bathe face with the milk, then gently rub with a slice of cucumber, or put on refrigerated mayonnaise for 15 minutes.

Mix equal parts of lemon juice and oatmeal and cover the affected parts the same night after you've been burnt. Leave until dry. Wash off with buttermilk and apply cold cream.

Tea will take the sting out of sunburn. Wring out a cloth in cold tea and apply to the area, or rub with a freshly cut tomato.

If all over body, pour a cupful of bicarbonate of soda or 2 tablespoons olive oil into the bath of cool water and soak in it. If only on back or arms, mix 4 tablespoons to 1¼ cups water, and pat on parts that are burned.

Rub sunburn (or cuts) with Calendula (Marigold) and they will heal quickly. Sunburn peeling is then prevented.

Laundry starch is a soother for a sunburned skin ; or, rub on a mixture of 2 tablespoons each of honey, glycerine and lemon juice, and 1 tablespoon alcohol, or, use evaporated milk, neat on the sunburn.

But the best plan of all is NOT to get sunburnt, and so prevent skin cancer.

"God bless the fools — but for them, none of us would succeed."

Teeth

Eat an apple after a meal and it not only cleans your teeth, but actually helps to preserve the body's store of calcium. To remove tartar, rinse mouth with diluted vinegar before brushing. Equal parts of salt and bicarbonate of soda also cleans teeth, as do sage leaves. If teeth are discoloured, dissolve 1 teaspoon each of peroxide and bicarbonate of soda in 4 teaspoons of water and soak teeth (false) in them.

Throat (Sore)

Slice 2 lemons and place in a jug. Add 1 tablespoon black currant jam and sugar to taste. Then pour over these ingredients 3 cups boiling water. Strain and drink. This gives quick relief ; or

Blend an equal part of lemon juice, honey and glycerine together and sip when required. Good for coughs, too. Or equal parts of lemon juice, honey, olive oil and glycerine mixed, or, boil the juice of a lemon, 1 cup honey and 30g glycerine for 10 minutes. Take 1 teaspoon three times a day. You can also soak a washer in ice cold water, wrap around neck, then wind a woollen scarf over the top and leave on all night.

Thrush

Plain yoghurt is very good.

Toe Nail (ingrowing)

Always cut nail level — not rounded — and pack a piece of cotton wool between the nail and fold of overhanging skin. Change frequently and wear properly fitting shoes.

Toes

After washing and drying thoroughly inbetween, dab some cottonwool into methylated spirit and rub between toes to finish the drying process. Do not use powder.

Toothache

Take 1 small teaspoon of bicarbonate of soda dissolved in a cup of boiling water. When cool enough wash out the mouth. Oil of cloves eases an aching tooth also.

Voice (loss of)

For loss of voice try (mixed together) ½ cup of cider vinegar, 1 lb. brown sugar and a beaten fresh egg. Put it in a basin in a hot oven for 2 hours, cool, then take a teaspoon 2 or 3 times a day. (Stand the basin in a dish of water, as you would a custard.)

Weight Watching

If you take 2 teaspoons of gelatine in chilled fruit juice, half an hour before a meal, you will find it a superb appetite depressant. Gelatine does not actually make you lose weight, but because of its high protein content it has a satisfying effect on a large appetite, and so weight is lost due to the smaller intake of food.

"Overweight is not actually a problem of old age, as fat people seldom live that long."

Warts Cure

Put banana skin on them, white side down, and leave for several days, or until they go away, or,

Warts disappear in 3 months if you rub them with castor oil before going to bed, or daub them with kerosene every day, or with a slice of garlic, or with 1 tablespoon of bicarbonate of soda dissolved in 2 tablespoons of water. Another hint is to melt a small piece of washing soda in vinegar and daub warts several times a day. I had them as a child and my mother told me to lick them on awakening and one morning they weren't there. Another sure cure is to put the juice from a dandelion root on them, or lay a slice on them and cover with a band-aid ; or, equal parts of discoloured iodine and castor oil mixed together. The latter cleans up boils too.

"Correction does much, but encouragement does more."

Watch Winder

If you have arthritis and find that even winding your watch is painful, save your empty ballpoint pen, withdraw cartridge, then cut, or get someone to cut, the narrow end to fit your watch holder. The pen will be easier to hold than trying to grapple with the tiny winder.

Whooping Cough

When whooping cough was raging in Campbell Town, when my two sons, Gerald and Ross, were chldren, they escaped it because I put slices of garlic on the soles of their feet (inside their socks), renewing it as the juice left it. In a few days, their breath smelt of garlic. It is a powerful cure of all manner of things.

Though it's not like her to settle for second best, Marjorie was perfectly proud when named runner-up Tasmanian of the Year for 1989.

5. COMMONSENSE HINTS

Like Voltaire before her, Marjorie Bligh reached the conclusion that commonsense is not especially common. During the decades when her advice column 'Tried and True Hints' appeared in the north-west Tasmanian newspaper the *Advocate*, Marjorie became the go-to girl for people in the midst of crises of home economics, and their phone calls often left her shaking her head.

What should I do, one caller asked, if I've put too much salt in the casserole? Well, obviously—Marjorie replied—you should divide the casserole in two, put more food in each half, and *don't add any more salt*!

What should I do, another caller enquired, if my son's new school shoes are too big for him? Well, obviously—Marjorie replied—you should stuff the toes with newspaper and wait until his feet grow.

But if Marjorie often provided straightforward ways to solve common enough problems, she also developed smart solutions for everyday irritations that many people would accept as unavoidable.

Thanks to Marjorie's commonsense brilliance, there's no need to put up with spectacles that slip down your nose on a hot day.

She can recommend a way of making sure you don't leave your perishables in your friend's fridge if you store them there while visiting after shopping.

You needn't tolerate the irritating ticking of your otherwise beautiful clock, nor suffer the exertions of manually blowing up a party's worth of balloons.

'Judging by your letters to me and verbal remarks,' Marjorie has written, 'I think you think that I am a sort of freak, a dictionary or a doctor—somebody who knows all the answers, but…I am only an ordinary person who has taught myself and learnt from my own and others' mistakes.'

—•—

There's no place like home: Marjorie celebrated her island home by writing Tasmania and Beyond *and was rewarded with a Bicentennial medallion.*

Baking Powder Test

If you think it is stale, put a teaspoon in hot water. If it bubbles it is O.K.

"A modern husband is a do-it-yourself man with a get-it-done wife."

Balloons

To blow up a large number of balloons, put the vacuum cleaner hose on the blowing end of the machine.

Bathing Hint

Powder yourself in the bath and save yourself from always dusting that room.

"Grecian ladies counted their age from their marriage not from their birth."

Beach Comfort

Pack all your beach gear and food in a shopping jeep if you walk to and from the beach. Saves carrying and lost gear.

Bed Table Substitute

Use the ironing board if someone is sick in bed. Ideal for meals, books and so on. Height can be adjusted and the sloping legs fit under the bed.

Biscuits Burnt

If your oven burns the bottoms of biscuits (or cakes), grate the burnt part off with the vegetable grater ; makes a neater job.

"Learn from the mistakes of others...you can't live long enough to make them all yourself."

Blistered Heels

To prevent blistered heels when going without stockings, rub your damp heel with a cake of laundry soap.

Bottle Top Tight

Try gripping the lid of the jar with a piece of coarse sandpaper.

Above: In the 1940s, as Mrs Blackwell, Marjorie aimed to be the perfect wife, mother and housewife.

Left: Marjorie has always been the architect and builder of a unique self-image.

Right: Marjorie was fond of using the banner from her Advocate *newspaper hints column, along with other magazine clippings, to brighten up the covers of her many notebooks. Photo by Gillian Ward.*

Below: Featuring seventy-eight eleven-inch squares, this knitted blanket dates from the late 1960s, when Marjorie and her second husband, Adrian, lived in the tiny northwest Tasmanian town of Redpa. Each square has a motif knitted in, or embroidered on later; and among the images are some of Marjorie's favourite pets, a map of Tasmania, and an image of lovebirds named Marjorie and Adrian. Photo by Gillian Ward.

With tulip petals for pockets, this apron is fashioned from sugar bags both dyed and natural. Photo by Gillian Ward.

Marjorie made this dress from 'exclusive blue ribboned lace, lined with blue taffeta' for her 1966 marriage to Adrian Cooper. It originally featured a scalloped hem, but this was later taken up to give the frock a different look when Marjorie wore it dancing. For the wedding Marjorie created a matching fascinator, and completed the outfit with long white gloves, white lace nylon shoes, and a trailing bouquet of artificial white satin roses, blue forget-me-nots and hyacinths. Photo by Gillian Ward.

Dreaming of exotic destinations, Marjorie used travel-magazine cuttings to decorate a sturdy reusable shopping bag. Photo by Gillian Ward.

A toilet roll implies a toilet-roll holder, and this one is fashioned from the bottom end of a soft-drink bottle, ribbon, lace and a fake flower. Photo by Gillian Ward.

Above: Upstairs at Marjorie's Devonport home a private museum displays her many treasures. The north wall holds her impressive thimble collection, as well as family photographs. Photo by Gillian Ward.

Right: The garden is the perfect place for Marjorie to find unexpected applications for materials she happens to have in abundance. She discovered that elasticised fabric could be made into protective nests for young strawberry plants. Photo by Gillian Ward.

Left: The iconic poodle soda-bottle cover was a 1960s crochet standard, and has been executed beautifully by Marjorie. Photo by Gillian Ward.

Below: Many of Marjorie's faultlessly knitted creations are on display in her museum. Photo by Gillian Ward.

Above: The recliner chair in her Madden Street living room is Marjorie's mission control. From it she answers correspondence, watches soapies and receives visitors. Photo by Gillian Ward.

Right: No waste item is too small to be beneath Marjorie's notice. Here, in bread bag tags, she combines her two creeds: Christianity and 'waste not, want not'. Photo by Gillian Ward.

Right: After being inspired by Marjorie's clever ways with used pantyhose, blogger Abby Fraser was moved to crochet this piece of hosiery art and send it to Marjorie for her ninety-fifth birthday.

Below: When composing her 1976 coffee-table book, Dame Edna Everage included Marjorie's party favourite Candlesticks, concocted from pineapple, banana, a glace cherry and a strip of orange peel. Edna added her own twist, incorporating a lettuce cup and some dribbles of mayonnaise to represent melted wax.

"The greater the difficulty the greater the glory"

Cordial Tip

Never leave Coca-Cola in the sun, or in extreme temperatures, as it is liable to explode.

Crayfish Tip

Use a nutcracker to break open the claws of crayfish and so prevent nasty scratches.

DOUBLE BOILER: Put marbles in bottom pot and you will know when water is getting low.

Drawers

If they don't move freely, rub bottom edges and sides with coarse sandpaper, then smear on a light coat of wax polish.

Fringe Cutting

When cutting a fringe, put sticky tape across forehead and cut on edge. Result will be straight line.

Gift Idea

If you do not like *useless* coloured paper, wrap your gifts in tea towels, hand towels or hankerchiefs.

"Rich gifts wax poor when givers prove unkind."

GLAD WRAP HINT: Glad Wrap is easier to handle and not so sticky if you keep it in the refrigerator.

Hair Dryer (One with Nozzle)

A hair dryer will not only dry your hair, but also the dog, wet shoes, defrost the freezer, dry out bottles, fabric lampshades, wet carpet and so on.

Hair Rollers

Put a shower cap on, before you put on, or take off, your clothes. Much easier.

"My hair looks great,
My dress is new,
Tonight's the first date
With you.
My eye shadow gleams —
A subtle grey,
My lipstick matt —
I'm on my way.
But will you tell me, please — if anyone knows...
Why a spot has appeared...on the end of my nose."

Hammering

Hold a nail firm, by pushing it through a square of paper before you hammer. By holding the paper, not the nail you are less likely to hammer your fingers.

Ice Trays

Prevent them sticking in the freezer section, by smearing bottoms with glycerine, or sprinkle salt under the tray. Waxed paper works too.

Laces (lost)

Prevent lost laces by stitching them together where they first cross after being threaded into the shoe.

Lamington Tip

Keep the cake in the freezer, then when you want it for lamingtons, cut frozen cake, dip in hot icing (keep icing over pot of boiling water) with carving fork, then into the coconut. Cake will thaw quickly and icing sets before penetrating the cake.

Letter Writing Tips

When writing letters, always use the back page of the pad, as this avoids any imprint being transferred to other pages, particularly when using ball point pens.

If you like writing long letters, write on both sides of the paper. On the underside write the opposite way to appear vertical then each side can be read easily.

Double the news for the same postage in overseas airmail letters by using blue or black ink on one side of the thin paper, and red on the other. The letter is easy to read and weight will be the same.

To someone changing their address, write new address on the front of the envelope, and the old address on the back as *"sender".* Either way the letter will be delivered.

The most bitter word is — Alone
The most beloved word is — Mother
The most tragic word is — Unloved
The most cruel word is — Revenge
The most peaceful word is — Home
The warmest word is — Friendship
The saddest word is — Forgotten
The coldest word is — Indifference
The most comforting word is — Faith.

Lid (tight)

Immerse screw top only in hot water, then tap lightly and unscrew.

Linen Storing

Wrap in blue paper to stop yellowing.

Linoleum (hole)

Warm a wax crayon, same shade, and press into hole.

Mascara Dry

Put a single drop of olive oil on it and it is ready for use again.

Mincer Trick

Attach a plastic bag to the opening to collect foodstuff. Good when making breadcrumbs.

Mirror Fogging

Mix equal parts of glycerine and methylated spirit together and rub on the tiniest smear, or rub mirror with a cake of dry soap and polish with a dry duster. See also Car Windows Fogged up.

Nail Polish

To dry quickly, place fingers in a bowl of cold water. Put a ball bearing in the bottle and it mixes more quickly. When lids become difficult to remove, turn bottle upside down and apply a few drops of nail polish remover to dissolve dried polish.

Nose Dry on Hot Day

Apply roll-on anti-perspirant to bridge of nose and your spectacles won't slide down.

Orange Peel

Dried orange peel is as good as kerosene for lighting fires.

Parcel Tying

Wet the string before tying the parcel and it becomes taut and firm as it dries, and put the string over twice in the first tie, instead of once to make it tighter.

Perishables Forgotten?

Have you ever left your perishables in a friends refrigerator after visiting on your way home from shopping? Solve the problem by putting your keys in the refrigerator too.

Pie Crust (in a hurry)

For casseroles or savoury pies, butter some bread, cover pie, then sprinkle with cheese. Bake until golden brown. For fruit pies, use raw sugar and cinnamon in place of cheese.

Scrabble Tip

Use the revolving base of a Lazy Susan for scrabble, or other games, where the board has to be turned to each player.

"Unless one is a genius, it is best to aim at being intelligent."

Shifting House

Put paper plates between your plates and saucers to save breakage.

"It is a woman, and only a woman — a woman all by herself, if she likes, and without any man to help her — who can turn a house into a home.

"Too many cooks spoil the broth, but it only takes one to burn it."

Sour Cream

If you are out, add lemon juice to light cream.

Spectacles (cleaner)

Put a few drops of eau-de-Cologne on tissue and your glasses will sparkle after a light rubbing.

String Dispenser

Use a funnel for quick and tidy service. Hang on a cup hook.

Telephone Book

Paste a suitably sized calendar to the inside of your telephone book. Saves many trips away from the telephone to verify a date ; saves minutes.

"Utility is one phone, luxury two, and paradise none."

Telephone Calls (S.T.D.)

Set the timer on your stove, when you are going to make an S.T.D. call, then you will know when to cease.

Telephone Tip

If you haven't an outside bell for when you are working in the garden, put the phone into a tin such as a biscuit tin, and you'll be sure to hear it then.

From bust support to plant protection: it takes genius of the Marjorie Bligh kind to recognise that a past-its-best bra can have a second life guarding tender young seedlings in the garden.

6. THRIFT FOR BEGINNERS

The first rule of Bligh-style thrift is not to buy a thing if you can make it yourself out of materials that are cheap or—even better—free. Yes, it may take time to settle yourself down at the sewing machine and transform a pile of newspapers into home-made garbage bags, but it will shave a few dollars off your grocery bill. Vacuum cleaner bags, too, are just another annoying expense that you can cross off your list with the investment of a few hours of your time. Why buy incense, kindling, shaving cream, hairspray, shampoo or toothpaste when the ingredients of perfectly adequate substitutes are likely lying around your home?

Be assured that when measured in cups per teabag, Marjorie's fuel economy is second to none, and rule number two of economising the Marjorie way is not to use more of a resource than is absolutely necessary. She can tell you how to make a candle burn slower, how to make a bottle of washing-up liquid go twice as far, and how—with the help of a thermos flask and a little discipline—to stop your power bill spiralling out of control.

Rule number three is to be alert to the possible uses of things you might be tempted to throw away. Under Marjorie's guidance, and with a newfound vigilance, you will find sometimes unexpected incarnations for your wrapping paper and soap scraps, your coal dust and your baby's bottle, your old floral frocks, and even your uneaten toast that's gone cold and soggy.

—•—

ABBY FRASER, FLAUTIST AND HAPPY (CROCHET) HOOKER

Abby Fraser's nimble flautist's fingers are never idle during breaks in orchestra rehearsals: in her bag there is always a whimsical crochet creation in progress. Abby, who became a Marjorie fan after seeing an exhibition of the renowned recycler's crafts, grew up in Port Sorell on the north-west coast of Tasmania, and had a grandmother who taught her to crochet and instilled in her a 'waste not, want not' attitude.

Flautist and crafty type Abby Fraser has followed in the footsteps of her heroine, Marjorie Bligh, and started crocheting with recycled materials.

'I suppose it was a natural transition for me to idolise Marjorie Bligh! When I saw the exhibition, I loved Marjorie's knitted dress, and her apron made from men's ties, and all the other remarkable things she crafted from plastic bags. I was inspired to incorporate more recycled materials into my own craft, and to read up on Marjorie's life.

'From reading *Housewife Superstar* I learned Marjorie's address, birthday and that she does not tolerate late presents. It was clear to me that I must design and make Marjorie a slice of cake for her ninety-fifth birthday, to show my immense esteem for her. I knew, too, that it must be made from used pantyhose and arrive on her doorstep on 14 April, not a day before, not a day after.

'I was thrilled to hear back from Marjorie, who wrote to me—appropriately—on the back of a recycled card. She said: "It's nice to be loved and it is especially great to be loved by someone you don't know...I'll treasure it until I die."'

MARJORIE'S CAKE

Ingredients

4 pairs of recycled stockings: 2 pairs in beige, 1 pair in cream and 1 pair in pink

1 piece of foam cut in the shape of a slice of cake: height = 7.5cm, length = 13cm, width = 10.5cm (do not despair, the odd looks from the person at the foam cutting shop will be worth it!)

A small amount of fibre fill stuffing

Pearls and assorted beads that resemble sprinkles for decoration

Utensils

3.5mm crochet hook

Scissors

Wool needle

Abbreviations

sk = slip knot

ch = chain

sc = single crochet

ss = slip stitch

Method

Cut stockings in a 5mm* thick spiral strip from the toe (this may take some time, so alternate between cutting and crocheting for variety).

*Cut stockings depending on their thickness. For example: thicker, higher denier stockings (like the cream/pink ones in my case) create a thicker ply, so spiral should be cut 5mm thick, whereas a thinner, lower denier stocking (like the common beige ones) creates a finer ply, so may need to be cut 10–15mm thick.

Cake base

Make a triangle beginning at the tip with beige stockings. Make sk, 1 ch, 1 sc into sk, pull sk to tighten. Turn, 1 ch, 1 sc into 1st sc from hook (this increases each row incrementally), 1 sc into next sc. Turn, 1 ch, 1 sc into 1st sc from hook, sc into remaining sc to end of row.

Continue in this fashion until the triangle fits the foam cake slice. (Always check against foam to shape as you increase the triangle. If you find it is becoming too wide, 1sc into the 2nd sc from hook for 2 consecutive rows to decrease sides evenly and continue increasing as usual.)

Sides

Make 2 sides with cream between two beige strips. 29 ch, turn, 1 sc into 2nd ch from hook, sc in remaining 27 ch. Continue in this fashion for another 6 rows. Change to cream for another 6 rows, then back to beige for another 6.

Icing

With pink stockings, follow instructions for base, adding a rectangular section at end of triangle to cover outer edge of cake. After making triangle, turn, 1 ch, sc into the back loop of the 2nd sc from hook and remaining sc to end of row (by crocheting into only the back loop of this row, a ridge will be formed, making the edge of the cake more obvious).

Continue in this fashion (crocheting into both loops of each sc, as usual) until this panel covers outer edge of cake (around 14 rows).

Cream

For blobs of piped cream crochet in the round, beginning at base. Make sk, 1 ch, 6 sc into sk, pull sk to tighten. Join with ss into 1st ch, 1 ch to start next round and continue in a spiral to end (pulling the tail through to the front will help to see where you started). 2 sc into each sc for 2 rounds, then 1 sc into each sc for a further 2 rounds.

Decrease after every 2 sc until a soft peak is formed. Stuff with fibre fill and sew remaining few stitches with a wool needle.

Make 2 more blobs and attach to the top edge of icing. (If one blob happens to be larger than the others—like mine—place it in the centre for a more balanced presentation!)

Combine

Sew all pieces together with a wool needle around foam and decorate icing with pearls and sprinkles.

Serve with a doily and enjoy!

www.smallcraftalert.blogspot.com.au

{SEE LAST COLOUR PLATE FOR AN EXAMPLE}

Baby's Bottle

Baby's bottle can be put to use when baby no longer needs it, for storing French dressing. The markings will tell you what proportions of vinegar and oil to use.

Bread—Keep the bread tin sweet by using blotting paper. Replace once a week. A sliced fresh apple or new potato placed in the bread box keeps the bread beautifully fresh.

"When a wife has a good husband it is easily seen in her face."

Candles

Burn more slowly and last longer if you put them in the freezer or refrigerator for a few hours before you use them ; or,

Before lighting, sprinkle salt on top.

Coat with lacquer to prevent drooping or dripping.

They will light more quickly if wicks are trimmed and tipped with a little methylated spirit.

If your candle is too thin to fit the candlestick, hold candle upright and sprinkle sugar (coarse) between candle and holder.

If it is too fat for the candlestick, scrape it to fit with the potato peeler or put it in very hot water until it softens, then wriggle it in.

If bent, place in a barely warm oven until wax softens slightly and candle can be bent straight again.

"All the darkness of the world cannot put out the light of one small candle."

CHEAP CHRISTMAS CAKE

4 ozs. S.R. flour, 5 ozs. plain flour, ½ teaspoon salt, 6 ozs. brown sugar, 2 eggs, grated rind of 1 orange, 4 ozs. white solid shortening, ½ cup milk, ¼ cup orange juice, 1½ lbs. mixed fruit, ½ level teaspoon carb. soda.

Method : Sift flours and salt and divide into two. Place in basin the sugar, eggs, half sifted flour and salt, and orange rind. Melt solid shortening until luke warm only, add milk, then pour onto ingredients in basin and beat 3 minutes. Add remaining flour, sifted with bi-carb. soda, orange juice and fruit and combine evenly with a wooden spoon. Pour into a paper lined 8-inch cake tin and bake in moderate oven 1¾ hours.

* * *

Never economise on luxuries.

"Joy's the perfect gift that can give your heart a lift."

Christmas Stockings (cheap)

Use the bright plastic net bags you buy oranges or onions etc., in for the children's Christmas stockings.

Christmas Wrapping Paper

Used paper can be made good again, by spraying with spray starch and ironing with a warm iron. Remove adhesive paper by pressing with a hot iron

Coal Dust

Put into cartons, pour on used tea leaves and they will form briquettes.

Cosmetic Tissues

A super quality toilet paper is as effective as the most expensive cosmetic tissue.

Cream (mock)

Stir over low heat, ¾ cup sugar, and ⅓ cup water until dissolved. Bring to boil. Boil 5 minutes. Let get cold. Beat 125g (4 ozs.) butter until white, and *gradually* beat in sugar-water mixture ; or,

Beat together in mixer, 2 tablespoons each of icing sugar, powdered milk and soft butter, and 2 dessertspoons of boiling water. Add a few drops of vanilla. Beat until white and fluffy.

Cream Gone Sour (make into scones or pastry)

Add some fairly hot water to thin it a little, then add sifted S.R. flour to make it of scone dough consistency. Pat or roll out, and cut into rounds. Bake in hot oven for 10 minutes. Makes good pastry too. (To prevent, add pinch bicarbonate soda.)

Dresses Worn

If you are sick of a flowered frock, you can make a pillow case for your daughter.

In August 1958 there was a National Council of Women Savings Exhibition in Launceston and I occupied the Thrift Hints stall, supplied all the articles, and spoke about each one to people as they moved along to my stall. On the stall I had patchwork shopping bags, mats, oven cloths and pot holders I had made from dyed sugar bags, face washers knitted from the string that closes a sugar bag, mats made from remnants of woollen material sewn onto sugar bag, trays from picture frames with material patchwork, under the glass, and other items. I won the prize for the best display – an electric jug and a silver jug, donated by 7EX – and had my picture and display taken for "*The Examiner*". Mrs. Margot Parker, who was then the President of the 7EX Women's Association, wrote and congratulated me, and invited me into the station so she could make the presentation to me.

In a sponge cake competition run by M. T. Jessup on the 30th October 1958, I was announced the winner of the first and second heats, but I could not enter the finals as I was away.

Tea Saver

Sometimes you accidently make the tea too strong. If you drain all tea off the leaves you can use those leaves for your next brew of tea. It will taste just the same. If you crush tea with a rolling pin, you'll only need half the amount you usually use in the teapot.

"Habit is the best of servants or the worst of masters."

Toast (cold and soggy)

Don't throw away, cut into small squares, brown under griller and use them as croutons for soup.

Raspberry Jam (stretched)

Stew 6 apples in very little water. When soft add 5 or 6 cups of raspberries and boil for a few minutes. Measure and use cup for cup with sugar, stirring sugar in until dissolved before putting back on stove. Boil quickly until it jells. Can't taste apples when cooked. Do it with strawberries, too.

Wine (light table)

Left-over wines can be kept for almost any length of time if a spot or two of olive oil is poured into the bottle before re-corking. This seals it by keeping out the air. It can then be used only for cooking, but is invaluable for this.

"The difference between a chef and a cook seems to be who cleans up the kitchen."

Margarine (home-made)

1½ cups sunflower or saffron polyunsaturated oil , two heaped tablespoons skim milk powder, 5 tablespoons liquid skim milk, ½ teaspoon salt. Beat milks together until smooth, then while mixing constantly *add the oil drop by drop*. Continue beating till smooth and thick. You must be slow in adding the oil or it will separate out again ; or,

500g (1 lb.) clarified beef dripping, 350g (¾ lb.) lard, 500g (1 lb.) butter, 2 dessertspoons lemon juice, 1 thick slice stale bread. *Method*—Melt dripping, add to it the butter and lard. Bring slowly to the boil. Add lemon juice. Drop in bread. This absorbs any scum as it rises. Boil briskly for 5 minutes. Remove bread. Pour into container to set. When using, shred with a potato peeler.

I guess the first forty years of life give us the text, and the next thirty supply the commentary. When I first married I was more intrigued with being my own mistress for the first time. What a new face courage puts on everything. Does anyone believe that moderation is a fatal thing and that it is better to be faithful than famous ? I guess circumstances alter cases. I have always been an economist, buying things in bulk when the items are cheap, made my own, and children's clothes and many of the husband's, soap, herb tea, muesli, grew fruit and vegetables for preserving, kept fowls, and preserved the surplus eggs, cut the boys' hair, and now Eric's, are but a few ways I save.

"Don't drink and drive. There is no cure for the mourning after."

Detergent Saver

Pour half a bottle into an empty bottle, then fill both up with water.

Garbage Bags

Make your own kitchen garbage bags from three double sheets of newspaper. Double fold all the edges and stitch on the sewing machine down one side across the bottom and up the other side. You will have a strong bag about 28cm x 35cm. The bag will not come apart or leak.

Incense (home made)

Take a tablespoon of fine sawdust and a tablespoon of spice, such as powdered cinnamon, and mix thoroughly. Add about a tablespoon of water which has in it approximately half a teaspoon of gum arabic (obtainable at chemists). Shape into sticks, and let dry out.

Shaving Cream

Dissolve a small packet of soap flakes in boiling water. Add a dessertspoon or two of olive oil and perfume if liked and beat 5 minutes until creamy.

"The man who makes no mistakes does not usually make anything."

Newspaper Logs

Fill a tub with cold water, add ¾ of a cup of dishwashing liquid. (This tubful will do an awful lot of logs.) Mix well. Roll newspaper into logs — about 2 newspapers placed together and rolled tightly should do for each log. Tie each one with a piece of string each end. Soak logs in tub for about 24 hours. Remove and place in sun to dry.

They take several days to dry. Make sure they are properly dry before using or they won't burn properly.

ELECTRICITY SAVED: If you indulge in many cups of coffee during the day, fill a thermos flask with boiling water when you make the teapot of tea at breakfast time. Boiling the jug for one cup all the time, runs up the power bill.

"Few minds wear out ; more rust out."

Steel Wool

Cut soap-filled steel wool pads into quarters with scissors. A quarter of a pad will clean several pots or pans. This is better and cheaper than using the whole pad and wasting it through rust.

Steel wool will not rust if put in a jar of water with a pinch of bicarbonate of soda, or soapy water.

If you run out of steel wool, use crushed aluminium foil

Vacuum Cleaner Bag Hints

Put a mothball into the bag, or spray with disinfectant to eliminate the stale smell of cigarette ash, etc. in the bag.

Put a cupful of used tea leaves into the bag and shake well. The dust clings to the leaves. Empty before vacuuming, then if you spill any, you can clean it up, as you go.

If you run out of the standard bags for your vacuum cleaner, you can use the ordinary bags in which groceries come from the supermarket. Fitted carefully, these bags are strong and very suitable, as well as being free.

Make your own by using three thicknesses of old nylon curtains (not the lacy type). The suction is better to.

Vacuuming

Put petroleum jelly on the ends of the vacuum cleaner connector pipes and they will slide apart easily.

"My home is clean enough to be healthy, and dirty enough to be happy."

Moisturizer

Blend all together 100g Sorbolene Cream, 10ml glycerine, and 150ml water.

The addition of 50g of Vitamin E cream, makes it even better and the above is especially good after exposure to the sun.

Hair Shampoo

Dissolve one cake of velvet soap in 2 large cups of hot water by putting it in a double saucepan. Cool, then add one tablespoon each of borax and sulphur and two tablespoons of bay rum. Separate an egg, beat white and yolk separately ; add each to the cooled jelly. Keep in air-tight jars ; or,

Mix together in a blender, 1½ cups warm water, 1½ cups grated velvet or toilet soap (or soap ends), 1 egg, or some glycerine. For an extra shine on your hair, mix some maize oil with an egg and shampoo your hair with it.

Hair Spray

Dip a small pad of cotton wool into some lemon juice and apply to your hair. Let dry, then brush into shape.

Toothpaste Substitute

If you have strawberries, mash a couple and put on teeth and brush vigorously. It removes stains and yellowing.

Soap (toilet) From Ends

Cut all small odds and ends of toilet soap, that get left over, into shreds. To each cup of shavings add 2 cups boiling water. Stir over heat until dissolved, then add enough fine oatmeal to make a stiff paste. Turn into moulds. Turn out next day and cut into suitable sizes ; or,

Melt odd pieces over stove with a little water, and juice of a lemon, and a teaspoon of glycerine, and mix well, or,

Soak ⅔ cup rolled oats, 1 cup soap scraps, 1 teaspoon glycerine in 1 cup water overnight. Place in saucepan with a teaspoon honey and bring to boil. Simmer until soap melts, stirring now and then with a wooden spoon. Turn into a mould to set.

"The difference between failure and success is doing a thing nearly right and doing it exactly right."

"My life is my message."

Soap Pieces Used

Put in saucepan, cover with boiling water, add a little borax, boil 5 minutes, stirring well and pour into a mould — old broken handle cups will do, or, take a cup of cut-up pieces, ⅓ cup of rolled oats, 1 tablespoon honey and simmer until melted, stirring often. Add 2 tablespoons glycerine and pour into moulds to set.

Marjorie has expressed her unique taste through her expertise in a wide range of handicrafts.

7. KEEPING UP APPEARANCES

Marjorie Bligh does not like rundown shoes, sarcasm, liars, social climbers, finicky eaters, smoking, sniffing or throat-clearing. Also on her 'out' list are fat women in trousers, low-cut bodices on frocks, painted toenails and people who don't thank you for presents.

She disapproves of people lowering their false teeth in public, children who interrupt adult conversations, dogs that yap, babies who cry and sockettes teamed with high-heeled shoes. She believes that manners, polished shoes, matching leather goods and clean fingernails go a long way towards keeping yourself nice.

All of which seems quite reasonable, really.

—•—

KAZ COOKE, AUTHOR

'I have so many Post-it notes ruffling out from the pages of my Marjorie books, each volume looks like it wears a DIY Elizabethan collar...hmm, now there's an idea. I'll need an ice-cream container and...where was I?

'My favourite Marjorie hint? What a preposterous notion, to choose just one. As I rifle through my riffling, ruffled pages, there are so many. Should I choose my all-time favourite, but for me unusable, tip? It's this: "Pigs (stomach disorder in). A friend of mine gave raspberry cordial to one of her pigs and it soon got better." That is a brilliant conversation stopper.

'Some hints are bald genius on their own ("If you are out of rouge, cut a beetroot in half and use cut side on your cheeks"), but in others, context is all: "Raw potato juice taken internally helps to improve the condition of the skin. I was given this hint when overseas at one time." One is so impressed by the ineluctable glamour of the source being *overseas*, one practically skips over the implications of "internally".

'Sometimes one can imagine Marj being struck by inspiration, in this case when lighting the griller, perhaps: "Eyebrow liner missing? Don't worry. Take a match, the bigger the better. Burn tip of it until black, then let it cool off. You can use it on your eyebrows like a pencil liner." It's the "let it cool off" that lets you know we are in the thrall of a very thorough person, or at least one imparting the fruits of bitter experience.'

Kaz Cooke, an expert on keeping yourself nice (in fact the author of a book called Keep Yourself Nice, *from her etiquette-advice column), has found many pearls of wisdom in the well-thumbed pages of her copy of* At Home with Marjorie Bligh. *Photo by David Johns.*

WAYS TO BEAUTY FROM YOUR KITCHEN

Take a lemon and drink its juice in warm or cold water every morning on rising to improve your skin. Rinse your skin with warm water to which has been added the juice of a lemon—for gleam and glisten.

Take an egg and separate the white and the yolk. Beat the yolk and rub it into your wet hair, then shampoo in the ordinary way. Beat the egg white until stiff and apply it to your face. Relax for 10 minutes till it dries. Rinse off with warm water, and you'll have the same result as you get from a facial.

Take some butter and clean your make-up off with it. It is a wonderful cleanser and nourishes the skin, too.

Take some olive oil and warm it in a cup. Soak your nails, then rub some into your hands, put on a pair of cotton gloves and go to bed.

Take some ice and wrap in a piece of gauze. After you have cleaned your face, before you have applied new make-up, rub the ice over it. It tones your skin, gives you a pretty colour, and makes you feel fine. Go to it, even the noblewomen of ancient Rome bathed in asses' milk for beauty. Best of luck.

41

* * *

There is no spectacle on earth more appealing, than that of a beautiful woman, in the act of cooking dinner for someone she loves.

* * *

In case of facial emergency simply follow these hints :

- Get rid of that tired wishy-washy look with a brush of blusher.
- Wrap a cube of ice in a handkerchief and massage it over those dark shadows under your eyes before applying concealing cream.
- If your complexion is dull with clogged pores, simmer a handful of sage leaves in some rain water. Leave to cool, strain, then dab into the skin and leave to dry. Sage is miraculous.

Complexion Improved

Rub into skin 2 tablespoons of milk mixed with 1 dessertspoon of salt. Dry. Leave all night, then wash off, or rub with a cut tomato. For blemished skin, or one with open pores and excess oil, squeeze juice from two very ripe tomatoes and mix with 2 tablespoons yoghurt. Spread on face. Leave 15 minutes. Rinse.

Bad Breath

Chew parsley to relieve.

Throat Attention

Sun and salt can ravage this delicate area. In the palm of the hand blend a few drops of lemon juice and a small quantity of nightcream. Massage into the throat with firm upward strokes.

Elbows

Salt mixed with oil, cold cream or petroleum jelly and used as a rub soon smooths elbows, or, blend a few drops of salad oil, lemon juice and honey and rub into elbows several times a day. To make elbows white rub them with half a lemon after the juice has been extracted.

Face Cleaner

Mix almond oil with lanolin and olive oil, and clean off your make-up with this. After washing face in the morning with cold water *only*, pat more on face ; or,

Wash with milk sometimes instead of water. Mix oatmeal with it, to clean away grime, or put oatmeal in a muslin bag and use it again and again, dipped in water, to cleanse the face.

"Keep your face always towards the sunshine, and the shadows will fall behind you."

Face Mask

Halt the formation of excess oil on the skin, if only by cleaning the skin deeper than soap and water can reach. Try mixing a teaspoon or so of brewer's yeast with enough plain yoghurt or milk to make a loose, thin mixture. Pat this thoroughly into all the oily areas of the face. Allow to dry and remain on face 15 minutes. Rinse with warm, then cool, water. Blot dry ; or,

Wear a fruit mask made of soft pulpy fruit, to correct a variety of complexion ills. A fresh ripe pear is a helpful mask for an acne condition. Watermelon offers instant stimulation and many in America claim it can remove fine-line wrinkles.

For a dry skin, cleanse your face with warm milk to which has been added a few drops of oil ; or,

Wash face. Warm a little honey. Then pat onto face, followed by some pineapple juice, then honey again, juice, finally the honey. Let each coat dry before putting on the next. Lie down for 20 minutes, then sponge off with clear water. Pat with cold water and apply makeup ; or,

Mix yolk of an egg with one teaspoon each of clear honey and oil (olive) and smooth over face and neck. Leave half an hour, then rinse off with warm water ; or use 2 tablespoons honey with ½ teaspoon of apple cider.

Eyes (bags under)

Cut in half a fresh fig and place directly on the area, whilst lying down. Let them remain for 15 mins. Pat in a film of oil afterwards rinsing away the fig juice.

Eyebrows Darkened

Use sage tea with a few drops of olive oil.

Eyes Sparkling

Place a used teabag over each eye and relax 10 minutes. (Keep bags in fridge so they will be cold.)

To maintain healthy eye condition, boil a teaspoon of fennel seeds in enough water to fill a cup. Use this as an eye-wash three times a day.

Eye

If something has got into your eye, put a drop of castor oil into it to float the intruder.

"Keep your eyes open and your mouth shut."

Eyes

If they show your worries, give them a rest by focusing on a distant object. Don't stare too long or too hard, at what is straight in front of you.

Eyes Puffy

Make small pads from a peeled grated raw potato covered with thin gauze, and relax with one on each eye for 30 minutes.

Eyes Tired

Bathe in cold tea (weak) or juice from a cucumber.

Face Tension

Purse your lips and then let go, to relax tight lips that are caused by stress, and shows in the face.

Fainting

Lie patient down, head low. Loosen light clothing, apply cold cloths to face, give smelling salts. If condition persists more than a few minutes, keep warm and call a doctor. If feeling faint, have patient sit with head bent between knees. Make the patient inhale strong vinegar ; also rub temples with it.

Feet Perspiration

Soak often in bicarbonate of soda.

Feet Perspiration in Shoes

Sprinkle boracic acid inside children's gym. shoes to check perspiration.

"Don't walk in front of me — I may not follow ;
Don't walk behind me — I may not lead ;
Walk beside me — and just be my friend."

Pimples

Mix 3 tablespoons treacle with 2 teaspoons sulphur and take 1 teaspoon after each meal.

Potato Trick

If dieting, squeeze lemon juice over your scoop of potato, instead of butter, tastes the same.

Hair Greying

Toss 2 tablespoons dried sage together with two tablespoons each black tea and rum into three cups of boiling water. Cover. Simmer for 25 minutes. Then steep for several hours and strain. Rub a little of this liquid into the hair and scalp every day. When right shade is reached, reduce the daily application ; or,

Put *one* drop of castor oil on top of your head every night. It thickens hair also and makes it grow long and glossy. (Another of my mother's secrets.) ; or,

Mix three tablespoons of instant coffee powder in a cup of boiling water. Allow to cool, add a little perfume, then pour over hair after washing, or, put a teaspoon salt in 4 tablespoons brandy and rub on hair twice a week.

Hair (highlighted)

Make a pot of strong tea. Let it cool, strain, then use as a rinse. It highlights dark hair, brightens fair and grey hair.

Bandana to hide curling pins : Take a piece of nylon twice the length of your head around, and about 6 inches wide. Taper both ends to inch wide. Shirr the whole length of nylon with shirring elastic on the machine after hemming all round material. Tie on two pieces of ribbon and when wearing your Bandana, tie the ribbon bow on top of head. Make it to match your nightgown and you won't look unsightly in bed.

Weight Watching

If you take 2 teaspoons of gelatine in chilled fruit juice, half an hour before a meal, you will find it a superb appetite depressant. Gelatine does not actually make you lose weight, but because of its high protein content it has a satisfying effect on a large appetite, and so weight is lost due to the smaller intake of food.

"Overweight is not actually a problem of old age, as fat people seldom live that long."

"A gold hammer will break down an iron door."

Because all *Aries* have amazing energy, I am always a bit impatient with anyone who has not. I have a positive approach to life, am unpretentious, and always in a hurry – striding instead of walking, and my whole attitude is one of openness and self-assurance. The publicity I have received I feel I have earned, and since the publishing of my first book in 1965 I have had a tremendous amount of it, for which I am grateful, as it has helped increase the sales of my books. Selling books is not easy, and worse still when you are your own agent, as I am.

Stockings (ladder)

Stop a ladder by spraying with hair lacquer.

On the 7th July I received a letter, with an Australian $10 in it, and a request from Barry Humphries' children's nanny in England to send one of my books to Lady Craigmyle, 18 The Boltons, London. She mentioned that she often uses my book that Barry bought from me, and because she thought it excellent she wanted one for her friend. But because Barry had bought two of my books – the " hint " as well as the " cook " book – I wrote back airmail and asked her which one. After several weeks of awaiting a reply, I wrote direct to Lady Craigmyle, and she did not have the courtesy to answer either. Early this year I gave the letter to our Post Master to see what he could do about tracing her. He had no luck either, and I still have not heard anything. I also wrote to the "Australian Women's Weekly ", and they passed my letter on to Barry when he was in Australia. Also in July I cut the legs of 92 pantyhose into strips, and knitted a man's pullover with some and crocheted the rest into 10 cm squares to fashion into a table cover when I had enough done ; and more stockings were given to me. I used up the tops by knitting them into slippers.

Pantyhose Tips

If a ladder spoils one leg, cut it off, then wait till a ladder spoils a leg in another pair, and wear the two legs with a double top.

If your panty-hose sags or they will not quite come high enough, wet hands and run them up your legs and you'll be surprised how comfortable they will be.

See under *Stocking Care* how to make them last longer.

Pearl Buttons

Pearl buttons or earrings that have lost their lustre, can be brightened by painting with iridescent nail varnish.

Pressing Cloth

If you soak your pressing cloth in vinegar and water you can remove shine from wool fabrics.

Sandals with Woven String Heels

Brush heels with clear gloss lacquer and allow to dry. This prevents fraying and protects the heels against dirt.

Sandshoes (dirty)

Take out laces, spray with stain remover, and put in washing machine for 10 minutes. Use spray starch to prevent soiling.

Wipe inside with a damp cloth to which a few drops of eucalyptus have been added. This also helps to stop socks from becoming stained.

Stop perspiration by sprinkling boracic acid inside them. Good for gym boots, too.

Stockings or Panty-hose (care)

Double the life of your panty hose or stockings by dissolving 1 level teaspoon gelatine in 1½ cups of hot water. Add cold water to make 6 cups. Squeeze panty hose through this mixture several times, and hang over towel rail (do not wring). Wash in normal manner after each wearing but re-dip after 7 wearings ; or

Soak them when new for 24 hours in a tablespoon of salt and 3 cups of water ; or

Wash in methylated spirit before wearing. It soon evaporates and can be worn without further washing ; or

Wet new ones, wring out gently, place in a plastic bag and toss in the freezer. Once frozen, you thaw them out in the bath tub and then hang them up to dry.

"Remember, a handful of cents pinched every day, will pay for a glorious extravagance once a week."

* * *

It is magnificent to grow old, if one keeps young.

* * *

36

To do with Clothes

::::::➧ Give an extra touch of glamour to your black evening shoes by adding a pair of your clip on glittering ear rings.

::::::➧ If your evening shoes are shabby, paint with liquid glue or nail varnish and sprinkle with gold or silver glitter while wet.

::::::➧ Re-stiffen your nylon petticoat after washing by adding a packet of gelatine to 1 gallon of water, and rinse garment thoroughly in it. Dry over an open umbrella. A tablespoon of white sugar to a pint of warm water is also good.

::::::➧ White hats : Equal parts of flour and salt rubbed in and left for a while before brushing off, will clean white felt hats.

::::::➧ If your jars of shoe polish have gone dry, add a few drops of olive oil to them and mix well.

::::::➧ Paint your jewellery with nail polish and the stones won't fall out.

::::::➧ To save the inside of your husband's trouser cuffs from wearing out, sew 3 or 4 buttons about an inch apart on the inside of the back of the cuff. The shoe then rubs on the buttons and not on the material.

MAKE YOUR OWN TRANSFERS . . . 2 teaspoons boiling water, 1 level teaspoon castor sugar and ½ level teaspoon washing blue all mixed to a paste. Apply with small brush and allow to dry, then iron on to material. Worn out transfers can also be used again this way.

::::::➧ Wrap gold and silver shoes in black cloth or paper when you put them away, and they won't tarnish.

::::::➧ Petroleum jelly is best for patent leather shoes. Polish with soft cloth.

::::::➧ To prevent lame or other fabric with gilt or silver thread from tarnishing, store in black tissue paper.

::::::➧ To dry wet gum boots inside, fill them up with warm bran kept for that purpose.

::::::➧ One aspirin crushed and soaked with perspiry articles will take out all odour and stains as well.

::::::➧ When making a dress with a tight fitting bodice and flared skirt, sew the side zip fastener in upside down. The closed end of the zip will save the side seam of the bodice from being torn when pulled over the head, and also it is less likely to come undone. The lower end of the zipper, coming into the fullness of the skirt, will keep fastened securely, because there will be less pull on it.

::::::➧ Prevent loss of ribbons from babies' bootees by threading the ribbon half way round following the slots, then double back one slot before finishing the threading. Use also in gloves. Baby cannot pull the ribbon out this way.

Shoes (leather)

If they have water marks, rub over with a banana skin, or wipe with brown vinegar. They will polish better, too, if you wipe them with vinegar first, when not watermarked. If they are brown and you want them darker, sponge well with ammonia.

Shoes (mildew on)

Clean off with a rag moistened in antiseptic mouthwash.

Shoes (new)

If they pinch your feet, put on a pair of thick socks, previously dipped in methylated spirit. Put on the shoes and walk about in them for half an hour. The spirit softens the shoe leather and moulds it to the shape of the feet.

Shoe Soles

Make soles last longer by giving them a coat of varnish or rubber solution, then cover thickly with sawdust. Let dry for a day or two to harden.

Shoes (open-work)

Slip you hand into a paper bag before putting the hand in the shoe to be cleaned.

"A little tender loving care, makes life better everywhere"

Shoes (patent)

Wipe over with solution of turpentine or vinegar and water (weak), then polish till dry. Vaseline stops them from cracking.

Shoes (red)

If toes are badly scuffed, try red nail polish (of exact shade). Three or four coats are necessary.

Shoes (school)

If they are scuffed, remove polish with methylated spirit, then put araldite glue over toe and around edges, then polish as usual.

"Instruction ends in the schoolroom, but education ends only with life."

Shoes (shiny)

Put polish on overnight, then polish off next morning.

Cardigan

When doing it up remember to start at the bottom, otherwise you could fasten it crookedly

Handbag (cleaned inside)

Wipe out the inside of your handbag with a cloth dipped in eau-de-Cologne to remove grease and powder marks.

Handbag (leather)

Give it a new lease of life by rubbing it all over with beaten egg white. When dry, apply a coat of the best floor polish, then polish with a dry cloth.

Handkerchiefs

Do not turn your drawer upside down when reaching for a hanky for special occasions. Fold the good ones in a square, and the ones for around the home, in a triangle.

Lint and Fluff

Lint and fluff can be removed from dark articles with a "stickytape brush". Put tape around bottle, sticky side out, then roll the "brush" over article on a table.

BREAD JEWELLERY

Jewellery, like earrings, is easy and inexpensive to make - from bread.

I have a brooch and a thimble decorated with bread flowers. Flowery jewellery with a 'Forties' look can be made very easily with fresh bread, poster paints, glue and glossy varnish. The following is another way how to make bread dough for use in jewellery etc.

Fresh bread is very easy to mould by pinching small pieces from a slice, rolling it round in the palms of your hands and moistening slightly with poster paint to colour.

To make flowers, pull the fresh centre from a slice of bread abd roll into a ball in your hand. Colour dough with poster paint directly from tube or water colours mixed to a thick concentration. This colours dough right through so if flower chips while wearing it doesn't show.

Make flower in steps by pinching small piece of dough from ball, flattening between thumb and index finger and curving first into centre part then into small petals. Join petals together as you go.

Keep ball of dough moist by contunially rolling in your palm while working. Add small amount of water with paintbrush if dough get dry.

Cut leaves from flattened piece of dough in contrasting colour. Pinch leaves at each end to give shape.

Dry petals and leaves slowly in sunlight or in warm room. Do not dry in front of fire or direct heat as they may crack. When completely dry, assemble with strong, waterproof glue. When flowers are dry, glue them to earring clip, haircomb, hair slide or brooch pin. Glue leaves into place and leave for 48 hours. Varnish with high gloss plastic. Using this basic technique, you and your children can make inexpensive, pretty jewellery for yourselves or for gifts. Coloured berries and other kinds of flowers are easy to improvise.

Another way is to use fine breadcrumbs. You can do this in your food processor. Put them into a bowl and then stir in enough PVA glue to make a sticky mixture. You can do this with your hands. Keep working at it until it is soft and smooth. Use it straight away as it will start to harden once left. If you have to leave it for a while place in a plastic bag and put in the refrigerator.

To make a rose, roll a small piece into a ball, flatten and shape it into a petal, roll into a spiral, then add more and more until it looks like the real thing. You can make pretty bows by rolling the dough out, then with the hands, rolling pieces into lengths the shape of a cord and tie in usual way. There are no end of things you can make yourself from this bread dough. I learned it when I was just married at a craft school. Paint the finished work with acrylic artist's paints.

"The world has enough for everyone's need, but not enough for everyone's greed."

SECTION 11

Jewellery Hints

"My crown is in my heart, not on my head. Not deck'd with diamonds and Indian stones. Nor to be seen, My crown is called content."

Carat

is a unit of weight used for gemstones. Traditionally it varied from country to country, perhaps because of its method of origin — the name carat derives from that of the seeds of the Mediterranean locust tree, which were once used to weigh gemstones. By 1913 the carat was fixed internationally at 200 milligrams. The carat measure of gold alloys (usually gold, silver or gold, copper) indicates the number of parts of gold in 24 parts. Thus 22-carat gold contains 22 parts of gold in 24 parts of the alloy.

Diamonds

Diamonds can be cleaned by washing with a soft brush dipped in soapsuds to which a little ammonia has been added. Dry by shaking in a small bag of bran.

"A millionaire's money is twice tainted — 'Taint mine and 'Taint yours!"

Emeralds

Get a jeweller to clean them.

Gemset Jewellery

Clean with cloudy ammonia

Gold Jewellery

Wash in soap suds (or diluted cloudy ammonia) and dry in a bag of bran, polish with a soft chamois, or rub with a cloth that has been dipped in vinegar.

Another way is to rub in between your hands with fresh breadcrumbs, or Epsom salts dissolved in water.

Jewellery Hints

Toothpaste and a soft brush will clean any type of jewellery from imitation to fine filigree. Rinse afterwards and dry with a soft cloth.

Ammonia and eau-de-Cologne are cleansers too.

Line your drawer with aluminium foil and keep a cake of camphor in it to prevent tarnishing.

Imitation jewellery that has tarnished can be cleaned by putting them in a basin and covering them with milk. Stand in a warm place for two days. The thick milk should have by then removed the tarnish. Rinse well in warm water, using a soft brush on any crevices.

Hang your necklaces on a coathanger on hooks, or drawing pins pressed into the hanger, or use a man's tie rack.

When grading and restringing beads, put them in corrugated cardboard.

Keep a safety pin on window sill and put your rings on it when washing up. Pin it to your frock for safe keeping.

"Live more simply, that others may simply live."

Jewellery Made from Bread

Cut the crusts from sliced, very fresh, white bread and roll out thinly. Cut out petals to any shape you require and roll again. After the second rolling you may need to tidy the petal shapes. Now shape a flower by joining the petals together. A tiny drop of water is all that is necessary to get them to stick. On a very hot day, the petals may harden as you work, so keep a kettle on the boil and just use a little steam to keep the work pliable.

Dry the flowers out by placing them in the sun, or in the oven, turned on low, with the oven door slightly ajar. When the formed flowers are dry, paint them with children's watercolours, then spray them with a clear lacquer. Any good fast-drying glue can be used to attach brooch, earrings or necklace fittings to the flowers. Larger flowers can be made to decorate vases, jewellery boxes, and so on.

Marcasite

Clean by dipping a stiff brush in dry whiting or powdered school chalk covering the jewellery with more dry whiting and brushing well. Polish with a soft cloth, or, clean with a soft brush dipped in a plate of cleaning fluid. Water must not be used in cleaning marcasite

Mother of Pearl

Wash with powdered whiting and cold water. Hot water and soap destroy the brilliance of the shell.

Put in linen bag. Throw on some salt and tie up. Rinse in lukewarm water until all salt has been extracted and dry them at an ordinary temperature (still in bag).

Necklace from Seeds

Thread nasturtium seeds on strong cotton while still green and hang up till dry. Then colour with lacquer and attach a clasp.

Opals

Opals can be polished by rubbing the surface with putty spread on chamois. Polish with powdered chalk. Wash with water. Polish with sweet oil, or castor oil, sparingly, or, wipe with a damp cloth, sprinkled with ammonia.

In her youth Marjorie loved nothing better than a night on the dance floor. Naturally, she made many of her own spectacular gowns by hand.

8. ROMANCE & MARRIAGE

The most famous of Marjorie's fans, Barry Humphries, notes with some relish that along with all of her other accomplishments our heroine is 'no slouch in the matrimonial department'. Indeed, she is a veteran of fifty-four years of marriage: twenty-seven with Cliff, five with Adrian and twenty-two with Eric.

Sadly, only the shortest of these unions provided her with all of the romantic sustenance that her dreamy heart desired. During the Adrian years Marjorie tackled the business of loving with unparalleled zeal. The Coopers served each other breakfast in bed, left little notes in pockets to be found and, from time to time, wore matching hand-knits. They danced cheek to cheek, celebrated anniversaries and hummed sentimental tunes. Over an eleven-month separation Marjorie penned 534 pages of love letters to her darling (his responses filled 322).

To women in search of a good man she offers this advice: 'You want a man who loves you for what you are. Look for a man who'll

Marjorie kept all of her husbands in hand-knits. Husband number three, bus driver Eric Bligh, was always willing to model for the camera.

bring you flowers and leave notes under the pillow. A woman can take any amount of that you know. You want a man who'll say "that was a lovely meal", and not just wolf it down.

'There's no sense marrying just for sex, you've got to have someone you can sit down with, after dinner, and talk things over.

'When choosing a husband, find one who is always on time and keeps his promises. Note his manners when taking you on a date, and pay careful attention if he has clean shoes and wears a shirt and tie. Beware if he suddenly says (when it's time for payment) *oh dear, my wallet is in my other coat pocket.*'

Wedding Anniversaries

1st, paper ; 2nd, cotton ; 3rd, leather ; 4th, flowers or fruit ; 5th, wood ; 6th, sugar or candy ; 7th, wool or copper ; 8th, bronze ; 9th, pottery ; 10th, tin ; 11th, steel ; 12th, silk or linen ; 13th, lace ; 14th, ivory ; 15th, crystal ; 20th, china ; 25th, silver ; 30th, pearl ; 35th, coral ; 40th, ruby ; 45th, sapphire ; 50th, golden ; 55th, emerald ; 60th diamond.

"War has to have a weapon,
Wisdom, a cap and gown ;
Work, tools with which to labour,
Power, a throne and crown.
Art has to have a canvas,
Flight, pinions true and strong ;
Morning, its sunrise colour —
But love must have a song.

Joy has to have its laughter,
Sorrow, its briny tear,
Beauty, its ready mirror,
And home, its fireside cheer.
Autumn must have its harvest,
Winter, its evenings long.
The heart, its nameless longings —
But love must have a song."

ABC OF HAPPY MARRIAGE

ALWAYS. No refunds if not satisfied, so choose carefully.

BOREDOM. The arch enemy of marriage. Root it out at first signs of growth.

CHILDREN. Marriage was instituted for protection and procreation.

DOMESTIC DUTIES. The most important work in the whole community.

EXERCISE. Physical — to keep you trim. Mental—to keep you interesting.

FOOD. Be imaginative, original, and appreciative.

GOSSIP. Don't gossip about your partner's failings.

HONESTY. Be honest with each other, but not brutal.

INTELLIGENCE. Allied with commonsense, it solves many problems.

JOB. A helping hand or listening ear when necessary.

KINDNESS. Be kind to each other.

LOVE. To marry for less is to invite disaster.

MODESTY. Something you can't afford to lose.

NAGGING. Never accomplishes anything. Try encouragement instead.

OTHERS. To live in a cacoon of self-centredness is not wise.

PRIDE. Something you can't afford to lose.

QUARRELS. Always apologize first, even if you are right.

RELIGION. The tie that binds, the anchor that holds.

SEX. Sexual compatibility is essential to a happy union.

TROUBLE. Meet it together with courage and loyalty.

UNDERSTANDING. When grounded in love it is never abused.

VINDICTIVE. Check it by a check-up on your physical relationship.

WEDDING DAY. A beautiful memory, but only the beginning.

XTRAVAGANCE. Stimulating occasionally, but must not become a habit.

YOU. Retain your personality. Refuse to become just Mum or Dad.

ZZZZZZZ. Unfortunately, there is no known cure for snoring.

"There is only one success — to be able to spend your life in your own way."

Party Tip

Wipe light globes with French perfume for romantic occasions.

"None but the well bred man knows how to confess a fault, or acknowledge himself in an error."

WHAT IS A HUSBAND?

A good husband is a man who treats a wife as if he isn't married to her. There is a particular brand of togetherness with husbands that you can never feel with anyone else. He is simply all the good things in life wrapped up in one, a lovely warm person – either small, medium or large sized. A husband is a man who understands you and loves you for the way you are, and not for the way he would like you to be. A husband is a man with whom to share a quarrel, with no hard feelings afterwards. A husband is a man who halves all your troubles and doubles all your pleasures just by being around when they happen. A husband has to be crafty enough to outwit women, but not silly enough to think they don't know it. A husband is the head, but his wife is the neck that turns it. A husband is a man who says "we" not "I". A husband is someone you cannot hurt without hurting yourself, who brings you the first rose from the garden, rubs your back, praises your meals, mows the lawns and chops the wood. A husband is someone who wakes you up when the baby is crying, hangs around hungrily when a meal is cooking – then disappears when it is served. A husband is a lover who never has to go home, or who never feels too old to hold hands or say "I love you". A husband is someone who forgets your birthday, forgets your anniversary, but also forgets your grey hairs and wrinkles. A husband is someone whose Christmas card takes 20 minutes longer to choose than anyone else's because the words never mean enough. A husband is someone who will watch cricket, football or cartoons on T.V. all day, but finds a job when news or something educational comes on. A husband is the one you hope to die before – so that you are never left without him.

"A wise man has long ears, big eyes, and a short tongue."

HOW TO PRESERVE A HUSBAND

Be careful in your selection. Take only such as have been reared in good moral atmosphere. Do not choose too young. Some girls insist in keeping them in a pickle while others keep them in hot water. This only makes them sour, hard and sometimes bitter. Even poor varieties may be made sweet, tender and good by garnishing them with patience, well sweetened with smiles, and flavoured to taste with kisses. Then, wrap them in a mantle of charity; keep warm with a steady fire of devotion, and serve with peaches and cream. When thus prepared they will keep for years.

Husbands, like peaches, will not keep the year round unless they are well preserved. First, select him carefully; be sure he is not too green, neither should he be over-ripe. He might look very tempting and mellow in the market, but if he is too old he will not stand the test of the preserving process, but will expose his hard stony heart.

Husbands grown in the tropics of pleasure look very fine, but are usually insipid. The home grown are the best. Select your husband, if possible from a family tree growing on the sunny side of a church. You will be sure then that he has a sound heart. Unsound husbands, like unsound peaches, often have to be sorrowfully cast away. Having selected your husband you should have a clear, steady, cheer fire of love. Your preserving pan (the home) must be clean and neat. Give him plenty of sweetness, much sugar is needed – vinegar is never used in sweet preserves. If you think he demands a little spice, use it with caution. Do not keep stirring him up, neither should you keep poking him with sharp points to see if he is done – it will spoil his looks. If you follow the recipe, love will be preserved.

"Never forget what a man says to you when he is angry."

"Matrimony – An insane desire on a man's part to pay a woman's board."

WHAT IS A WIFE?

When a little girl puts aside her dolls and games for dreams, dates and boys, she becomes a young woman and when she seriously concentrates all the dreams and all the dates on THE boy, it's only a matter of time before she turns into a wife. A girl becomes a wife with her eyes wide open. She knows that the sweetest words, "I take thee to be my wedded Husband," really mean, "I promise thee to cook three meals a day for years and years, thee will I worry about, brag about, and talk to, even when thou art not listening." A wife is a girl whose doll is wrapped in tissue and packed away in the closet, a girl with a packet of letters at the bottom of her glove box, and a snapshot album that is never opened – each a fragile link with girlhood, each so treasured and so forgotten. She has stepped from the leisurely, lovely period of girlhood into the hurried world of domesticity.

A wife is a Jill of all trades. She is a painter, judge, nurse, banker, secretary, and treasurer, a gardener, laundress, cook, and bureau of information. She can repair a toaster, put up a shelf, unstop a sink, remodel last year's coat, let down a hem, paper a wall, and make supper for a guest out of scraps from the refrigerator. When the going is really tough and something has to be done in a hurry, she can become a delicate flower, a siren, a lady wrestler, or a Mother Superior.

A wife likes new dresses and hats, going places, teas, shows, neighbours, furniture (provided it is moved sufficiently), soap, babies, parties, lettuce, novels, chatting, rainy nights, kittens, tub baths, other people's birthdays, a husband who comes home on time, and surprises that are gift-wrapped. She is cool towards boxing matches, moths, mice, men drivers, cluttered workshops, grey hairs, telling her age, fried foods, unwashed children, camping trips, and the kind of women she knows her husband stares at.

As the years roll on, many a hope and dream will be packed away tenderly with the doll, the letters, and the snapshot album. Time will soften her beauty and strengthen her "intuition". She will understand that the touch of his hand . . . or a "peck" on the cheek. . . mean that she is the most wonderful girl in the world! And, when a wife has a good husband it is easily seen in her face.

"Matrimony is something that the batchelor misses and the widower escapes."

I loved Adrian's integrity. He didn't nag, always strove to please, had a streak of romantic chivalry in him, his physique was great, he always looked neat and tidy, his hair receding at the front. *"A hair in the head is worth two on the brush."* He answered intelligently, because he was intelligent, and was unfailingly courteous. With him I could talk without restraint. He listened intently to all I said and this I liked, so was it any wonder I loved him? (Only thing I regret in writing this book is that he isn't alive – he would have given me such encouragement and reassurance.)

" The gentleman will always be gentle – the crude man crude, whatever the task he is performing."

SECTION 39—

VALENTINE DAY STORY AND RECIPES

Valentine's Day is February 14th, the day lovers pledge their affections by exchanging cards, and admirers spring a surprise by sending a Valentine to girls who have caught their eye. Whether you are 15 or 50, or just wishing your husband was more gallant, try a Valentine. History tells us that the original Valentine was a very gallant saint, who was executed for his faith in A.D. 270. On the night before his death he is said to have written a farewell note to his gaoler's daughter, whose sight he had restored, signed 'From your Valentine'. That's the best that traditional stories can do to trace the origin of St. Valentine's Day cards. A Shakespearean couplet suggested that birds began their courting on February 14th, the day set aside for the martyred St. Valentine, and this might have had something to do with the romantic association St. Valentine's Day came to have.

In Leap Year, girls have their chance to send cards too, and may if they wish, and are brave enough, declare quite openly their feelings for some lucky fellow. Wives romantically inclined, who have perhaps let their marriage become a little monotonous, may send a Valentine to their husbands, to remind them that they would love a little of the glamour that existed in their courting days. Husbands may, of course, do likewise.

This is the verse about the first Valentine that I will include as well:

From the Tower of London in the 1415's
Came the first 'Valentine' signed, 'Duke of Orleans'
His lady love thought this was a wow
And millions of folk are sending them now!
He, of course, wrote nothing new—
Just old-fashioned words like 'I love you'.
The card which on MY doormat plops
Nowadays, tells me I'm 'the tops!'
One I've seen says 'Who'd have us?'
(If I get THAT, there will be a fuss)
All the same, if a card wasn't there
I'd really feel a frightful square.
Just in case I'm not quite in your heart,
I'm trying out some of this Valentine's Art.
Things like pinning bay leaves on my pillow,
And just to be sure, I'm adding some willow!
Then, of course, I'll take up that Valentine treat
And marry the first chap that I meet.
So just make sure you toe the line
And send me a card, my Valentine.

* * *

Here are some recipes that will win his heart on Valentine's Day

LOVING CUPS

¾ cup lemon juice, 2 cups raspberry topping, 2 quarts of soda water, 2 quarts of dry ginger ale, ice cubes, thin lemon slices, strawberries.

Mix lemon juice and topping in a large basin. Stir in soda water and ale. Add plenty of ice cubes and float lemon and strawberry slices on top.

SWEETHEART SHAPE

1 large tin tomato juice (2 cups), 1 cup chopped tomatoes, 1 tablespoon vinegar, 1 teaspoon Worcestershire sauce, salt and pepper to taste, ½ lb. pork luncheon meat, 2 hard-boiled eggs, 1 oz. gelatine, 2 tablespoons stock or water, stuffed olives, salad greens to garnish.

Mix tomato juice and tomatoes together, add vinegar, sauce and seasonings. Chop meat into cubes and slice eggs. Soften gelatine in stock, place over hot water to dissolve. Dilute 1 teaspoon of this with another tablespoon of stock and pour over base of wetted (or lightly oiled) heart-shape mould. When beginning to set, arrange over the slices of egg. Allow to set, then fold in gelatine and meat into tomato juice. Spoon carefully over egg slices in mould. Chill, and when firm, turn onto serving dish. Garnish with salad, vegetables and olives.

PASSION FLUMMERY

Dissolve 2 tablespoons gelatine in 1 cup of water. Blend 2 tablespoons flour in another cup of water. Pour both mixtures into a saucepan, add ¾ cup sugar and bring to boil. Boil 5 minutes, stirring continuously. Add 1 cup of passionfruit pulp and reheat to boiling. Cool and allow to partially set. Whisk until set and frothy.

TENDER KISSES

Cream 4 oz. each of butter and sugar with ½ teaspoon vanilla. Add an unbeaten egg. Work in 8 oz. plain flour that has been sifted twice with 3 teaspoons baking powder and pinch salt. Put into bag and pipe small rosettes on to a greased tray. Bake in a moderate oven 7 to 10 minutes. Allow to cool on trays. Join with jam or butter icing and dust with icing sugar.

LOVERS' KNOTS

Sift 6 oz. plain flour with ½ teaspoon baking powder. Rub in 4 oz. butter and add 2 oz. sugar. Beat 1 small egg with a tablespoon cream and add to make a stiff dough. Leave in refrigerator 15 minutes. Cut into small pieces and roll into thin strips. Tie each strip into a knot, brush with milk and dip in crushed sugar. Bake 20 minutes in moderate oven.

VALENTINES (Prize Recipe)

7 oz. butter, 4 oz. of pure icing sugar, 1 egg-yolk, 10½ oz. plain flour.

Cream butter and sugar. Add egg-yolk, beating well. Mix in the sifted flour. Knead until smooth and roll out on a slightly floured board. Cut into heart shapes. Cut smaller hearts and bake in a slow oven, about 20 minutes. When cold, add a dab of butter cream to the large biscuits and put the smaller one in the centre. Ice the small heart with pink glace icing. Pipe a scalloped edge around each biscuit and pipe two small birds in blue icing on the smaller biscuit.

BUTTER CREAM: 6 oz. sifted pure icing sugar, 2 oz. butter, beaten together and mixed with hot water to make a cream. Add vanilla to taste.

SWEETHEART CAKE

This one was a favourite with my beloved husband

Beat 3 eggs with 1 cup of sugar for 10 minutes. Sift together 3 times, ¼ cup of cornflour, ½ cup of plain flour, 1 teaspoon of cream of tartar, ½ teaspoon of carb. soda, add add to egg mixture, folding in lightly. Add lastly 3 tablespoons milk that has been boiled with 1 oz. of butter. Pour into heart-shaped greased tin and bake 20 to 25 minutes in a moderate oven. Split when cold, and fill with whipped cream. Ice the top appropriately.

* * *

Lay up for yourselves treasure in Heaven . . . for where your treasure is there will your heart be also—(Matt. 6:20 - 21).

Gerald and Ross Marry

Marriage!
It's rough. It's tough. It's work.
Anybody who says it isn't
Has never been married.
Marriage has far bigger problems,
Than toothpaste squeezed
From the middle of the tube.

Marriage means ...
Grappling, aching, struggling.
It means putting up
With personality weaknesses,
Accepting criticism
And giving each other freedom to fail.
It means sharing deep feelings
About fear and rejection.
It means turning self-pity into laughter.
And taking a walk to gain control.

Marriage means ...
Gentleness and joy.
Toughness and fortitude.
Fairness and forgiveness
And a walloping amount of sacrifice.

Marriage means ...
Learning when to say nothing
When to keep talking
When to push a little
When to back off
It means acknowledging
"I can't be God to you –
I need him, too."

Marriage means ...
You are the other part of me
I am the other part of you.
We'll work through
With never a thought of walking out.

Marriage means ...
Two imperfect mates
Building permanently
Giving totally
In partnership with a Perfect God.
Marriage, my love, means us!

Marjorie and her third husband, Eric, cut the cake, 1976.

All the time Adrian was at Margate we wrote to one another. All told he wrote 322 pages in letters to me and I wrote 534 to him. So that I wouldn't have to keep them all I wrote excerpts from each one into my scrapbooks – here, there and everywhere, so as to confuse any "sticky-beak" who happened to read one of them. I'll share some sentences with you, so you can judge some things for yourself, and I'll put breaks between the sentences. Here are some – "If you love me, really love me, then whatever happens darling I won't care – One of these days I'll have the pleasure of telling him what I really think of you – Even when my back was turned I could see you, and all the time was the desire to claim you as my own – I hope I shall never have to wash *your* undies when we are married – I want all the things you are to be mine – It's wonderful to know you are there, and that you love me and are mine, and it pleases me to know that I won't have to ever buy any more unnecessary expensive clothes – I know where my happiness lies and where I must go for a chance to live, instead of just being alive, and it will be Heaven to be able to think for myself – The future is big enough for us not to worry too much about it. The present is not so bad that it couldn't be worse – Why I love you so much is that *you* don't humiliate me, you stay until the end of a dance (don't leave about 10 p.m.), we share things, and, the way we look at life – when two people like doing things together, then there must be love – Rest assured, you fill my mind and heart at all moments of my waking life, but I hope my darling *you* don't wake me at night with the clickety click of knitting needles from 3 a m., or with endless cups of tea until dawn, as I don't like light beaming in my eyes when I want to sleep – The times I spend with you are like an oasis in a desert – when I am writing to you there is so much in my heart and head that my pen can't keep up with my thoughts – I could never get you out of my system whatever happened – I do love you so, but just how much is beyond my power of speech – I feel quite proud to think that you are mine, that I won't be under a petticoat government, and that I'll be able to do all the things that I've wanted to do without restriction. There is no other woman who could claim distinctions that you can claim – We were made for each other and you are one of the best things that have happened to me. My father, a minister of religion, taught me to put woman on a pedestal, so I have. You haven't been on that pedestal, darling, so look forward to that treat – True love thrives on difficulties. Driving something underground doesn't get rid of it, but only makes it grow – There is much more to find out about you yet. What I am learning about you only makes me more aware of my good fortune and your husband's stupidity – All the wonderful things that have been sung or said, or written about love I could say to you with interest – Understanding comes first ; understanding of the loved one's weaknesses and faults, wishes and desires. Trust comes next, perhaps Love and trust go hand in hand. Qualities best in women are ; Patience, an affectionate nature, companionship, ability to respond to a mood – You have missed so much of what you want out of life. It reminds me of the Bible verse about children asking for bread and being given a stone (Matthew 7 : verses 9-10-11) – I love you so much darling that it hurts me so much to see you unhappy, and pleases me so much to see you glad."

Though now estranged from her eldest son, Gerald, Marjorie has fond memories of taking him down the street and being complimented on his spruce appearance.

9. CHILDREN

Despite her undisputed talent for economising, it is doubtful that even Marjorie Bligh could have planned and pulled off the perfectly timed births of her boys, Gerald and Ross. 'Both sons are born on same day and month, the 20th January it falls,' she writes. 'It comes in handy at party time as for only one cake it calls.' But what a cake it would be! Whether a train, merry-go-round, farm scene or garage, the annual cake was always an extravaganza of patience and skill, kept as a closely guarded surprise until the very last moment.

Marjorie enjoyed the trappings of motherhood, making sweet little outfits to keep her boys as spruce as two active boys could be kept, and proudly walking her offspring down the main street of Campbell Town. Some of the child-rearing methods Marjorie describes in the chapter of her autobiography titled 'My Two Sons Gerald and Ross (both conceived on my birthday)' are no longer widely accepted. Naughty boys were sin-binned, Harry Potter fashion, in the cupboard beneath the stairs; if it was raining when the time came for Marjorie to bring in her cows from the streets, she would tether her boys to the legs of the kitchen table to keep them out of mischief while she was gone. Yet some of her child-related tips transcend the generations, such as her tried-and-true method for preventing children squabbling over the bigger portion of a divided treat.

Children bring with them particular challenges. Marjorie knows how to avoid the embarrassment of your child wetting a bed when you put him or her down for a nap at a friend's house, and has devised a cunning way to keep your little one occupied while a thermometer registers their temperature. There is nothing she doesn't know about the management of hems and how to make children's garments last longer. She has thought out how best to cut a baby's fingernails, discovered which household cleaning product is best for filthy little hands and knees, and uncovered the role of sticky tape in getting a winning photograph of even the least co-operative toddler.

—•—

Rachael Treasure is too busy writing novels, training kelpies, wrangling her kids and looking gorgeous on horseback to think much about housework, which is why she is grateful for Marjorie's handy tip on keeping carpets clean. Photo by Helen Quinn.

RACHAEL TREASURE, AUTHOR AND COUNTRY CHICK

'To be honest, floor cleaning's not really my thing. My solution to the mess my babies made under their highchairs was to acquire a Jack

Russell pup, call her Indie—because she comes *indie* house—and get her to clean up the scraps.

'Nevertheless, I do fear dirty wheel marks on my carpet and think Marjorie's genius tip for saving carpet from pram wheels could be readily adapted for the wood barrow.

'I'm wondering now if I might further adapt Marjorie's brilliance to solve the problem of Indie's mucky paws. What about a condom (unused, of course), secured with a small bulldog clip, on each little paw?'

Pram Hint

If you want to bring baby's pram into the house but fear dirty wheel marks on carpet, try this: — Buy four shower caps and pull them over the pram wheels. There will be no marks and the plastic caps last for ages.

—*M.B.*

The Parent's Prayer

" O, Master, make me a better parent.

" Teach me to understand my children, to listen patiently to what they have to say, and to answer all the questions kindly. Keep me from interrupting them, talking back to them, and contradicting them. Make me as courteous to them as I would have them be to me. Give me the courage to confess my sins against my children and to ask them forgiveness, when I know that I have done them a wrong.

" May I not vainly hurt the feelings of my children. Forbid that I should laugh at their mistakes or resort to shame and ridicule as punishment. Let me not tempt my child to lie and to steal. So guide me hour by hour that I may demonstrate by all I say and do that honesty produces happiness.

" Reduce, I pray, the meanness in me. May I cease to nag; and when I am out of sorts, help me hold my tongue.

SECTION 3

Children (to do with)

"In childhood be modest, in youth temperate, in manhood just, and in old age prudent."

Apple Trick for Children

To settle the old argument over the bigger piece of apple, allow one child to cut it in halves and the other to have first pick.

Apron from Child's Frock

If your child has outgrown her frock, remove sleeves and bind armholes, enlarging them first. Cut back down centre and add ties, or open up sides, and add ties at the waistline.

Baby Cool

Wet a mosquito net, wring out, and drape over bassinet.

Baby Entertained

I kept my babies entertained whist busy, by putting them in front of a mirror. They "talk" away to the other "baby".

"Blue — the colour of sunny skies and of a new-born baby's eyes ;
Of magic distances and space, of placid seas and dress of lace ;
Of kingfisher, and blue tit, too, who proudly flaunt their heavenly blue ;
Of smiling bluebells in a wood on Summer eve when life is good.
No other colour is so kind as blue for bringing peace of mind."

Baby's Cot (when visiting)

Ask your hostess for a drawer out of their chest of drawers, add a pillow etc. and baby will be comfortable all night.

Bedding Kept Dry

If visiting, take along some aluminium foil and place it under the sheet, when you put baby down for a nap.

Bedroom Curtains etc., for Daughter

Make them of gingham, and add a matching strip also to the top of her sheets.

Child's Frock Hint

When making a frock, make a handkerchief to match, then if your daughter happens to tear her frock you have a piece (the hanky) to match the dress, for a patch.

Child's Frock (outgrown)

If it is too short or too tight in the bodice, unpick bodice from skirt, then cut the bodice vertically from the shoulder to the waistline, both sides (back and front), then insert braid or lace. Then add braid to bottom of bodice, and sew back to skirt. This looks like a belt when worn ; or, you can cut off the hem and add braid or lace to cut edge, then sew back the hem.

D'oyleys (lace)

Can be made into little girl's collars and cuffs by snipping from outer edge to centre, then by cutting out a circle to fit child's dress. Bind edges if you want a detachable collar. Make cuffs the same wav.

Dough (play)

Keep children amused and entertained at holiday time and weekends with home-made equipment.

Playdough will keep children interested for hours modelling all kinds of things. You need 2 cups plain flour, 1 cup salt, 2 tablespoons cooking oil, 2 tablespoons cream of tartar, 1 cup water. Sift dry ingredients into a medium-sized heavy based saucepan. Make a well in the flour and add the oil. Slowly add the water until it is a smooth paste. Cook over gentle heat stirring continuously until the dough leaves the sides of the saucepan. Turn out, add food colouring and knead until smooth. Stored in an airtight container, it will last for months, or,

Mix 1 cup salt and ½ cup cornflour with 1 cup of boiling water to a thick paste. Allow to cool, than add 2½ cups fine sawdust. Put in plastic bag and knead until well mixed. Leave 3 days in bag before using., After modelling an article it can be painted or varnished if desired ; or,

Tear newspaper into small pieces and soak in water overnight ; then, wring out the water and rub into a pulp. Next, add 1 cup of flour and ⅓ cup of salt, and it is ready for moulding into animals, etc. Paint articles when dry ; or,

Moulding clay for children can be made from 6 cups flour, ½ cup salt, 3 tablespoons alum. Mix to stiff paste with cold water. Leave articles made to dry in the sun. Paint or varnish when dry.

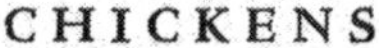

CHICKENS

Make your own Easter chickens, they're quite simple to make.

Materials : 1 oz. of wool—a few strands in a contrasting colour ; small black beads for eyes, pipe cleaners and small pieces of yellow felt.

Cut two circles of cardboard, each three inches in diameter then cut out a small circle in centre of each piece about the size of a 3d. Place the cardboard pieces together, then thread bodkin with wool, using four thicknesses, put the bodkin through the centre hole and wind wool over and over circle till centre hole is filled, introducing other colours here and there.

Take a sharp pair of scissors, cut through wool between outer edges of circle, slip a double strand of wool between the circles and tie at centre very tightly.

Remove cardboard and trim large ball to oval shape. Make a smaller ball, using smaller circles of cardboard. Place the small circle on large one for head of chick, and secure. Bend the pipe cleaners at centre, shape foot by adding a spur and two claws to the one which forms the leg. Stitch to body. Attach beads for eyes and felt for beak.

Children's Frocks on the Line

Hang them inside out, then the hem fades in the sun, and when the frock has to be let down, there's no tell-tale hem mark.

Children Sick

Give them a whistle they can blow when they need attention, as a child's voice is weak and difficult to hear if they are sick.

"A kind word's never gone — it just goes on and on."

Children's Jumpers

When knitting children's jumpers, commence from top of sleeve instead of cuff. In this way, cuff can be unpicked and lengthened quite easily. Follow the knitting pattern by reversing the directions, increasing where decreases are shown and vice versa.

Children's Knees and Hands

Children's knees and hands that are dirty are easily cleaned by rubbing them with a cloth dipped in brass cleaner.

Fingernails (baby's)

Cut them whilst baby is asleep.

"Advice after injury is like medicine after death."

Finger Paint for Children

Make a paste with cornflour and cold water. Add boiling water and stir until it thickens. Divide, and put different food colourings into several portions.

Little grubby finger-prints on the painted door ;
Cotton reels and saucepan-lids on the kitchen floor.
Nothing neat about the house, much as Mummy tries ;
Things are scattered all around, right before her eyes.

Fast as she can tidy up, there's a mess again ;
On the carpet broken cake leaves a nasty stain :
Clothes are dragged from room to room ; shoes are thrown about ;
Everything is hard to find when we're going out.

Mummy's running all the time, putting back in place
All the treasures pulled about ; she has quite a chase.
Mummy has to keep a watch sharper than a hawk.
Things are changed about our house — Baby's learned to walk.

"Keep the corners of your mouth up and the tone of your voice down."

TEMPER: Try whispering in your child's ear; he'll stop crying so he can hear what you are saying and then calm down without realising it.

Shampooing the Children's Hair

Put an inexpensive pair of swimming goggles on them and they will look forward to their hair being washed.

Jumpers (children)

Sew a small loop of elastic inside the cuff edge of your child's jumper so they can slip their thumb in the loop as they put on their coat, making it an easy matter to keep the sleeves from riding up with the coat as they put it on.

Jumpers for Children

Join in a second ball just below the elbows, and knit double wool for several cms. to give it longer wear.

Medicine Taken

Give a child a piece of ice to suck first. He will then experience very little taste.

Napkin Bucket

Put a teaspoon or two of bicarbonate of soda in with the water, when you are soaking baby's napkins. It prevents odours, cleans and deodorizes, removes soap and ammonia, and prevents nappy rash.

Overcoat

Make a loop at the back and pass his or her scarf through the loop, to save losses.

Painting (children's)

Hang behind their doors on the clip-type skirt hangers.

Tablet Taking

Crush, then mix with jam, preferable raspberry — the powder pieces will be camouflaged with the seeds.

Temperature Time

Give him an eggtimer to hold and he will not become restless, as he watches the sand run through.

Wetting the Bed

Sprinkle stain immediately with talcum powder. When dry, brush with a hard clothes brush and the stain should disappear without leaving a mark on the mattress.

HOW TO FOLD A NAPPY

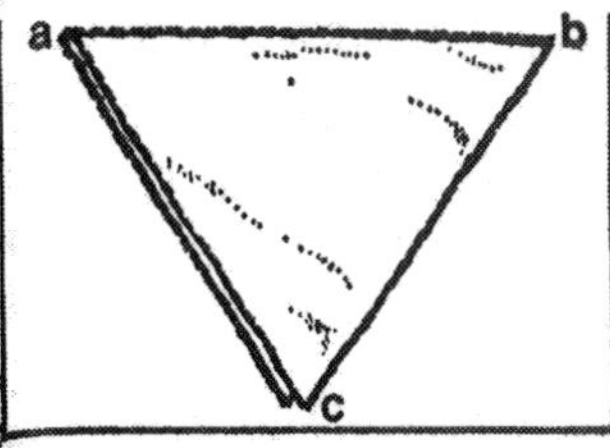

The triangle nappy. Bring 'A' and B' round the baby's middle and 'C' up between the legs. Pin with one safety pin.

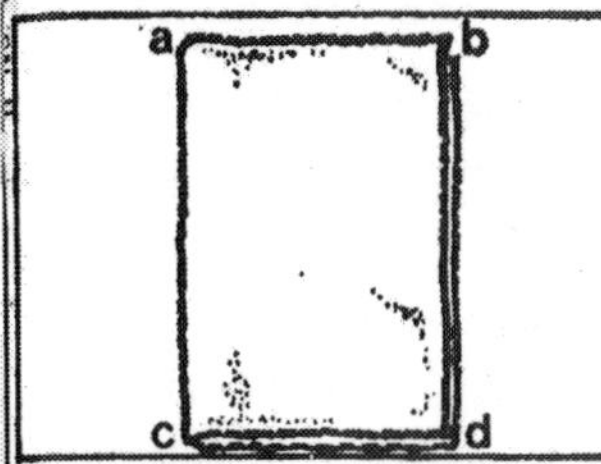

The oblong nappy. 'A' and 'B' are at the back, bring 'C' and 'D' up between the legs. Pin 'A' to 'C' and 'B' to 'D' with safety pins.

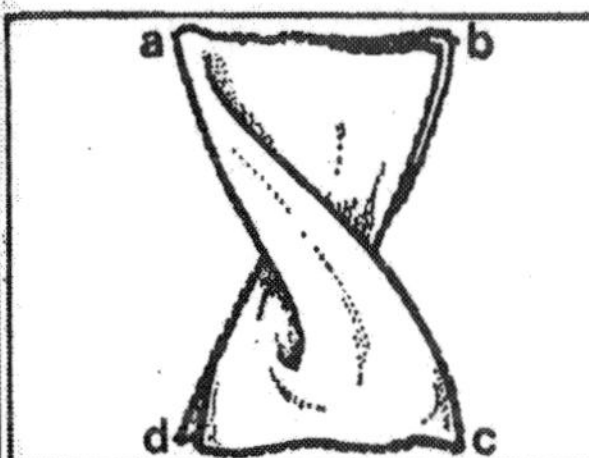

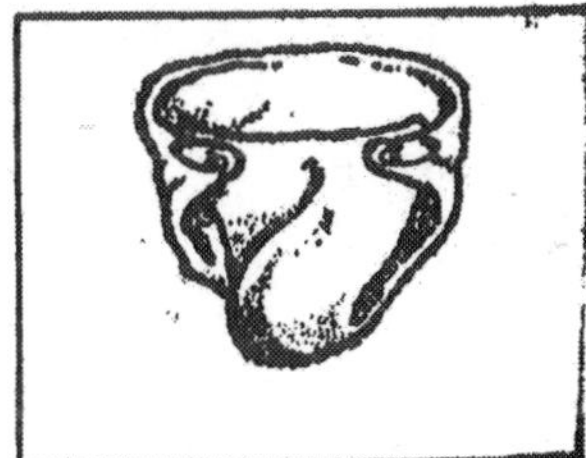

The twisted nappy. As for the oblong nappy, but twist before bringing up between the legs and then pin 'A' to 'D' and 'B' to 'C' with safety pins.

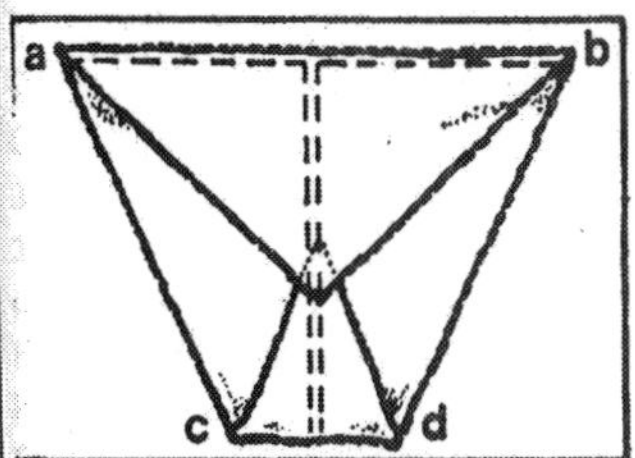

The kite nappy. Fold the sides of the nappy in so that it is wide at the top, narrow at the bottom. Pin 'A' to 'C' and 'B' to 'D' with safety pins.

"Do you know what thought did? He didn't, he only thought he did!"

HANDY HINTS:

BABY'S BOOTEES: Instead of using ribbon, thread with shirring elastic.
BABY'S DRESS: When putting sleeves into a baby's dress, sew the sleeves into the armholes, them sew the sleeve and side seams in one operation. Less fiddly.
BABY'S KNEES: Protect baby's knees when crawling by making a pocket inside the knees of overalls and slipping a piece of foam rubber inside.
BUTTON HOLES ON CHILDRENS CLOTHING: Make horizontal not vertical, and they are less likely to pop open.
CHILDREN'S KNITTED SOX: When casting on, put double number of stitches on, then, on first round knit two together in rib to give sock extra strength.
CHILD'S JUMPER: After completing, thread a few lengths of yarn up the side seams to repair a hole later.
CLOTHES TIDY FOR CHILD: If your lass has outgrown her skirt, sew up botton, put two loops at top, and hang behind her door on a coathanger for a tidy.

At Christmas time, right from their very first, they received far too many toys and this used to confuse them. You name it, they had it, so I'd take some from them after the event, and put them away for their birthdays. When Gerald was four he had his first two-wheel bike and learned to ride it immediately. That was passed on to Ross when he was four, Gerald receiving the next size. A few months beforehand we would sneak the bike away, paint it, then hide it until his birthday and they'd think they had a new bike. (When Ross was four – 22nd September 1949 – the Soviet Union exploded its first atomic bomb.) I remember once when they were sleeping upstairs, and visitors downstairs, and both had received their full size bicycles on Christmas morning, the boys were riding them in the bedrooms at 5 a.m. and, of course, running into the furniture. Quite often the three of us would ride the seven miles to Ross to see Aunt and Uncle and return after lunch. Ross (even at the age of four) would ride in front, Gerald next and me behind, and we'd rest halfway. Aunty Amy made Ross his first long pants suit. It was a pair of riding breeches, split back coat, and cap, in brown donegal tweed. He looked so cute in it riding to Ross, or when he rode our Shetland pony. And was that pony a devil ! When he didn't want the boys on his back, he'd race through two petrol drums standing in the paddock, to drag them off that way, or he'd lie down to throw them off. The trouble began when school children came to play with him, and teased him as well. (When Gerald was twelve the Coronation of Queen Elizabeth II took place on the 2nd June, 1953, and the same year Sir Edmund Hillary, New Zealand explorer and mountaineer, with Sherpa Tensing Norgay, who I met later at Campbell Town, made the first ascent on Mt. Everest. Hillary was born on 20th July 1919).

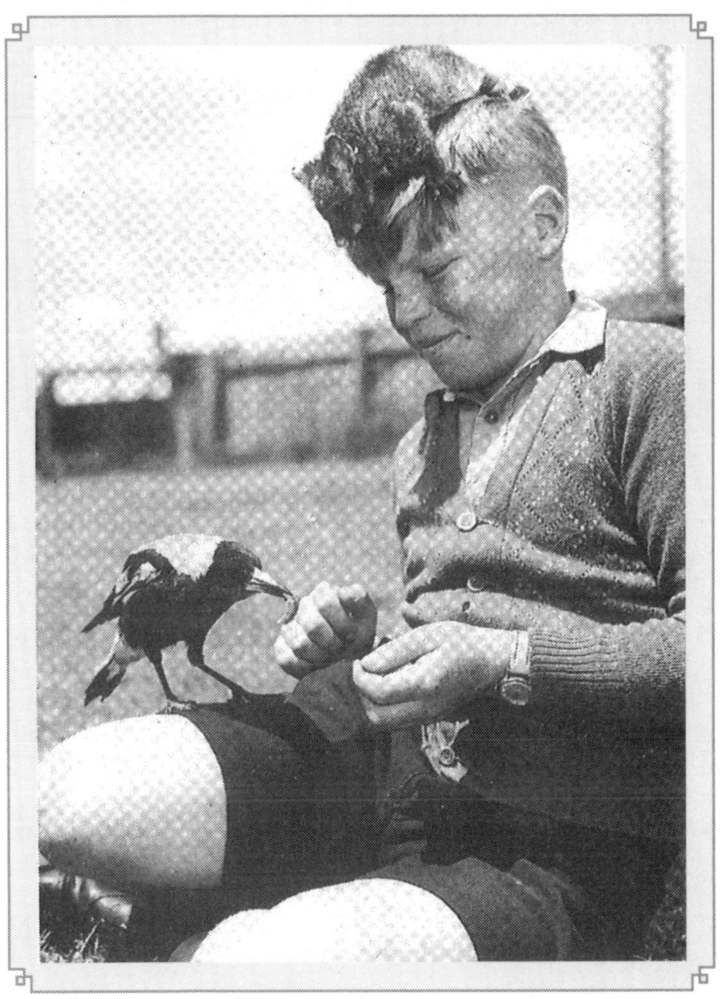

One of my favourite photos of my son Ross Blackwell of Ross, taken when he was 12 years of age by The Mercury in December, 1957. On Ross's head is Possy the possum, and Butch the magpie is taking morsels of food from him. Ross's sons are Damien and Phillip.

A Mother's Love

" It is patient and forgiving when all others are forsaking,
And it never fails or falters even though the heart is breaking . . .
It believes beyond believing when the world around condemns,
And it glows with all the beauty of the rarest, brightest gems . . .
It is far beyond defining,
It defies all explanation,
And it still remains a secret
A many splendoured miracle man cannot understand,
And another wondrous evidence of God's tender guiding hand."

Photograph of Baby

When he's able to sit up for a photograph, stick some cellulose tape on the palm of his hands. The antics while trying to remove it are delightful.

MB

"The teeth are smiling, but is the heart."

Picnic Treat

A picnic treat for youngsters would be frankfurts (small ones) on arrival at destination. Put them in a thermos with boiling water and have a hot dish immediately.

"He who eats till he is sick must fast till he is well."

I had to bring the cows from the streets every afternoon and would take the boys with me, but if it was raining I'd put on their leads and tie them to the table legs. Of course, when Gerald was about six, he didn't require tethering. When I was vacuuming the bedrooms upstairs the boys came with me so I could keep an eye on their whereabouts, and our bedroom window seemed always to fascinate Ross, as he could see out. I often caught him trying to lever himself up, and was always terrified that one day he would over-balance and fall out onto the roof of the workshop,

Shoes (children's)

After buying new leather shoes for children, paint the insides of them with clear nail varnish and their socks won't discolour. Coat the soles with linseed oil and you'll be surprised how much more wear you will get from them. Use raw potato on scuffs.

Toffee Apples

Boil 1 cup of each of brown and white sugar in 1/2 cup each of water and vinegar until it crackles when a little is dropped into cold water. Remove from heat and dip the skewered apple in mixture. Put on a greased plate to dry and wrap each in greased proof paper.

Marjorie, in her Campbell Town days, with just a few representatives of her menagerie.

10. PETS & PESTS

There are creatures that are useful and adorable, such as sheep, rabbits, canaries and newly hatched chicks. And there are creatures that are useless and irritating, such as sparrows, starlings, slugs, silverfish, leeches, cockroaches, mosquitoes, wasps and cocks that crow before dawn.

Just occasionally, the good and the bad can be the same beast. A dog dozing contently by your hearth is a thing of beauty, richly deserving of home-made biscuits, jackets made out of the sleeves of your old jumpers and having its coat deodorised with a liberal sprinkling of bicarb of soda.

A dog that digs in your garden or fouls your nature strip, though, is nothing but a menace and should be dealt with accordingly. White mice in an aquarium are delightful pets, but if you have brown mice in skirting boards you'll need to convince them to walk the plank. Possums in the ceiling? Get them out with Marjorie's ingenious, incendiary method...but make sure you have a fire extinguisher on hand, in case it all goes wrong.

"He who sows courtesy reaps friendship, and he who sows kindness gathers love."

Shrubs (dog deterred)

Put a few mothballs around, or pepper, or cayenne pepper, or ammonia in small bottles pushed in soil.

"Sometimes the message has to be blunt so you will see the point."

Animals

HINTS ON LOOKING AFTER YOUR PETS

Pets I have at present, include a cat, dog, gold fish, rabbit, guinea pig, deer, two kangaroos, pigeons, love-birds, canaries, two magpies, a black jay, two possums, a wallaby, as well as cows, calves, fowls, etc.

I have had numerous others, too, in my time—even to swans—but all need loving care, like a child, to live to the full length of their lives. Clean water daily, warm beds, and sufficient appropriate food and careful handling soon make animals love and cherish their masters.

Guinea pigs make lovely pets, and can be kept outdoors all the year round. They should have a run in a sheltered position away from wind and direct sunshine.

Cockatoos or any parrots are very destructive, but make excellent pets if you have suitable cages. Do not let them have the run of your yard or garden as they will bark the trees ; and if they pick up small pieces of glass, it is fatal to them. That is how we lost our white cockatoo. Cockatoos live for about 70 years and other varieties from 20 to 30 years. Add a little codliver oil to their feed occasionally to keep them healthy. Do not give a parrot milk as it sets up a skin irritation. They need plenty of sunshine and shelter from wind as they catch cold easily. Cover the cage at night if it is outside. A young bird can be taught to talk in three to four months, and males are the best talkers, although females do talk.

Cod-liver oil is a good conditioner for most animals. It is a good substitute for sunshine in winter or for tropical animals in cold climates. Dosages range from ½ teaspoon weekly for a cat or small dog to a dessertspoon a week for an Alsation dog. Mix the oil with your pet's food. Most of them will like it because it has a fish taste. Glucose is also a vital conditioner for most animals and can be bought in a concentrated form—either as liquid or grain.

A most important thing is **do not overfeed your pet.** Healthy animals should always be a little hungry, as they are in their natural state. If an animal is pregnant she should be allowed to use her own judgment and eat as much as she likes. A change of diet is as important to your pet as an occasional visit to a restaurant is to you. White bread is not good for any animal, but there is an ingredient called "agene" in most white bread that is particularly bad for wild animals. Brown bread on th other hand is quite safe.

Pets will be far happier and healthier if you use a little common sense with them. Their needs are basically similar to ours in many ways. It is our responsibility to try to understand their simple needs and to care for them accordingly. Remember the golden rule.

Fish :

3 or 4 grains of Conde's Crystals in the tank each week will keep tank clean. This is most important if you want healthy fish. A pinch of Epsom salts once a week stops the fish from becoming constipated. One meal a day in the summer and one every week in winter is what a fish requires. As much as will lie flat on a threepence is sufficient for a 3-inch fish.

If the water turns green in aquarium the light is usually too bright. Try pasting some tissue paper on the side facing the light or introducting more plants.

Indigestion is the most common ailment with fish and is caused through constipation brought about through feeding the fish with too much starchy dried food. Give finely cut up earth worms occasionally or scraped lean raw meet. They also like boiled cabbage or spinach and finely cut lettuce.

Remember that the most important thing when selecting gold fish is that they

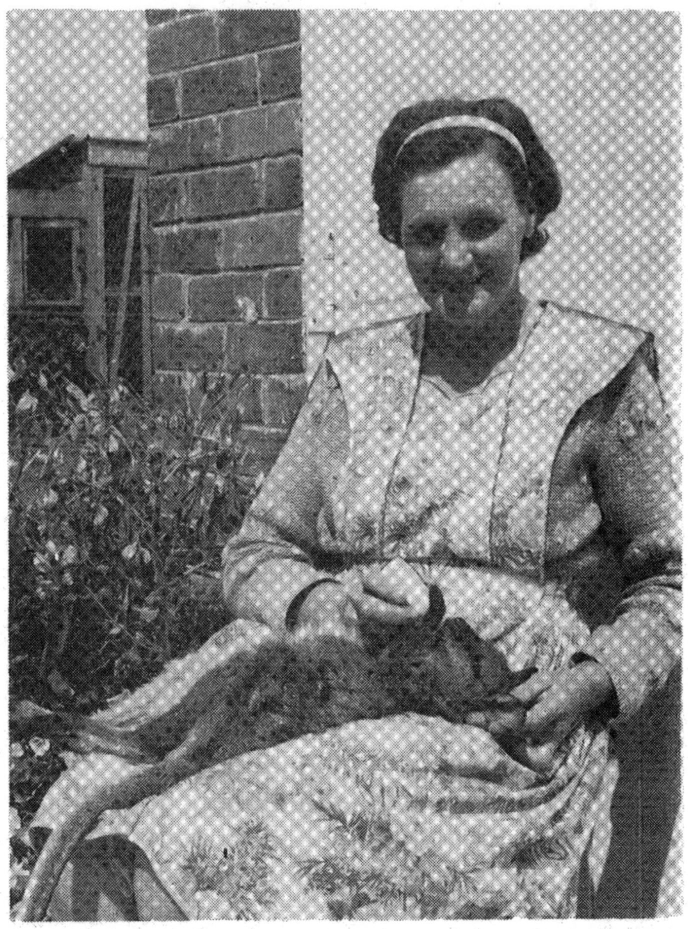

Mrs. Blackwell feeding her baby kangaroo "Mick".

* * *

Those who love deeply never grow old. They may die of old age, but they die young.

Sheep (fly blown)

I know a friend who lathered a sheep with my wool mix, found in "Washing and Ironing" section, and it was cured.

Freda Fi Fi

In May 1966, Mrs. Kirk gave Adrian and me five fowls to add to our menagerie of two wallabies, rabbit, cat, and canary, then on the 21st January 1967 we went to Devonport and Adrian bought me a poodle pup for $30 from a Mrs. Simms. The pup was seven weeks old, a ball of fluff, and we called her Freda Fi Fi (Freda after my second name Alfreda). Next, Adrian arrived home with a lamb, so she was called Willis, after my third maiden name. Adrian went into raptures over that dog, and was really upset when we had her de-sexed on the 8th May, same year. Every night after he came home from school he would sit on the floor and bowl a ball down the long passage into the sunroom, and wait till Freda Fi Fi brought it back, then he would repeat it for half an hour. Every 4th December – her birthday – he bought her an icecream and a chocolate frog, and I made her a patty cake, and she sat at an out-doors table and ate them. Whenever he had a spare moment he took her for walks, bought her a plastic chair, made her a pine box bed, and a tick, then had a builder make her an expensive kennel ; that was never used until 1980, but more about that later.

Once, when she killed one of our fowls, I was wondering how he was going to deal with her, but he hung the fowl around her neck for several hours, and it cured her. In May 1968 we ordered boots for Freda to wear outside when it was raining, so that her feet wouldn't dirty the carpets inside when the boots were taken off. I also made her a raincoat. However, when the boots arrived there were four, not two of course (we'd forgotten about that) and it took ages to put them on when she wagged her tail to go out, because they had to be all laced up as well. But, oh, the first time we put them on, we nearly died laughing. She lay down, stood up and held both back legs off the floor, then one leg, shook her legs, and the performance was as good as a circus. Our only regret was that we forgot to film her antics.

Adrian was really angry one day at the Polling Booth. Freda Fi Fi was with us, but out of sight in her basket behind Adrian, and when a voter came in, she barked. This particular voter then said, as she walked towards him, " Get out of my way you b–, mongrel," and that really stirred Adrian. He rose to his feet and shaking his hand at him, said – " Look here Mr. – if you were as well bred as this dog you'd be a gentleman." *" Before a fight, two men are boasters ; afterwards, only one."*

Woollens (washing mixture)

In a screw top jar put 2 cups of soap flakes (Lux), 2 tablespoons of eucalyptus oil and ¾ of a cup of methylated spirit. Shake well. Use in the proportion of 4 teaspoons to 20 cups of water. (The flakes remain visible in the mixture.)

DOG COAT FOR FREDA FI FI

MATERIALS

2 balls 8ply (50g balls); 1 pair No 8 (4mm) Disc knitting needles; cable needle; 12 buttons; stitch holder.

MEASUREMENT:

To fit an average-size miniature poodle.

TENSION:

22 1/2 sts to 10cm over st-st.

ABBREVIATIONS:

Cable, slip next 2 sts on to cable needle and leave at front of work, k 2, then k 2 from cable needle; Inc, pick up loop which lies before next st, place on left hand needle and knit through the back of it.

COAT:

Cast on 110 sts.

1st Row: K 2, * p 1, k 1, rep from * to end.

2nd Row: K 2, *p 1, k 1, rep from * to end.

3rd Row: K 2, cast off 2 sts, rib to end.

4th Row: Rib to last 2 sts, cast on 2 sts, p 1, k 1.

5th Row: Rib 7, *p 2, k 4, p 2, k 3, rep from * to last 15 sts, p 2, k 4, p 2, rib 7.

6th Row: Rib 7, inc, *k 2, p 4, k 2, p 3, rep from * to last 15 sts, K 2, p 4, k 2, Inc, rib 7.

7th Row: Rib 7, k 1, * p 2, k 4, p 2, k 3, rep from *to last 16 sts, p 2, k 4, p 2, k 1, rib 7.

8th Row: Rib 7, p 1, * k 2, p 4, k 2, p 3, rep from *to last 16 sts, k 2, p 4, k 2, p 1, rib 7.

9th Row: Rib 7, k 1 * p 2, cable, p 2, k 3, rep from * to last 16 sts, p 2, cable, p 2, k 1, rib 7.

10th Row: Rib 7, p 1 * k 2, p 4, k 2, p 3, rep from * to last 16 sts, k 2, p 4, k 2, p 1, rib 7.

Cont. in patt (as in last 6 rows), inc (as before and taking extra sts into patt) at each end of 2nd row and foll 6th rows until there are 122 sts, at same time working buttonholes in foll 9th and 10th rows from previous buttonhole.

Work 12 rows, working a buttonhole in 7th and 8th rows.

DIVIDE FOR LEG HOLES

1st Row: Rib 7, patt 8, k 2, turn. Work 14 rows on these sts, working a buttonhole in 4th, 5th and 14th rows and keeping rib 7 and k 2 border correct.

Leave sts on a stitch holder, join yarn to rem sts.

1st Row: K 2, patt 38, turn.

NOTE: When turning, bring yarn to front of work, slip next st on to right hand needle, take yarn to back of work, slip st back on to left hand needle, then turn. This avoids holes.

2nd and Alt Rows: Patt to last 2 sts, k 2.

3rd Row: K 2, patt 33, turn.

5th Row: K 2, patt 28, turn.

7th Row: K 2, patt 23, turn.

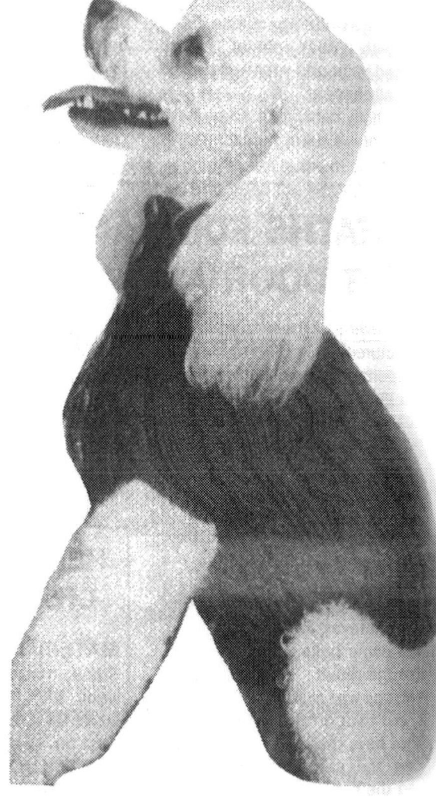

9th Row: K 2, patt 18, turn.

11th Row: K 2, patt 13, turn.

13th Row: K 2, patt 8, turn.

15th Row: K 2, patt 86, turn, cont on these sts.

Rep rows 1 to 13 incl once.

Joker

Once when Cliff was away camping and I kept Joker home for company, he didn't greet me when I opened the back door in the morning so I went to the gate and whistled him. I heard Joker's faint bark somewhere, so ran northwards in the direction of the bark and found him on the side of the road opposite Doctor Pugh's residence. He was badly injured – had been hit by a car – so I carried him across to Doctor Pugh, and after he examined him, informed me that he could do nothing for him – he would not get better. I carried Joker home and rang Ruth and Max who came up from Moonah and took him back to a vet. where he stayed for three weeks. Then the vet. rang me and said that Joker would have to be destroyed as he didn't respond to treatment and continually cried. I told him I didn't want Joker destroyed, so he rang Ruth and Max and they collected him and brought him back home. He was helpless, couldn't stand, but could eat and, my goodness, he was pleased to see me! He licked and licked my hand and tried to move. I found a large wooden box, knocked out one side so I could attend him, put a layer of plastic, then paper, next an old bag and finally straw and Joker, and there he stayed on the hearth mat until he got strong enough to walk. I massaged him every day, fed and kept him clean by renewing the straw, and kept him in the box for a couple of weeks before I stood him up for a minute or two. After doing that a few times I obtained two kerosene boxes, put bricks inside to keep them firm, then stood Joker in between them for ten minutes or so. I did that for about a week, then one morning when I got up, Joker wasn't in his box. He was out on the mat. I was that excited because I knew he could at last move his limbs. Each day he improved, and moved a little more, sliding along on his side, then one day when I stood him up he took a step forward, then later two steps and so on, until he walked, even ran, although one of his back legs was stiff. It was a miracle, and a victory for me, as I loved him dearly. He lived a long time after that.

" The good we never miss we rarely prize."

" Lord, help me live from day to day in such a self-forgetful way,
That even when I kneel to pray, my prayer shall be for 'Others'.
Help me in all the work I do to ever be sincere and true,
And know, that all I do for you must needs be done for 'Others'.
And when my work on earth is done, and my new work in Heaven's begun,
May I forget the crown I've won while thinking still of 'Others'.
'Others', Lord, yes, 'Others'! Let this my motto be.
Help me to live for others that I may live for Thee."

" Count your garden by the flowers,
Never by the leaves that fall;
Count your days by golden hours,
Don't remember clouds at all.
Count your night by stars, not shadows,
Count your years with smiles not tears,
Count your blessings not your troubles,
Count your age by friends, not years."

Dog Bandage

Discourage your dog from tearing off the bandage by wetting a cake of soap and rubbing over the bandage.

"Love me, love my dog."

Dog Biscuits

Mix 500g (1 lb.) each of bran and pollard, 250g (1/2 lb.) blood and bone, 1 cup powdered milk, 375g (3 lb.) grated suet or dripping, 1 teaspoon salt. Add warm water and mix to a stiff paste. Press into a greased baking dish and mark into squares. Bake in a slow oven until cooked, or,

Mix to a stiff dough with water, 9 cups bran, 6 cups pollard 3 cups blood and bone. Add 2 tablespoons skim milk powder. Cook as above. Another recipe is to boil 2 kg. of liver, cut small, add 6 cups each of bran, pollard, oatmeal and blood and bone, and 3 cups linseed meal. Mix with water off the liver and bake as above.

Dog (coat cleaner)

Rub in some bicarbonate of soda, then comb it out. It is deodorizing too.

Dog Food

Sprinkle parsley onto your tinned dog food and stir in. Keeps their liver and kidneys healthy.

Dog Kennels

Wash out with kerosene to keep fleas from entering. If fleas are already there, put salt in the kennel and they will leave.

"Diplomacy — The art of saying 'Nice Doggie' till you find a rock."

Dogs Bowl (ants away)

To keep ants away, place bowl inside a larger one of water.

Dogs Coat

Make from the sleeve of a discarded jumper. Cut holes for armholes.

Dogs Fouling Lawn

Dogs won't foul areas where there is fresh water, so place some in containers, if you are troubled by roaming dogs.

Cat Food

Finely dice and boil 3 sheep hearts, or similar amount of other meat or fish, 2 medium carrots, small cup soaked soya beans, and any green vegetables, small cup rice. Boil all in 6 cups water, adding more water if needed. While mixture is still hot, dissolve 1 heaped tablespoon gelatine, and add to mixture. Cool, and refrigerate. When dishing out portions for their meals, add ½ teaspoon of cod-liver oil, once a week. It is a good conditioner, and substitute for sun in the winter time.

Cats or Dogs

Cats hate the smell of liquid ammonia, eucalyptus and cayenne pepper, so if you are worried by them, sink a few small uncorked bottles, each containing a teaspoon of ammonia or eucalyptus (or sprinkling of pepper) into the soil where they frequent. Renew occasionally or if they are a nuisance in the garden, blend chillies in water, add a teaspoon of detergent and spray on the plants.

Cat Shampoo

Bicarbonate of soda is an excellent dry shampoo for cats.

Cats (hair balls in)

During shedding season, many long-haired cats accumulate hair balls in their stomach. This can cause such symptoms as loss of appetite, vomiting, coughing, sneezing and bad breath. To prevent, or cure hair balls, give cat some oil to lap once a week. The oil from a sardine tin will not only be therapeutic, but a treat for the cat. Cod liver oil is also suitable, adding it to food in small amounts — ½ teaspoon — is a good method. Combing the cat weekly usually gets rid of most of it.

"Animals are such agreeable friends — they don't ask questions, or pass on criticism."

Cats (ruining wire on windows or doors)

Spray the wire mesh with ammonia, but repeat it if it rains, or, rub with a little oil of cloves.

Cockroaches

Put the peelings of cucumber about the house if you have cockroaches. Generally they get in kitchen cupboards or behind refrigerators. Why cucumber is so effective has to do with the chemistry of the cucumber. Remember pigs won't eat 'it', or,

Mix equal parts of borax and sugar and put in containers where they are, or, mix 1 tablespoon each of borax, flour and sugar to a paste with water and bake in moderate oven until dry. Put small pieces under the refrigerator, in cupboards etc. where they are. Keep out of reach of children as borax is poisonous.

Mice

Push steel wool, not paper into their hole (not the soap impregnated kind). They cannot chew steel wool.

Moth Preventative

Mix about ½ cup Epsom salts with 20 whole cloves, and put in corners of cupboards etc. Paint inside cupboard with oil of cedar.

Mouse or Rat Trap

Sprinkle vanilla essence on a crust of bread and tie on. They won't resist it, or put a raisin on trap, as it is a good decoy, or, put chocolate on a mouse trap. Never fails. They can't smell your fingers for the chocolate. They also like coconut.

He told Mum once of a "perfect" way of killing mice. First you put some cheese in a thimble, then you take a basin, turn it upside down, rest the thimble under the brim, so that when the mouse went under and tried to get the cheese, the thimble would go under the basin, the basin would drop to the floor and you'd have a mouse. To get the mouse out, you wriggled the basin around until you found the tail, grabbed it, took the basin off, then flung the mouse to the cat. This is all right if the basin was of no further use, and you weren't frightened of mice. I think Mum's method was better. She filled a kerosene tin with water, sprinkled the surface with chaff, then rested a piece of board against it, so the mice would venture up it, walk on the chaff and drop to the bottom.

MOUSE BAIT: A pumpkin seed is a good mouse bait on the trap.

"A good rooster crows in any hen house."

WHITE MICE

A square fish aquarium is an excellent place to keep mice, as you can watch their antics and enjoy them better. If you cannot afford an aquarium, a square box with fly-wire front and door would be as good. Have a revolving wheel and a ladder, as mice like to play.

Use sawdust or hay on the floor for cleanliness. The important thing is to clean their cages often to stop any unpleasant smell. They will eat anything you leave from the table except meat, and love wheat or bird seed.

They need fresh drinking water and love bread and milk occasionally.

If you have more than one buck in the cage, they will fight, but you can have several does. I would advise to have only one pair, or better still, a buck, as they breed quickly. Do not forget to give greens occasionally, such as lettuce. Mice live for two years in captivity.

Fowls (eating eggs)

Fill an empty shell with mustard. Seal and put in nest. Be careful when you are making the hole in the egg. Then blow out the egg before filling. Some burn the sharp tip of the fowls beak or snip it off, which does not seem to harm them.

"You make your living out of what you eat, but you make your life out of what you give."

Here I am feeding my pet hens in the garden at our home in Devonport.

Fowls (scale on legs of)

Dip the feet and shanks in a mixture of equal parts of kerosene and sump oil in early morning. You can help loosen the scales, if you scrub them first in warm soapy water and let legs dry, before dipping in above solution. Keep pen racked, clean and spray with Malathion in case there are scales and mites laying around. The scales are caused by an infestation of an itch called Chemidosoptesmutans or the scaly-leg mite.

The mite lives mainly on the birds and it burrows into the skin where the females deposit their eggs. As scales drop off, it spreads to other birds. The first signs are found between the toes, and then spreads.

Cock Crowing

Prevent them crowing in early morning by suspending loosely a small lath above the perch, so that when he stretches his neck to crow, his comb will come gently in contact with it. This will soon stop his noise.

"Sometimes the message has to be blunt so you will see the point."

CHICKENS HATCHED IN AN ELECTRIC FRYPAN

This is a worthwhile substitute when the hen leaves the nest.

METHOD 1: For this you will need the frypan with the glass lid, an asbestos mat, a dish large enough to hold 5 eggs and some wadding in a small dish for water. Thermometer. Place asbestos mat in frypan, which has been previously heated to 99.9 degrees, at which temperature the frypan should remain until hatching is completed. Place dish filled with wadding on mat and arrange eggs comfortably packed but not touching each other in the dish of wadding, standing them on their pointed ends and slightly slanting. Place another small dish of water in the frypan, and put on the lid. Every 12 hours turn eggs and allow them to slant the opposite way. Hatching takes approximately 3 weeks. As chicks emerge from the shells, raise the lid of the frypan very slightly to allow ventilation. A second frypan, heated to just warm and inverted but propped up to allow air to pass through, may be used to cover the chicks when hatched, or failing that, a box with holes in lid put near the fire will do.

METHOD 2: Line frypan with aluminium foil, then half fill with sand, over which a clean tea towel is placed. Place eggs on tea towel as in method 1. The lid of the frypan is put on with vent slightly open and the temperature at just warm, turning the eggs as before mentioned, every 12 hours.

A man who won numerous prizes with poultry at shows, gave me the following tips. Don't feed chickens for 24 hours after they are hatched. Nature provides for this period. Brown bread soaked in milk, then squeezed dry, makes the best 'first foods' for them. Sunflower seeds are perfect food for poultry

A good disinfectant for your fowl house can be had by putting sulphur in a tin and setting alight to it. It will keep germs at bay in the home too.

* * *

POULTRY HINTS: To cure lice on fowls, dip a feather in nicotine sulphate and run a thin line of it along the perch, just before they go to bed at night. Repeat after a fortnight, if exceptionally bad.

Or, burn the pest out with a blow lamp, then paint the house out with creosote. Dust the fowls with derris dust or spray with pyrethrum. Hold fowl upside down to do this.

To keep laying hens disease-resistant give them a good feeding of raw onion at least once a week. Cut onions finely with a sharp knife and add to the morning feed. Do not mince as that only squeezes out the juice, the main food value.

Put 1 teaspoon of cider vinegar into 5 cups of their drinking water to keep them healthy. It also promotes quicker feathering. Add kelp meal to their starter feed to ensure swift, healthy development.

Starlings

Cut strips of foil and hang about in fruit trees. Give each strip a twist. They don't like the rustle.

Swallows in Garage or under Verandah

Hang a plastic bird there and they will soon leave.

BUDGERIGARS AND CANARIES

Birds :

Canaries or budgerigars like spinach or lettuce leaves in their daily diet, as well as their seed. Seeding grasses and dandelion are excellent too. A tuft of grass, roots and all, is a favourite with my budgerigars.

If they will eat an apple they will benefit by doing so. Do not leave uneaten pieces lying in the cage.

A budgerigar kept indoors as a pet and deprived of access to direct sunlight may suffer from a deficiency of Vitamin D, but this can be made good by the use of cod-liver oil, especially during winter months. Mix 1 teaspoon of cod-liver oil into a pint of their seed, well stirred through. Do not mix this all at once as it tends to turn rancied. The above would do for a cage of about 20 birds outside that do not get much sunlight. About one-eighth of a teaspoon would do one bird in a cage indoors. It will keep sweet for about 3 days, so you'll know by the quantity above how much your birds will need at a time.

Fine shell grit is another essential and cuttlefish bone, which provides calcium.

You can easily tell a male and a female budgerigar by the pad above the beak with the two small apertures. It is called the cere, and the two openings are the nostrils. In young birds the ceres in both sexes are pale blue, but as the male bird grows older it turns to a deeper blue and the female bird goes a rich brown. It is easy to tell if the budgerigar you have just purchasd is young or an old bird : the young bird's eyes are large and black, the older birds have smaller black circles, with a white ring around them. This does not develop until the bird has reached 5 months old.

If you want your pet to talk, a budgerigar must be no older than 4 weeks when purchased. Do not go near its cage for a week ; it must have sufficient food and water for that period. By then it will have come accustomed to its surroundings and all fear and fright will be gone. Commence by saying one sentence such as "Hullo Joey," or "Good morning, boy," or whatever his name may be. Always say the same sentence until he has said it, then you can go ahead and teach it other sentences. In the evening is the best time, with the lights lowered. Place a cloth over the cage and insert your hand and tickle the bird's head, all the time repeating the one sentence. Keep your hand perfectly still if he takes fright and flies about his cage. Wait until he settles down and do it again. It will soon learn to enjoy it after a few nights.

The chicken is a useful bird a little laddie said,
Cause folks can eat him 'fore he's born and after he is dead.

Cockatoo Rearing

Give porridge if the bird is too young to crack and consume ordinary parrot seed. They will nibble fresh greens and grated carrot and it is an ideal start to teach a young bird to feed for itself.

Fruit is another good standby, as it is soft enough for the youngest cockatoo and contains sufficient vitamins to compensate for anything which is lacking in the sustitute diet. If your cockatoo appears dopey, he probably has indigestion, so give him smaller seed — canary, linseed, safflower — and crumbled biscuit mixed with honey and cod liver oil. Farex baby food is excellent for any parrot.

Marjorie is a great bird-lover. She is expert in getting budgies to talk, and hatching chicks in an electric frypan.

Canary Tips

Canary babies start to warble on the 14th day. To get deep yellow canaries mate a deep yellow with a light yellow — never two deep yellows. Strawberry baskets make good nests.

When canaries neglect their young it is because both are young parents. It is better to have at least one parent 2 years old, preferably the female. If the male is younger than the female the chances for producing a large number of males are greater. Put plenty of building material in the cage, for, if you don't, the parents will pick feathers from the heads of their young. If you want 50 per cent white canaries, mate a white with a pale yellow. It makes no difference which mate is white.

Insect in ear

If someone around smokes, a puff into the ear will make the insect crawl out.

Cabbage Moths

Beat them without sprays by using gauze cages. Drive a few stakes into soil and wrap around a non-metal gauze and tie with fine wire and it will keep out all pests and let plenty of light in, or ;

If you cannot make cages, sprinkle salt in centre of plants. You can also spray them with salty water — about a dessertspoon to ½ bucket of water, or ;

Spoon a little sour milk into the centre (vinegar added to milk will sour it). If they have already landed make a powder of ½ cup salt and 1 cup flour and shake a little of the mixture on plants in early morning. The grubs will eat this, bloat up and fall off dead. Cabbage moths do not like rosemary, sage, nasturtiums or tomatoes, so grow one or two of them near your cabbage plants.

Leeches

When bushwalking take a jar of Vegemite with you. It puts the leech out of his misery faster than salt will ever do.

Codling Moth

Stop codling moth, by placing round a tree trunk a sticky substance which will prevent the ascent of the wingless females. Put it on grease proof paper which has been securely tied to the tree both top and bottom. Periodically inspect it and destroy all you find. Band about April and leave on all the winter. The ideal grease should remain "tacky" throughout the winter. Or, put corrugated cardboard or hessian around trunk and main branches in November. Take off and burn in summer. The larvae spin their cocoons inside the corrugations; or,

Put a little vinegar into a bottle and hang it on your apple tree. Codling moth enter and have no way to leave, and the vinegar adds the finishing touches to them; or

Mix 1 part molasses with 9 parts water and half fill tins or plastic cups with this mixture and hang in your apple tree by wire loops. Spray tree twice with clensol and white oil.

SILVERFISH

Half fill a tumbler or small bowl with flour and dangle some strips of flannel in the flour, letting it come well over the sides, so silverfish can climb up the flannel and into the flour where they will smother.

Silverfish

Do not like cloves or salt, so sprinkle some in kitchen cupboards or drawers, or a mixture of sulphur and Epsom salts. (Put salt on carpets if they are eating them. Leave all night, before vacuuming). To catch them in a cupboard, put a small glass, half filled with flour into the cupboard and it is a sure catcher. To prevent them entering your cupboards and wardrobes, paint the inside with oil of cedar, or, wipe over with kerosene.

To deter them eating the paper after making scrapbooks, etc.; mix some ground cloves and a few drops of turpentine in with paste.

Sparrows in the Ceiling

Sprinkle a little cayenne where they get in, and they'll soon leave.

Wasps

Sprinkle liberally with an insecticidal dust around the entry to their nest and they will carry the dust through the nest and destroy it. European wasps were first noticed in Tasmania in the late 1950's and have since spread to Victoria.

Another way to eradicate them is to pour diesel oil into their nest or spray with kerosene, or, sprinkle Lane's Rose Dust in their nests. If you cannot get to their nests put derris dust in vacuum cleaner, put the hose on opposite end and turn on, or, place a container of oil — any kind, near their entrance and they will end up in the "soup".

> *"When we feel someone else's pain we can help to lesson it."*

Cockroach tip: Rub vaseline on the inside neck of a jam jar; add a piece of banana. The cockroach goes in but can't climb out, or, mix sugar and bicarbonate of soda 50-50 and put in a jar. See also silverfish.

Cows: Give a cow a dessertspoonful of apple cider vinegar a day for 3 weeks before calving (pour over the concentrates). Organic farmers claim it is a "cure-all" and that it helps in cases of mastitis. At the first sign of a clot in the milk or the feeling of heat in the udder, apple cider should be given and within a few hours you should see a noticeable improvement. (Give cider vinegar to pigs too, if they get sick.)

Apple cider vinegar brings out everything in the original apple except the changes that take place in the sugar content of the apple juices. These are altered into the acid which is vinegar. The best product is made from the crushed whole apples but it is possible to obtain an apple cider vinegar from peelings and cores after the pulp has been extracted. This is less valuable medicinally. The vinegar also contains traces of calcium, phosphorous, sodium, potassium, iron, copper, zinc, riboflavin and nicotine acid.

An old gypsy remedy for cows having off-spring is to give them draught beer to help them expel the afterbirth.

> *The cow is a useful animal that gives us milk and meat,*
> *Hides to make our boots and shoes, gelatine from its feet;*
> *And there's no waste in nature for how often, to be sure,*
> *Are we told to mulch our gardens with well-rotted cow manure.*

We were never without pets

We were never without pets as Cliff periodically brought home rabbits, possums and baby kangaroos from the bush. Mr. Frank Dowse, M.B.E., the then curator of the Launceston City Park, and his wife, were friends of mine and he gave me angora rabbits too, as well as our first gold fish (Mr. Dowse died at Devonport on the 16th May, 1983). We built a lovely cage with wire netting a foot under the ground. Ross's favourite pet was the rabbit. One we had at one stage was almost human. It was cunning and liked playing hide and seek. It ran about the house and outside, but if you tried to catch it, it would get behind a hedge, then you would go behind the hedge to get it, and Nipper, as we called him, would walk through to the other side, and this would go on for some time, until tempted by a piece of carrot or biscuit. Ross often sneaked him into bed too, but after one instance (which gave him the name of Nipper) he wasn't allowed to any more. Ross always put him back in his cage about 10 p.m. but this night he forgot, and the result was that next morning I found several holes in the blanket and sheets. Another time Nipper disgraced himself properly, *and* on a Christmas Day! My sister Beatrice, brother-in-law Tony, and their boys Barry, Ashley and Danny, were at my place for the day, and Tony was sitting back on the sofa with Nipper on his chest, stroking him. When he put him down, there was a big hole in the lapel of Tony's sportscoat. But he was a wonderful pet and although Joker, our dog, was a good rabbiter, he never touched Nipper. They sat together on the couch, or stretched out on the mat together in front of the fire. A pet possum was just as friendly with them inside, but he became too mischievous, so in the end we had to keep him in a cage.

to constantly watch them when they were small. We were never without pets as Cliff periodically brought home rabbits, possums and baby kangaroos from the bush. Mr. Frank Dowse, M.B.E., the then curator of the Launceston City Park, and his wife, were friends of mine and he gave me angora rabbits too, as well as our first gold fish (Mr. Dowse died at Devonport on the 16th May, 1983). We built a lovely cage with wire netting a foot under the ground. Ross's favourite pet was the rabbit. One we had at one stage was almost human. It was cunning and liked playing hide and seek. It ran about the house and outside, but if you tried to catch it, it would get behind a hedge, then you would go behind the hedge to get it, and Nipper, as we called him, would walk through to the other side, and this would go on for some time, until tempted by a piece of carrot or biscuit. Ross often sneaked him into bed too, but after one instance (which gave him the name of Nipper) he wasn't allowed to any more. Ross always put him back in his cage about 10 p.m. but this night he forgot, and the result was that next morning I found several holes in the blanket and sheets. Another time Nipper disgraced himself properly, *and* on a Christmas Day! My sister Beatrice, brother-in-law Tony, and their boys Barry, Ashley and Danny, were at my place for the day, and Tony was sitting back on the sofa with Nipper on his chest, stroking him. When he put him down, there was a big hole in the lapel of Tony's sportscoat. But he was a wonderful pet and although Joker, our dog, was a good rabbiter, he never touched Nipper. They sat together on the couch, or stretched out on the mat together in front of the fire. A pet possum was just as friendly with them inside, but he became too mischievous, so in the end we had to keep him in a cage.

Slater Bait

Mix 30 to 60g. (1 to 2ozs.) of arsenate of lead with 5kg. of bran and 140ml. of molasses, or 110g. of brown sugar and 0.5 litres of water, or, dip pieces of sliced potato in arsenate of lead and place under timber or pots where slaters congregate. Keep away from pets, children or birds.

Slug and Snail Baits

Mix one heaped tablespoon wholemeal flour and one teaspoon of gluten flour with water. Put in a margarine container until ⅔ full. (This concoction also attracts earwigs.) Cut a hole in the lid as big as a 50 cent piece. Put in their haunts, sunk into the ground, or surround with mulches.

Stale wholemeal bread crumbed with water works too ; or,

Grated potato peeling, mixed in water. They are attracted to foods containing or producing yeast.

Possums in the Ceiling

Put some flowers of sulphur in a foil dish in the ceiling and set it alight, and you won't be troubled again.

Puppy (new)

Wrap a ticking clock in an old jumper and put in the puppy's bed if you want a good nights sleep. The pup will think the tick is the mother's heart beat. Add a hot water bag, ½ filled with warm water too. Do not add a cover — the water moves as the skin of its mother.

Puppy Urine

Sponge carpet with ¼ cup white vinegar, 2 cups warm water and 1 teaspoon of detergent (mixed together). Rinse in clean water. Pat dry. If an old stain, leave mixture on for ½ hour. Sprinkle with talcum powder.

Rabbits as Pets

Cabbage and lettuce leaves have no food value for rabbits, except perhaps vitamins and moisture. Do not give them parsnips, rhubarb leaves or potatoes. Give them thistles, carrot tops, grass and some crushed oats and bran made crumbly with boiling water, and (as a special treat) apple.

RABBITS

Give your rabbit a mixed diet and do not let it have cabbage or lettuce leaves; cauliflower leaves sometimes, and oats, fresh grass and sow-thistles; carrot tops, but not parsnips or raw potatoes. In winter, a crumbly warm mash of poultry meal is relished, and a special treat is an apple. Don't forget to give fresh water daily and don't believe anyone who says that rabbits don't drink! Rabbits are mature at 6 months and one doe can produce 58 young in a year.

In the garden, where you can make something out of almost nothing, Marjorie is in her element. Here, she poses with the roots of her labour.

11. IN THE GARDEN

Marjorie Bligh is not in favour of lawn. At least, not in her own backyard. Given nature's abundant variety of flowers and fruits and vegetables, who in their right mind would choose merely to grow grass? In the 1970s Marjorie's beloved second husband, Adrian, attempted to protect some of the remnant lawn in the Madden Street garden by erecting a cyclone fence around it, but Marjorie and her rampant flower and vegetable beds eventually proved the stronger force.

In the realm of the garden, where this year's tomato seeds are next year's tomatoes, and where new plants are just a neighbour's garden and a secateurs' snip away, thrifty Marjorie is in her element. Here, where discipline and know-how are rewarded with such tangible signs of success as fruit and flowers, she thrives as happily as her roses, lemons, hippeastrums, aspidistras, daphne, lilies, silverbeet, jonquils, apples, passionfruit, figs, apricots, persimmons, loquats, blueberries, grapes…

It's easy to spend a lot of money on a garden, Marjorie cautions, but far from necessary. Why buy plastic plant protectors when an old brassiere and a handful of stakes will serve? Umbrellas at the end of their street life can be rigged up to provide shelter for frost-tender plants—just cut off the curving part of the handle before pushing the spike into the soil. You can cut up perished garden hoses into lengths and fasten them together for a nifty mat to save your knees while weeding. And don't forget your discarded pantyhose—they're good for protecting bunches of grapes against the ravages of birds, and for holding some scraps of soap next to your garden tap.

'Flowers are the beautiful thoughts of nature with which she indicates how much she loves us,' Marjorie instructs. 'Go into the garden when the sun is out as sunlight is the breath of life, and when you are indoors, sit by the fire and enjoy my books.'

—•—

Photographing your Garden

Hose your flowers before you take a photo, and the photos (or slides) will look 100 per cent better when they come out.

"Don't put off till tomorrow what can be enjoyed today."

Finger-nails Clean

Dig them into a cake of soap, before you go into the garden, then the soil won't get under your nails.

Tools (garden)

To remove rust, dip a soap-filled steel wool pad in kerosene or turpentine and scrub well. When you have removed most of it, and while it is still wet, rub briskly with crumpled aluminium foil.

Paint handles a bright red, if they are the small type used for weeding, etc. I lost many, before I hit on the idea.

A Helpful Philosophy for the Gardener

1. In the need of the times I shall take my gardening seriously and try to broaden my knowledge of horticulture, particularly in the matter of vegetables, fruits and such foodstuffs.
2. I shall set a definite plan and programme for each season, and keep to a regular working time schedule within the reasonable limits of my ability.
3. I shall strive to make the best use of my land by sound methods of cultivation.
4. I will economise space by discarding superfluous or unworthy plants or trees.
5. I will seek to grow only best varieties obtainable, for these require no more attention than the common types, and yield more satisfaction.
6. I realise that plants are living things, and as such must be adequately nourished, otherwise they are not likely to become anything more than puny specimens.
7. I must be at all times ready to prevent the ravages of insect pests and disease by timely attention to spraying, etc.
8. I shall be careful to avoid planting any kind or variety of seed or plant out of season, for this causes disappointment, and the waste of both time and garden room.
9. Realising the value of humus to plant life, I shall consistently conserve all waste matter from garden and kitchen to improve soil fertility.
10. Only as I aspire to better understand shall I come to really learn and love gardening and you might as well fall flat on your face as lean over too far backwards.

Bird Bath Hints

In the winter, add a few drops of glycerine to the water and it will stop it from freezing.

To stop algae forming put a sprig of mint in the water.

If the birds are shy to drink in your bird bath, put a few coloured marbles in it to attract them.

Barrow Garden

If you have bought a new barrow, do not discard the old one. Paint it white, line with plastic ; add stones for drainage, fill with soil, and put plants in that do not require much water, such as succulents or small cacti.

It is so easy to be good-natured, I wonder if anybody takes the trouble to be anything else.

* * *

About Pot Plants

Firstly, **light** is most important to indoor plants. The more glass you have in your home, the more successful you will be with your **indoor** garden. Of course, whilst some plants thrive in a sunny window, others like half shade. Most indoor plants are not immune to disease, and must be watched for the appearance of fungi, bacteria and virus diseases which is generally caused by insufficient light, too much, or too little watering, and food.

The Philodendron is about the only one that I have that seems to escape all diseases at one time or another. Be careful when you repot your plants . . . Do not water plants before repotting. **Do not** shake off all the dirt around the root, and when you repot it in the following mixture, stand the pot in a bucket of water with the chill taken off for 10 minutes.

This mixture will suit 95 per cent of all your plants for indoors : ⅔ peat moss, ⅓ sharp sand and ¼ teaspoon of complete fertiliser to each 3-inch pot, that is if you want to give your plants the very best, but good garden loam, leaf mould and rotted cow manure mixed is also excellent for the majority.

All foliage plants benefit from monthly waterings of weak liquid manure or sulphate of ammonia. Rotate pot plants in windows so that all sides of the plants get a fair share of the light, or they will grow lopsided.

Humidity, which is essential, can be obtained by standing your pot plants on pebbles in their saucers or by softly spraying smooth leafed plants with tepid water.

Fresh air is essential also, and no draughts. Serious damage will be done to your plants by drowning a plant one day and letting it dry out completely afterwards. Keep just moist. Immersing in a bucket of water once a week until bubbles disappear is a good idea for plants that are not grown near the window in the hot sun. They require, of course, more frequent waterings. If the sun penetrates too much, it is better to pull the blind or have a shade fitted on the window outside for protection, or else you will have scorched plants.

Indoor plants must be kept clean to be healthy. If you have a shower, stand your plants under it, and spray with luke warm water about twice a year, or sponge the leaves with clear water or white oil and water (1 teaspoon to a pint of tepid water). Don't use olive oil as it attracts dust and prevents plant breathing. Under the hose on a warm day will do if you have no shower in the home.

A cloth dipped in soapy water or methylated spirits will remove insects, etc., from under leaves. Nicotine spray can also be used to kill them.

Repotted plants do better if, after repotting, you do not stand in the hot sun in a window for a few days.

Feed, about once a month in summer, and every 2 or 3 months in winter with ½ teaspoon sulphate of ammonia to a pint of water ; for bigger and greener leaves. (Use 1 tablespoon to a 4-inch pot). Never pot from a very small to a much larger pot. Big pots allow roots too much freedom and make for smaller leaves and flowers.

Asparagus Dressing

Put ½ cup or a little more to a square metre at end of September and when finished cutting in December, of the following :— 3kg. (6 lb.) common salt, 1 kg. (2 lb.) of sulphate of potash, 1½ kg. (3 lb.) sulphate of ammonia, 750 g. (1½ lb.) each of super and lime. Leave ferny tops on from December until they die off.

Asparagus Grown Easily

Lay crown on top of soil and heavily mulch them, instead of going to all that trouble preparing bed beforehand.

Asparagus Hints

Plants should not be cut until 3rd or 4th season. Do not cut any spears later than mid-December, or you'll weaken the crown and reduce next year's crop. After cropping, let fern grow until it turns yellow, then cut off 5 cm above ground. Then, lime the bed and apply a good layer of compost, plus 125g of complete fertiliser to the square metre. Asparagus likes so much food that it is hard to overfeed. Keep bed moist at all times and use a special asparagus knife to cut the spears as soon as they appear through the soil. Asparagus has male and female plants. Female plants have fronds almost to the round and bear berries in 2nd year. Male plants are taller with foliage higher up the stems. Male plants yield most so keep them for transplanting.

BONSAI

You can grow a bonsai from a seed placed in an orange or grapefruit skin, cut in half and filled with suitable soil. When roots come through the skin, cut them off. When root bound, transfer to a small pot. Yearly, when dormant, take them out of the pots, trim their fibrous roots to shape of pot and cut out the long thick roots altogether. The purpose of root pruning at any stage is not to weaken the plant but to encourage the formation of a mass of active roots in a small space. A little weak liquid fertiliser may be given every 2 or 3 weeks in the growing period, especially in the early years. Leave bonsai outside in the open to harden to slow down the growing process, that also reduces the amount of pruning needed. With firs and spruces, nip out some swelling buds, leaving only the bud that seems to be pointing in the direction in which you would like the new branch to grow. Never put a plant dead centre in a round bowl, and always toward one end of an oblong. Flowering or fruit trees need repotting every 1 to 2 years, conifers every 4 or 5 years. Loosen roots by jabbing with a wooden skewer. Bend branches into shape with copper wire and leave in position for 6 months. Water every day in summer, but very little in winter.

Bonsai means—bon, meaning a tray-like pot; and sai, meaning to plant.

* * *

Toads are among the best friends the gardener has; for they live almost exclusively on the most destructive kinds of vermin.

* * *

Compost of Newspapers

8cm (3 ins.) of newspaper, double handful of fertilizer, 25mm (1 inch) soil. Repeat until bin is full. Make concave in centre to collect water. In 9 months it should be rich black compost.

Compost

Anything that has lived can go on a compost heap ; organic refuse from the house, and this may include not only the vegetable peelings, fish heads, left overs and tea leaves, but also paper, rags and dust and fluff from the vacuum cleaner. Any other soft organic matter can also be used such as leaves, straw, bracken, sawdust, feathers and manure of any kind. Put a layer of soil and a sprinkling of blood and bone between each layer of refuse. Compost must be kept neither too dry or too wet. If moisture can be squeezed out by squeezing with the hand, it is too wet. Keep heap covered to prevent rain entering, but as each layer is added, moisten it thoroughly. Ashes from open fire seem to speed up the breaking down process.

"When a man eats his words — that's recycling."

Cuttings (collected on holidays)

Take a plastic bag and some sphagnum moss. When someone gives you a cutting, rinse bag with water, dampen moss and put cutting into moss. Put back into bag and tie the top, after blowing it up.

"A man may be found with a garden that's vast,
Very dandelioned, daisied, and shivery-grassed ;
But if it's a picture you can bet your sweet life
He has all sorts of gardening tools...and a wife."

Daphne Bushes

If the leaves are turning yellow give a good watering first, then sprinkle ½ cup of Epsom salts on leaves, and water again. In less than a week the leaves will be green again.

Daphne (sick)

Paint limbs (not the young, but the older ones) with castor oil, or put 2 teaspoons around the roots and water in. Tea leaves from your pot is good too. Mulch with peat or tan bark.

Bulb Tips

If they are diseased, dust with sulphur and transfer to different soil, some distance away.

Bulbs store well in old nylon stockings, or the nylon mesh bags you buy oranges, etc., in at the supermarket.

Flowers of spring bulbs are best broken off, not cut with scissors. Scissors may seal the cut so prevent the absorption of water.

Cabbages Galore

After cutting the first cabbages, leave the stumps in the ground. Each will sprout 4 or 5 smaller cabbages. When these are cut they will sprout again, but pull out the root to prevent, as leaving it in the soil can cause club root.

Brick Path

If you have moss on your brick path you can kill it by painting it with methylated sprit or spraying it with sulphate of iron.

"Time moves steadily, time moves fast.
Before one's ready, youth has passed.
But fruit grows not on a withered bough,
The fruit for eating is the fruit of NOW.
Yesterday's harvest has mouldered to waste;
It's the fruit of today I lust to taste."

Fruit Trees

Fruit trees can be transplanted any time of the year, and best results are obtained if you do it at night — so my mother used to say. To prevent birds pecking the fruit from trees tie small plastic bags on a few of the branches. A light breeze will make them rattle just enough to frighten the birds away without harming them, or,

To frighten them away, hang your blown electric light globes in the trees and the glittering frightens them.

Fuchsia (striking)

Fill a thick plastic bag with a moist mixture of half sand and half peat moss. Tie the top tightly and hang in a shady wind-free place. Push holes in the bag about two inches apart and poke the stems of the cutting into the holes. Mist the cuttings occasionally. Do not water the sand and peat moss mixture.

Hanging Baskets

After filling with moss, put a saucer in bottom, then fill with compost. The saucer collects water, and soil doesn't dry out as quickly, and it cuts down dripping.

SECTION 36—

GARDENING AND INDOOR PLANT HINTS

'When the world wearies and society doesn't satisfy, there is always your garden'

GARDEN LOVER

When crippling age has loosed my grip
On secateur and hoe
When clouded eyes can't focus flowers
In multi-coloured show,
When auction signs are on my fence,
Lord grant the highest bid
From one who knows plants by their names
And loves them — as I did.

A GARDENER'S TEN COMMANDMENTS

(1) THOU SHALT: Keep it clean at all times; even unto thy speech, when frost killeth vine and flower, and insect-plague doth ravage thy seedlings.

(2) THOU SHALT: Feed the Soil abundantly, according to thy means. Yea, and water it, even with buckets, as the law of the land, and thy conscience, doth permit.

(3) THOU SHALT: Sow and Plant according to experience and the word of experts, and not on the say-so of sidewalk superintendents, who have less understanding of thy problems.

(4) THOU SHALT: Prune thy Trees, and the branches thereof; yea, and the roses and shrubs in their season. Cut them not back in the wrong month, lest ye be deprived of their full flowering and fruiting.

(5) THOU SHALT: Spray constantly, but with caution, remembering that a fool sprayeth in the heat of noon, when the bee visiteth the flowers. Neither shall thou use the pump in a high wind, lest thou spread poison on thyself and others.

(6) THOU SHALT: Gather the fruit of thy toil when it matureth, not waiting until it be over-ripe. A fool wasteth, but a wise gardener subsidiseth not his greengrocer.

(7) THOU SHALT: Share the Garden Crop with thy neighbours. Yea, verily, the tight-fisted gardener is an abomination to his fellows. (Also they remember him not in the hour of their abundance.)

(8) THOU SHALT NOT: Envy thy Neighbour, even though he winneth the Show Championship, and his pumpkins are mightier than thine.

(9) THOU SHALT NOT: Abandon thy Tools to the elements, by day or by night, lest thou expose them to rust and rot, and set thy neighbour's feet on the path of temptation.

(10) THOU SHALT NOT: Leave thy Plot untended for many days, while relaxing in slothful ease in a place of holiday. Rather, thou shouldst help they neighbour in the months before, so that he returneth the favour in thine hour of need. Thou shalt Keep these Commandments—and thy fingers crossed—lest thy garden perish. Yea, verily, and thou thyself become a byword, and without honour in the eyes of thy neighbour. (Amen)

GLOSSARY

ALTERNATE: The term is applied to leaves to indicate that they are arranged on different levels on opposite sides of the stem.
AERATION: The exposure of soil to the action of air.
ANNUAL: From seed to maturity, produces seeds, then dies in 12 months.
AXIL: The angle formed at the junction of a leaf with the stem of the plant.
AXILLARY: Designates that a growth or flower stem arises from an axil.
BASAL: Attached to, or arising from, base of plant.
BUDDING: The act of taking a healthy well-developed leaf bud from one plant and inserting it in a rooted cutting, to form a new plant.
CALYX: The protecting outermost leaves of a flower, usually, but not always, green.
CILIATE: Hairy.
COMPOUND: A term indicating that a flower is made up of a number of single flowers, or that a leaf has two or more leaflets.
CORDATE: Heart shaped.
COROLLA: The total petals of a flower.
CORYMB: A nearly flat head of flowers.
CROSS POLLINATION: The act of transferring pollen from one flower to that of a different variety.
CYME: A flattish flower cluster, the inner flower opening first.
DECIDUOUS: Losing the leaves annually.
ENTIRE: Whole; applied to leaves which have no indentations or waves at the edges.
FIBROUS: Containing fibres. Specially applied to roots of a stringy appearance.
GRAFT: To insert a piece of wood into a stem of a growing plant to form a new plant.
HERBACEOUS: A plant with perennial roots, but with annual stems.
HYBRID: A plant resulting from two related, but more or less unlike, plants; produced by cross-pollination.
INFLORESCENCE: The arrangement of flowers on a stem.
LATERAL: A side branch, rather than a main stem.
LOBE: A section or part division of a leaf, or petal.
OBLONG: Longer than broad, with sides nearly parallel. Applied to leaves.
OVATE: Egg shaped, with the broader end at the base.
PALMATE: Leaves which are divided into hand-like lobes.
PANICLE: A branching flower head, each flower having a pedicel.
PEDICEL: Stem of one single flower of an inflorescence.
PEDUNCLE: The stem of a solitary flower; or main stem of an inflorescence.
PERIANTH: The combined sepals and petals hardly distinguishable, as in a daffodil.
PERENNIAL: Living more than two years, whether it retains its leaves or not.
PETIOLE: The leaf-stalk.
PINNATE: Feathery, applied to leaves made up of narrow, opposite leaflets, as in many wattles.
RACEME: An inflorescence with stemmed flowers arranged along the peduncle.
REFLEXED: Turned back abruptly, as the petals of some flowers.
RHIZOME: A fleshy root-like stem, which grows partially above, or wholly beneath the soil. Example: Bearded iris.
SCAPE: A leafless flower stem, which arises directly from the ground, as in a daffodil.
SEPAL: The outer protective leaves of a flower, they are usually, but not always, green.
SET: To plant.
SHRUB: A woody plant, no more than 12 ft. high, which produces near or at the base, having no main trunk.
SPIKE: An inflorescene of usually stemless flowers, which are arranged in an elongated manner at the top of a stem.
STEM-ROOTING: A term applied to bulbs which produce roots on the stem above the bulb.
SUCCULENT: Fleshy; a term applied to a group of plants with juicy stems and leaves.
TUBER: A fleshy swollen stem with buds on its surface, or on the stem at its neck, as in a potato or dahlia.

UMBEL: An inflorescence with the flower stalks arising from one point, and radiating somewhat as the spokes of an umbrella.

WHORL: An arrangement of flowers, leaves, or branches arising in a circle from one central branch or stem.

THE LANGUAGE OF FLOWERS

ANEMONE: Forsaken.
APPLE BLOSSOM: Preference.
ASTER: Variety.
AZALEA: Temperance.
BACHELORS BUTTONS: Single blessedness.
BEGONIA: Dark thoughts.
BLUE BELL: Constancy.
BROOM: Neatness.
CAMELLIA: White, loveliness; red, unpretending.
CANDYTUFT: Indifference.
CANTERBURY BELL: Acknowledgement.
CARNATION: 'Alas, my poor heart'. White, disdain; striped, refusal.
CHESTNUT: Luxury.
CHRYSANTHEMUM: White, truth; yellow, slighted love.
COWSLIP: Pensiveness, winning grace.
CYCLAMEN: 'You fill me with uncertainty'.
DAFFODIL: Send 'my regards'.
DAHLIA: Good taste.
DAISY: White, innocence; coloured, beauty.
FERN: Sincerity.
FORGET-ME-NOT: True love.
FOXGLOVE: Insincerity.
FUCHSIA: Red, taste.
GERANIUM: Melancholy.
GLADIOLUS: Strength of character.
GOLDEN ROD: Be cautious.
HOLLY: Foresight.
HOLLYHOCK: Fecundity.
HONEYSUCKLE: Sweetness of disposition.
IVY: 'I have found my one true love'.
JASMINE: Amiability.
LARKSPUR: Lightness.
LAVENDER: Distrust.
LILAC: Humility.
LILY: White, purity; yellow, gaiety.
LILY OF THE VALLEY: Return of happiness. 'You've made my life complete'.
MICHAELMAS DAISY: After-thought.
MIMOSA: Sensitiveness.
MORNING GLORY: Affection.
NARCISSUS: Egotism.
NASTURTIUM: Patriotism.
ORANGE BLOSSOM: Chastity.
PANSY: 'You occupy my thoughts'.
PEACH BLOSSOM: Confesses 'I am your captive'.
POPPY: Silence, consolation.
PRIMROSE: Early youth or sadness.
RANUNCULAS: 'I am dazzled by your charm'.
ROSE: Red, various meanings from 'I love you' to 'You are young and beautiful'.
SNOWDROP: Hope.
STOCK: Lasting beauty.
SUNFLOWER: Tall, haughtiness; dwarf, adoration.
SWEET PEA: Depart.
SWEET WILLIAM: Gallantry.
TULIP: Declaration of love.
VERBENA: Scarlet, sensibility.

Lynn met us at the Devonport airport at 10.40 a.m. and it was good to be home nice and early in order to air our beds. Next day we went to see Rod and Jean and pick up eleven ferns they were minding for us and stayed for tea.

"I love the cool green look of ferns, their elegance, their twists and turns ;
I love them for their slender grace, their tendency to float in space ;
The ladder fern that climbs so high, its limit seems to be the sky ;
The lovely, gentle maidenhair – perhaps of all its kind most fair –
And many others, all designed to lift the heart and ease the mind
Of those like me, whose pleasure springs, from contemplating growing things."

On the 1st April we went to Bridport to collect Freda Fi Fi, attend Cheryl's 17th birthday party, and to visit Faith's father – Horrie Ewans – in the Scottsdale hospital. I went to church with the Cooper clan on Easter Sunday and we came home next day – the President of the C.W.A., Mrs. Leslie Duff calling the same afternoon with a Gloxinia I had won with my knitted waist coat made from stockings.

Gladioli All Year Round

Stagger their growing by keeping them in the refrigerator and by bringing them out in succession every month. In winter, plant in a warm spot.

Gladioli Hints

Lift corms 8 weeks after they flower. Cut tops off fairly close to corms. Dry them in a shady place for a few days, then dip in a Lysol solution (or Clensol) — 5 teaspoons to 4 litres of water — coverings and all. Leave 3 hours, then wash in clear water. Dry. Leave 6 weeks, then clean off last year's corm. Don't remove natural covering. Plant from August to end of February. The earlier you plant them the more likely you are of beating the thrip.

Another method is to dust sulphur or napthalene flakes through the box you have them stored in.

Before planting, keep soil pests at bay by watering the soil with a weak solution of permanganate of potash. When planting gladioli make a hole, add a teaspoon of blood and bone and cover with soil. Place the bulb on top and add more soil. Blooms will be better manured this way. Put bulbs in hot water (125 degrees) for 20 minutes to kill diseases. Growing them near iris, calendula, sweet pea, dianthus, dahlia, delphinium, aster or potatoes will complicate control of thrips as they feed on these host plants.

Gladioli Opened Quicker

Soak in warm water and put under a neon light.

Lawn (brown patches)

Brown patches in lawn are caused by lack of food and hard soil. Go over lawn with a sharp fork, driving it in at intervals and gently loosening the soil. Follow this with a dressing of fertiliser, provided the grass is still growing. If the roots are still active a dressing of sulphate of ammonia will help it recover swiftly. Apply the fertiliser at the rate of 30g (1oz) to the square metre, and water it in immediately.

"Though nothing can bring back the hour of splendour in the grass,
Glory in the flower,
We will grieve not, rather find strength in what remains behind."
(taken from 'Splendour In The Grass' from William Wordsworth
'Ode On Intimations of Immortality')

Lawn Clipping Manure

Put in a drum or bucket and fill with water. Leave to ferment, and then give it to any plant.

Lawn Edges Against the Fence

Pour a little kerosene round lawn edges which grow against the fence. The grass will die, then you can pull away the dead grass and make it tidy.

Take time to Work — it is the price of success.
Take time to Think — it is the source of power.
Take time to Play — it is the source of youth.
Take time to Read — it is the foundation of knowledge.
Take time to Worship — it is the highway of reverence and washes the dust of earth from your eyes.
Take time to Help and Enjoy friends — it is the source of happiness.
Take time to Love — it is the one sacrament of life.
Take time to Dream — it hitches the soul to the stars.
Take time to Laugh — it is the singing that helps with life's loads.
Take time to Plan — it is the secret of being able to have time for the first nine things.

Pond for Garden

When making a lily pond cover the soil with paper before pouring on the cement as this absorbs the water from the cement and not the soil. 1 part cement to 3 parts sand, and depth 8cm. (3ins.). Pond needs to be 45cm. (18ins.) deep ; or,

Turn the children's outgrown swimming pool into an attractive pond by inserting into the ground a little, and camouflaging the sides with stones. Perhaps your handy man can add a little rustic bridge ; or,

Make one from an old cement washtrough. Knock out central division carefully, as low as possible. Set in ground and arrange stones and plants around top edge. Keep ponds sweet by adding charcoal and replacing it from time to time.

As time went on I became more greedy for flowers and less lawn and Adrian never knew what to expect when he came home from school. In fact, I dug up that much of the back lawn for flower beds that he erected a cyclone fence around what was left, to stop me. Now, there is no lawn at all, but a huge pond, bridge and more plants. Sometimes, when he walked in, he would say, " Where's that shrub from the front lawn ?" and I would say, " Oh. I shifted that today to around the back " – and I am afraid that is still going on. I am " Mrs. Shift-It ". It's a disease.

We have only an average size block here at 163 Madden Street, but it is overflowing with trees, shrubs, creepers, a vegetable garden, glass house, garden shed, chook yard, wood shed, pond, a bridge, pergolas and nooks. We have a Lady in the Snow apple, an espalier Red Delicious, and another with three grafts – Granny Smith, Jonathon, and Golden Delicious. In the citrus we have a Meyer, Lisbon and a variegated lemon with brutal thorns (that I purchased from Rarer Plants in Queensland), a Valencia orange, a cumquat, and another we once bought from a nursery at Ulverstone in 1969 for a miniature orange, and as yet has not had a flower or fruit – only gulps up food. In the peaches, one is a semi clingstone, the other, eating (I grew them from stones) and a third is a miniature, with outstanding double pink flowers each year, but fruit not as nice as the ordinary peach. Mrs. Overton gave us a nectarine that she grew from a stone and that is a good bearer ; we also have a dwarf nectarine. In the plums there is a D'ager Prune, and a Greengage. We also have Chinese Gooseberries, Cape Gooseberry and ordinary Gooseberries. Our apricot tree has three grafts on it – Newcastle, Blenheim and Tilton, and the pear has also two grafts – Beurre Bosc and William's Bon Cretien. We also have a Feijoa, Persimmon and Tamarillo (Tree Tomato) and all three have their fruits ripening during the winter, so we gather fruit nearly all year round. I don't think there is a sight that can equal a Persimmon tree in June and July with its orange fruit smothering bare branches. Our Loquat is 14 years old and has never had fruit – too cold I guess, and the last, and my favourite, is the Fig tree I grew from a cutting.

In the bushes and climbers we have black, red and white currants and blue berries ; also grapes, black and banana passionfruit, and summer and winter rhubarb to add to a pudding list. So I guess by now you are wondering how on earth I crammed all those into an ordinary block, but I did, and all are flourishing. Besides those, I have 190 shrubs, 44 climbing plants, 83 different kinds of bulbs, and lots of roses and perennials.

On the 13th March, when the carrier brought a huge parcel to the door, I wondered what on earth it could contain as I had not sent for anything. But on opening it I found that the McCarthys we met at a Caravan Park in Coburg the year before, had sent us a large banana plant, a variegated pineapple, and variegated leaf Hippeastrum. We were very excited with their generous gifts.

Our garden is a combination of joy, work, friends and money. Joy watching each plant perform, the perfumes, colours, habits etc. As one grows older there are fewer joys elsewhere, but more interests, but I enjoy my own life and do not compare it with others. Work done in a garden is never ending - there is always something you can find to do, and like, but I don't believe the world owes me a living — the world owes me nothing — it was here first. I love the quotation — "Happiness is - something to do, something to love, and something to hope for." Sometimes what we see in life depends mainly on what we look for. My garden always reminds me of my friends as lots of my plants are from friends, some having passed on. The language of friendship is not only words though, it is also meaning. In prosperity our friends know us; in adversity we know our friends. Friendship is not dependent upon performance or perfection. To have a friend is to be one, and a true friend loves unconditionally. We are a friend not for what we can get but for what we can give. I have given more plants and books away that I can count, because, not he who has much is rich, but he who gives much. A true friend is one to whom you can tip out all the contents of your heart, chaff and grain together, knowing that the gentlest hands will take and sift it, keep what is worth keeping, and with the breath of kindness, blow the rest away. There is another kind of friend too - a friend while you are giving and a foe when you stop. And having a garden means money. Money for plants, seeds, water, soil, mulches, tools, hoses, manures and so forth, but if you save your seeds, build a garden shed, make some compost or potting mix etc., you can cut expenses to simplify things. Simplicity is a jewel rarely found nowadays. Do have a place for everything and have everything in its place!

I get numerous letters from people, even children, asking me questions, or giving me praise. I judge folk on their questions, rather than by their answers, as I answer all letters. Children are so truthful in what they say and I tell them not to pass the days in idleness, as youth will not return. Most of us long to have someone hear what we are saying and what we mean beneath the level of words. Today we have too many people who live without working, and on the other hand we have altogether too many who work without living. But he who is willing to work will always find employment. Money is not everything, and as you mature you will find that good health is more important. I'll never be rich as I don't make enough profit on my books, but I am rich in other ways. God has given me the skill and dedication that a gardener needs.

So, friends and readers enjoy my book and use it as a bee does a flower. Flowers are the beautiful thoughts of nature with which she indicates how much she loves us. Go into the garden when the sun is out as sunlight is the breath of life, and when you are indoors sit by the fire and enjoy my books and a piece of Rocky Road. So many folk have asked me for the recipe, that I'm going to include it at the end of my letter. When you are shopping or out walking, pause a minute and you will find you have helped mankind if you give a smile or cheerful word as it makes their life and yours worthwhile.

Even in her mid-nineties, Marjorie's greatest pleasure is to get out into the garden, do a spot of weeding and see how her many plants are progressing.

ROCKY ROAD

Melt 300g milk chocolate, 90g copha and 90g butter; add 200g of (chopped) pink marshmallows, 100g (chopped) white marshmallows, 1 cup unsalted roasted peanuts, ⅓ cup coconut all together. Spread into a foil lined tin and refrigerate until set. Turn out and cut into squares.

I am yours sincerely

Marjorie A. W. Bligh

Marjorie Alfreda Willis Bligh

My dearest mother tended her flower garden well,
And each petal's perfume I still seem to smell.
Daffodils and iris bloomed with snowdrops so small,
While chrysanthemums stood tall by the ivy-clad wall.
Catmint and pansies massed closely beside,
Lily of the Valley and pretty London pride.
Sweet honeysuckle rivalled night-scented stocks;
Old roses and lupins jostled tall hollyhocks.
And near the backyard grew fruit trees galore,
Whose blossoms in Spring shed their fragrance - and more.
Oh how I yearn to see them again,
And wish it would happen at the stroke of my pen.

"Beware of little expense ; a small leak will sink a great ship."

Lemons

Pick when pale yellowish green. Cut off, don't pull it off. Don't pick when wet, because oil cells in rind will break down and fruit will go rotten. Lemons will develop plenty of juice if held in a brown paper bag for several weeks. To store, wrap in tissue and pack in a case and store in a cool dry place, or,

Store by putting them in a sawdust or sand-lined box. Do not let them touch one another. Cover with more sawdust.

Another idea is to rub over with vaseline and store so they do not touch one another.

Lemons (scale on)

Spray with (mixed) starch or what is left after washing day. If they can't breathe, they die, or, use white oil.

Lemon Tree (pruning)

Take off all small limbs, twigs and leaves and leave only main branches. Result is better limbs — stronger — and bigger fruit. Give plenty of blood and bone.

Lemon Trees

500g. (1 lb.) of washing soda applied dry around the trunk of your lemon tree every year causes profusion of blossoms followed by luscious juicy lemons. Epsom salts act the same.

Lettuce (about)

Lettuce seed goes dormant if temperature rises above 30° Celsius and will not germinate until temperature drops considerably. If this is a problem in your garden, moisten some seed and put it in the refrigerator for a week or two. Sow immediately on removal, and keep well watered till the plants emerge.

Lettuce plants should be watered weekly with a tablespoon of Epsom salts to a bucket of water.

They will move quickly too, if you put your lawn clippings into a container and cover with water and leave for several days, then water them with the brew, or,

When planting out the seedlings put a handful of meat meal, or blood and bone around each plant, and cover with soil.

Wireworms completely destroy the young plants. Place naphthaline around them.

Summer House Trick

Use a pair of wagon wheels as *"windows"* at the end of your summer house. Novel and attractive.

Miniature Garden in a Dish : A large earthenware saucer or an old meat dish, or a floating bowl you can purchase in the shops, are all ideal for this fascinating hobby. I won a prize each year I entered with one of these dish gardens at our local show, and of course worth all the trouble I went to, to make it.

Start with the drainage by placing at least 1 inch of crocks or small stones over the base. Cover this with fibre or moss or skimmings off old turf, then make up the following and add : 1 part sifted good quality loam, 1 part washed sand, 1 part of decayed leaf mould and 1 part of gritty material such as granite chippings. Choose some nicely shaped stones and place in position. Place suitable succulents or small growing cacti against stones, but be sure they stay miniature by asking your nurseryman the right plants to use. Coloured marbles add a splash of colour. Water with a tiny spray watering can and keep near a window. Place outside occasionally. Small ornaments can also be used.

Gloxinias : These plants prefer subdued and indirect lighting to get the best from them. They grow easily from cuttings.

Mulching

Use seaweed all the year round as a mulch. There is a great range of trace elements in seaweed in addition to the main plant foods, nitrogen, phosphate and potash. It is impossible to apply too much to light soils.

When your mulching shows signs of decay, sprinkle some blood meal or other nitrogen rich material on it, then apply more mulch. This avoids taking too much nitrogen from the soil. Damp newspaper makes a good mulch around plants. Especially good if leaving them for a few weeks to go on holiday.

Grass clipping are rich in nitrogen.

A leaf mulch is good for the acid loving plants.

The best time is November when the soil is warming up, but before it has lost most of its stored moisture,. If applied too early in the season while the soil is too cold, it may slow down growth.

If you use sawdust, mix it with grass cuttings, poultry manure or other material that contains nitrogen and compost it first. The grass will provide the ammonia needed to break down the sawdust and stops it packing tightly. Large dressings of sawdust directly on soil can depress plant growth for years by tying up the soil nitrogen. Before you lay sawdust (which must be well rotted) spread a handful of blood and bone over each square metre of soil. It is a good mulch for tomatoes when it has nitrogen in it.

Pond for Garden

When making a lily pond cover the soil with paper before pouring on the cement as this absorbs the water from the cement and not the soil. 1 part cement to 3 parts sand, and depth 8cm. (3ins.). Pond needs to be 45cm. (18ins.) deep ; or,

Turn the children's outgrown swimming pool into an attractive pond by inserting into the ground a little, and camouflaging the sides with stones. Perhaps your handy man can add a little rustic bridge ; or,

Make one from an old cement washtrough. Knock out central division carefully, as low as possible. Set in ground and arrange stones and plants around top edge. Keep ponds sweet by adding charcoal and replacing it from time to time.

Pumpkin Tips

Plant the seed of pumpkin and squash in a central hollow and train the vines to grow away from it. You can then soak the root area without wetting the foliage and fruit ; or,

To water pumpkins and plants that do not like overhead watering sink a coffee tin in the ground with holes punched in the sides. No need to trench, no erosion, less weeds. Drains slowly and confines water to the roots.

Roses (about)

Soak roses overnight in water before you plant them. Next day, dig a hole, fill with water, mound earth in centre, and then lay roots of rose carefully over this rounded heap of earth. Add more earth, more water, then finally rest of earth, remembering to plant the rose no deeper than the mark on the stem when you bought it.

Be sure not to cut off roots as they will sucker if you do. If you *have*, cut suckers off below the ground as they appear.

They can be successfully moved at most times of the year, even in full flower. Remove all leaves, buds and flowers, shorten stems, then cut back any long roots. Replant immediately and *"puddle"* them in. Firm the soil and keep wet.

"The rose is fragrant, but it fades in time :
The violet sweet, but quickly past the prime :
White lilies hang their heads and soon decay
And white snow in minutes melts away."

Watering (quick)

If you have a plant container garden and the plants are side by side, here is a quick and efficient method for watering them. Get a piece of roof guttering the length of the row of pots and cap it at both ends. Now punch a hole in the bottom of the trough for each container. Lay the guttering on the pots and fill with water. It will irrigate the plants slowly and all at once.

Seed Tips

Seeds when not sufficiently ripe, will float if placed in a pan of water ; when they have reached full maturity, they will uniformly sink to the bottom. This is said to hold true of all seeds from the coconut to the orchid.

Line your seed box with plastic foam or newspaper; prevents soil drying out too quickly. A salt shaker makes sowing seed easier; or,

Use a cardboard egg carton. At night, shut the lid. When seeds are big enough, cut out each section and put into soil, as cardboard rots in the ground ; or,

An ideal place to grow seeds for planting out is a not-in-use foam picnic box or cooler. Punch holes in the bottom, half fill with potting mix and sow seeds. Cover the top with clear plastic.

Strawberries (about)

When taking strawberries from runners, only take the first from the parent plant, as it's the strongest. If growing in a strawberry pot, put a cylinder of wire netting down centre and fill with small stones. Water the strawberries by pouring into the cylinder.

Make sure that you do not cover the crown, otherwise rotting and disintegration sets in. Incidently, they thrive on bone dust if you can obtain it.

Lay boards between your strawberries for the slugs to crawl under, and each morning turn them over and sprinkle the slugs with salt to eradicate them. If blackbirds are taking them, hang some rubber snakes in the patch, and unless they are more crafty than the average it will keep them off them, or

Cover with mesh bags from supermarkets, such as the bags which the oranges are sold in.

If you are short of space, get a length of guttering and drill holes at uneven distances in it. Fill with soil, plant your strawberries, then fasten the guttering to your garden fence. Water well, when needed and feed them too.

Geese are good destroyers of grassy weeds in the patch and they do not relish strawberry foliage. Remove them, of course, when berries begin to turn pink, as they love the fruit.

Stump of Tree Unsightly

Nail a circle of 15cm. (6 inches) wide pieces of wood to the stump so that they are about 10cm (4 inches) above the top of the stump. Fill the gap with bark then add soil and plant flowers in this.

Tool Hint

Ordinary tools are too clumsy to carry in one's pocket around the garden, but if you carry a pair of old scissors and a 50mm putty knife you will be able to prune tomato plants, thin carrots and so on by snipping rather than pulling. The knife acts as a spade, cultivator or hoe.

Throw your plastic milk and juice bottles on the tip? Not on your nelly! With a little creativity, and some ribbon, lace and fake flowers, the top end of your bottle can become part of a fetching floral arrangement. The bottom bit can be covered with crocheted plastic bags for a useful trinket holder.

12. THE NITTY GRITTY OF HOUSEWORK

It is true: Marjorie Bligh does *not* like housework. Our queen of the domestic scene may love a spotless home, with a place for everything and everything in its place, but this is not to say she relishes the work that makes it so. Housework, in Marjorie's book, is best approached with economy, pluck and foresight.

Cleaning ought not require recourse to expensive cleaning products—in many instances a good sprinkle of bicarb, or splash of vinegar, will do the trick. You will not find yourself having to wipe from your walls the unsightly marks left where broom and mop handles rest if you have thought about how to prevent this kind of staining in the first place. Nor will you ever again need to sweep beneath your doormats, if you observe Marjorie's pre-emptive practices. Dust will slip from your dustpan; silver cutlery will sparkle for longer.

With a little forward planning, you will be prepared in the event that you are called away to the telephone while in the middle of sponging your venetians, and you'll avoid getting drips down your arm while cleaning the ceiling. Scrub your house the Marjorie way and you'll be back to your knitting in no time.

—•—

35 Hints on Washing, etc.

- Do not use a detergent and a powder together in washing machine ; they act against one another.
- For best result in washing nylon, use warm water and a detergent ; rinse only once. Hang out to drip-dry without wringing. Nylon will not discolour if you use detergent. If it has gone yellow, wash in very hot water to bring it white again.
- All good detergents on the market are better for washing of all dscriptions, because they have a petroleum base which does good to the clothes. You have to use twice as much soap as a washing powder on wash day, and soap is difficult to get out of the clothes. It mats woollies because of that.
- You can boil discipline cottons ; pinwhale velvets or velveteen wash well. Rinse in warm water. Do not wring. Hang inside out and shake occasionally on the line.
- Do not wash chamois gloves with a detergent—wash with a pure soap on your hands. Rinse in two clear waters, then finally in a soapy one. In the last rinsing water put 1 dessertspoon olive oil or glycerine. Put some of the rinsing water in the fingers before hanging out to dry to inflate them and stop them sticking together. The fleecy-lined leather glove can be washed likewise if labelled so.

*　　*　　*

Time and chance can do nothing for those who will do nothing for themselves.

Our bathroom is graced by this verse which is in picturesque surroundings within the frame :

A BATHROOM HINT

A BATHROOM should be full of grace—
Don't disarrange its shining face !
Remember, those who use this place
Like nice things to surround them.
So be a tidy soul ;
Come, swill (not fill) the bowl,
And leave things as you found them.

"Always take on more than you can possibly handle, and you'll never do all you can do. But you must hurry — time passes."

Bathroom Tidy

Put a plastic kitchen cutlery tray in the medicine cupboard and keep small bottles in it. The partitions keep all manner of things upright.

Bathroom Tiles

Wipe over with a kerosene cloth occasionally to prevent mould. Clean them with liquid window spray and they will take on a new lustre.

To keep mildew from forming, rub undiluted bleach over the tiles occasionally. It will remove it too, if it has formed.

Blinds (venetian)

Keep a plastic peg in your pocket, then if you are called to the phone, you can peg the slat you have just cleaned.

Paint one of the two blind cord knobs a contrasting colour to avoid the nuisance of pulling the wrong cord. Clean with 1 part kerosene and 2 parts of methylated spirit. Grease and dust are removed easily.

Broom Hint

Put plastic foam on tops of handles, so that when they rest against the wall, they won't leave marks ; or,

A finger cut from a rubber glove slipped on top will act the same.

Cards (playing)

Clean with hot bran, or, sprinkle talcum powder through them. Stir the cards well in the bran and grease will be removed. Keep cleaned with a little wax polish, rubbing it off well.

"We tire of pleasure we take, but never of those we give."

Ceiling Cleaning

Put a bracelet of plastic foam around your wrist, so drips won't run down your arm.

If mildewed, wash off, then paint with one coat of size (available at the paint suppliers).

If it is smoked, paint with a solution of starch in water. When dry, rub off with a soft brush.

Chrome Taps Cleansed

Soak terry cloth in cider vinegar and *"snuggle"* it all around, over and under, then pour over more vinegar. Let soak over night. It removes spots and left over cleanser in hard-to-get-at places. Rinse. Ammonia is also good.

There is one fool at least in every married couple.

* * *

Household Hints

IN ALPHABETICAL ORDER

Antique Furniture : Old and new will respond well to a polishing with brown nugget.

Book Mark : Emergency book mark can be made from cutting the corner from an envelope and passing over top of page.

Bath Cleaner : Take 4 tablespoons flour, 4 tablespoons vinegar, and 8 tablespoons peroxide. Mix to a paste and spread over the bath ; leave for a few hours and wash off with cold water. Over-night is an excellent idea. Repeat in four days' time.

Blankets : When storing blankets for summer, sprinkle them with powdered alum and roll up. Bitter apple from chemist crushed and sprinkled among clothes is effective remedy for keeping silverfish and moths away ; or make a bag out of newspaper and sprinkle in epsom salts.

Brooms : Or dusters . . . sprinkle with kerosene—it gathers dirt easier.

Brass : If your brass is very tarnished, rub it first with hot vinegar or lemon juice dipped in salt. Especially good for ornaments, too, as it doesn't leave a white mark in the crevices like some cleaners do. Wash and polish in usual way.

Carbon Paper : If carbon paper is worn, hold near fire until warm. The heat will spread the carbon evenly on worn patches and so give it a new lease of life.

Curtain Rods : Slip a finger from an old glove over rod for easy threading of lace curtains.

Chrome : To keep all chrome ware like new, wipe it with a soft cloth dipped in kerosene, then rub it with a dry one. Ammonia or methylated spirits are also good. Every two months is sufficient if you use the kerosene. Dry flour will polish chrome and aluminium too.

Carpets : Brighten by sponging them with 1 cup of vinegar added to a quart of warm water or cleaning them with ammonia (1 tablespoon to a quart).

Chamois Leather : Retain its softness by adding a teaspoon of carb. soda to ¾ of a washbasin of warm water. A few drops of olive oil added to last rinsing water is also good.

Combs and Brushes : Will be cleaned in a jiffy if you add 1 tablespoon of ammonia to enough water to cover.

Duster : For carved furniture and pleated lampshades can be had by using your husband's discarded shaving brush.

Dusters : Soak in turpentine and allow to dry. They will dust better. Kerosene is also good. There will be no fluff left on tables, etc.

Dust Pan : Keep your dust pan polished with ffoor polish and the dirt will glide off and on more easily. If no dust pan, dampen the edges of a piece of paper : it will adhere to the floor and allow the dust to slide on easily.

Doors : When painting wire screen doors, paint one side only ; use dry brush on other side, which will work paint through the mesh.

Dirty Greasy Clothes : Put a cupful of kerosene in trough. It will dissolve the grease.

Earrings : or pearl buttons will renew their lustre if you paint them with irridescent nail polish.

- White kid gloves can be cleaned, if put in a bottle with screw-top lid and some cleaning spirits fluid and shaken vigorously. Take out and put on hands and rub with a clean towel until almost dry. Spirits make them dry quickly.
- When washing woollens, add a dessertspoon of glycerine to last rinsing water. This prevents shrinking and keeps them soft.
- Vinegar is good when you over-blue clothes on wash days. Soak in a strong vinegar solution to remove excess blue.
- Add a small handful of salt when making blue water to prevent streaking and keep clothes snowy white. Good for hard water, too.

★ One nylon stocking usually ladders and leaves one perfectly good. Keep these good ones until you have four (or more). Place them in a saucepan of cold water with a pinch of salt and bring them to the boil. Boil a few minutes and leave in pan till cold. Rinse and hang in shade to dry. All stockings will be the same shade—a fashionable shade.

★ When marking linen, take a blunt pencil, write name, etc., then follow over pencil mark with ink . . . it will not run on material and writing will be neat.

★ Mix starch to a cream and use as a substitute for cleaning white shoes.

★ When ironing tablecloths, iron the four ends first, then the cloth will be straight when finished.

★ Add a tablespoon of salt or ½ a packet of Epsom salts to the starch on wet, windy washing days, then the starch will not blow out. Starch your ironing sheet too, for a smooth surface that will not wrinkle.

★ Prevent nylon (white) from yellowing by putting as much cream of tartar as will cover a sixpence into the washing and rinsing waters.

★ If you still boil your clothes in a copper, and it is stained, fill up with water and add 1 tablespoon cream of tartar. Stir until dissolved. Let stand all night. Next morning empty and wipe your shining copper.

★ Equal quantities of salt, starch and soft soap will remove mildew stains on cotton. Soak in milk all night. Wash in detergent next day. Repeat if stubborn. If not removed then, put paste on one side and place in sun to dry ; put on other side and then let dry again. Wash thoroughly.

★ **To clean white needlework** without washing (to make it look like new again) soak it overnight in a strong solution of borax and cold water. Next morning squeeze out as much water as possible (do not rinse) and wrap in a towel for an hour, then iron on the wrong side only.

★ An excellent cleaner for woollens, suits, or perspiration and grease stains can be had by mixing together the following : Dissolve firstly 1 tablespoon of soap flakes in a pint of hot water. When cool, add 1 tablespoon cloudy ammonia and 1 teaspoon powdered borax. Store in bottles and shake well before using.

★ When ironing and you accidentally scorch an article, dampen a cloth with peroxide, put it over the mark and iron. The scorch will disappear.

★ Re-stiffen your taffeta frock by sponging over the wrong side of garment with a solution of one teaspoon of borax dissolved completely in 1 cup warm water. When nearly dry, iron also on wrong side.

★ Sponge mildewed clothing with eau-de-Cologne and rub gently. Use it also on all leather articles that have gone mildewed.

* * *

My simple recipe for living :
Shut out the past—the dead yesterdays. Shut out the future—the unborn tomorrows. Do with all your might what lies clearly at hand today.

Coathanger Tricks

Always tie the instructions to the coathanger, and hang the dress or coat always on that hanger, then you will know how to deal with it when it has to be cleaned.

Cut a small V-shaped notch on the top of hanger 25mm from the end. The notches will hold the loops on top of skirts better than an ordinary coathanger, if you haven't the proper hanger. To make a wire coat hanger serve the same purpose, curve the hangers upwards at the ends.

"as contrary as a handful of coathangers."

Dish Cloth Hints

Soak in 1 part bleach to 20 parts of water.

Dishcloths will be cleaned and sweetened by the addition of bicarbonate of soda to the water in which it is soaking. Use it for tea towels too.

Use bright face washers to match your colour scheme for dish cloths, they wear longer, can be boiled and are cheap.

Doors can be made Burglar Proof

Doors can be made burglar proof by slipping a wooden or rubber wedge in at the bottom. This makes the door impossible to open from the outside.

"Have you ever noticed how, in all books, people coming into a room always gently close the door behind them. I suppose the reason for this is that if they closed it in front of themselves they'd still be outside."

Egg Dropped

Scoop up a dropped raw egg into two pieces of cardboard (one on either side of egg). Quick, easy and no mess ; or,

Pick up the bulk of it with a piece of newspaper, then sprinkle salt on rest which can then be swept into a dustpan.

Lunch Wrap Cylinders

Are good for storing valuable documents.

Mat (door)

Place a newspaper under the door mat to collect the dust that falls through.

"My home is not a palace, it's neither rich nor grand,
But in the stakes of happiness, I'm the richest in the land,
For I have friends a-plenty — I see them every day,
They help me, and I help them, along life's busy way."

Dustpan

Polish with floor wax, so dust slips quickly off it. If you do not have a dust pan, dampen edge of newspaper and it will adhere to the floor and allow the dust to slide on easily.

Electric Jug

Put lemons sliced (or peels) into electric jug. Bring to boil. Cool, boil again, then the brown scum will shift quite easily off inside of jug. Always keep element covered in water — lasts longer.

Electric Kettle (stainless steel)

If you notice flakes in the bottom it needs cleaning. Fill with water, add 1/2 cup brown vinegar, bring to boil and continue for several minutes. Repeat if necessary, or, use sliced lemons.

Refrigerator Hints

To clean underneath the refrigerator wrap a cloth around a fly swat, fix in place with an elastic band, then go to work.

Keep dirt from collecting under the refrigerator by putting a square of linoleum underneath. This can be pulled out and washed more easily than trying to get underneath.

To remove mould use a dry dishcloth or toothbrush dipped in lemon juice and rub firmly.

Clean inside monthly with a solution of bicarbonate of soda in water — 3 tablespoons in 6 cups of water.

Put a jar inside with a small amount of vanilla in it and you can put foods in your refrigerator without fear of tainting each other.

Mustard mixed with water acts the same, so does coffee grounds or crushed charcoal, or, a teaspoon of bicarbonate of soda in a glass of water.

Marks often respond to a rubbing with a soft cloth moistened in cooking oil. Use that on rubber as well.

Clean the rubber with methylated spirit every few months. It will help to preserve it too, or clean off with 2 parts bleach to 6 parts water.

Turn the dial to a warmer setting when you go away for extended periods. Since the refrigerator won't be opened, it will stay as cool.

Cover all liquids stored in the refrigerator to prevent moisture being drawn into the air from them. Moisture in the air makes the motor work harder to maintain the set temperature.

Take care of your refrigerator by defrosting regularly ; thick ice is hard on the motor and uses extra power. Try not to let more than 6mm collect on the inside before defrosting.

When defrosting, put several layers of newspaper on each shelf and it will help sop up the water.

White Shoes : Add milk instead of water with the cleaner for white shoes. The white will not rub off so easily.

HINTS IN RHYME

TO GET THAT SCREW

When a screw is in too tight,
And you've tried with all your might,
Though 'twon't loosen, don't resign,
Try this happy thought of mine :
Your screw-driver, get it hot—
This you'll find will help a lot.

STOP THAT LEAK

Leaking pipe is something you
Can't put off attending to.
With this trouble you can cope—
Use a piece of softened soap.
Soap will plug the leak, I've found,
Till the plumber comes around.

METHYLATED SPIRITS

Mixed with whitening 'tis a wheeze
To clean and shine your piano keys.
With methylated and soft duster,
Clean all the glass that you can muster,
And don't forget that mirrors, too,
When polished thus will shine like new.

43

Stains and their Treatment

(in alphabetical order)

Alcohol : Add glycerine to washing water, then rinse with vinegar or use bleach.

Adhesive Tape : Apply kerosene, eucalyptus, or eau-de-cologne.

Biro : Methylated spirits will remove in quick time on cotton, linen and wool ; or petroleum jelly, then wash in hot suds.

Blood and Meat Juices : Use cold water and rub briskly with a brush until blood dissolves, then sponge with ammonia water for cotton and linen. For wool, cold water, then wash in suds.

Bluing (from wash) : Rinse in warm vinegar water.

Beer : same as above.

Chocolate, Cocoa, Coffee : For cottons first soak in cold water with a bleach that is now on the market. Then wash in hot suds as usual. For wool, wash in luke-warm suds (use peroxide if necessary). Borax and cold water is also good.

Cod Liver Oil : Household Bleach. Remove before washing or will brown when ironed.

Cream or Milk : Cold water first, then soap and tepid water, or if stubborn, cleaning fluid.

Chewing Gum : Rub with an ice cube until brittle enough to scrape off. If any remains, then use nail polish remover, scrub, then leave to dry.

Carbon Paper : Carbon tetrachloride.

Egg : Cold water only.

If stain is old, apply warm glycerine to stained area. Stand for a few minutes, then rinse thoroughly with warm water and soap.

Frocks : Remove dye from underarms of silk frocks by soaking stained parts in cold water, and gently rubbing in bicarbonate of soda. Leave about an hour before rinsing in clear, cold water.

Grass Stains : Alcohol, then wash in soap and cold water or rub warm glycerine into stain until it fades in colour. Then apply soap powder and work into the stain. Apply water until glycerine and powder have disappeared. On woollen materials, wash in lukewarm suds and sponge with methylated spirits. On tennis, cricket or bowls trousers, use glycerine and egg-white mixed. Leave 2 hours, then wash off with a soapy lather.

Grease and Oils : Blotting paper, then warm water and soap, or petrol or benzine.

Ink : Soak first in fresh milk, then flush with cold water. Wash lastly in warm water and soap. For cotton and linen, rust remover will also shift, then wash in suds. **For wool,** sponge with methylated spirits, then lemon juice. Use Oxalic for old stain.

Ice Cream : Carbon tetrachloride or household bleach.

Iodine : Alcohol or ammonia, then warm water and soap, or try a bleach that is on the market. Wash in luke warm suds. This is for cottons and linens. For wool, wash in luke warm suds.

Kerosene : Warm water and soap.

Lipstick : On cottons, sponge with lighter fluid and soap together until it disappears. Rinse with warm water ; on woollens, use eucalyptus.

Medicine : Alcohol.

Mildew : For cottons, moisten both sides with lemon juice, and salt and dry in the sun, or soak in sour milk. Another method is bleach or peroxide.

Mustard : Glycerine, then methylated spirits.

Nail Polish : Nail polish remover, then household bleach.

Paint and Varnish : On linen and cotton materials, hands or floor etc., turpentine, chloroform, or alcohol or floor polish. Soak for a while, then wash with hot water and soap. For woollens use floor polish or turps only, then wash in warm suds.

Perspiration : Apply ammonia to the stain, then flush with warm water. Watch colour of garment as it might run while the ammonia is in action. If so, rinse in cold water and apply table salt to hold the colour. An alternative suggestion is to soak the parts affected in water in which an aspirin has been dissolved. Another method, add vinegar to last rinsing water.

Pitch, Tar or Wheel Grease : Rub with lard, and wash with soap and water. Kerosene rubbed into stain and stood for an hour will remove tar too. Wash in usual way. Another good remover is petroleum jelly or eucalyptus.

Pencil Marks : Indelible. Do **not** use water first. Spreads dye. Use cleaning fluid.

Rust : For cottons, a paste of lemon juice and salt. Leave in the air for an hour before washing ; or boil in 1 teaspoon of cream of tartar to 1 pint of water, then oxalic acid if still persists ; for wool, lemon juice with carbonate of soda rinse.

Soot : First cover the carpet with dry salt, then sweep.

Scorch Marks : When ironing, always keep a bottle of peroxide handy and when you scorch any article, dampen the cloth with peroxide, place over scorch and iron. Scorch will disappear, or bleach in the sun.

Shoe Polish : Black—turpentine or cleaning fluid and wash in a detergent ; coloured—cleaning fluid or household bleach.

Soft Drinks : Household bleach.

"A man's true wealth is the good he does in the world."

Concrete (oil on)

1 part detergent, 6 parts kerosene. Leave on 5 minutes, then hose off.

Concrete (rust on)

Use equal parts of spirits of salts and water. Use gloves to apply.

Concrete (stains)

Mix equal quantities of household bleach and hot water, and scrub vigorously. Add washing soda if the concrete is muddy.

Cutlery (stainless steel)

Clean with a damp cloth that has been dipped in cream of tartar.

Cutlery Drawer

Line with aluminium foil and your silver will stay cleaner longer. Place a sheet over top as well.

Lavatory

Pour half a litre of vinegar into the bowl overnight to remove the calcareous deposits which are found in the bowls, if you live in an area where there is a lot of calcium in the water.

Instead of using strong-smelling deodorants in the lavatory, try a bowl of herbs from the garden. Mint, rosemary, thyme, parsley, and verbena are good. They absorb unpleasant odours and your lavatory will always smell fresh and clean.

Washing Up (greasy)

Add a couple teaspoons of bicarbonate of soda to the water.

A dash of vinegar in the water helps to remove grease from dishes.

If water is getting greasy, let it out slowly, then wipe sink with kitchen paper towelling, so grease won't go down the sink.

Shower Curtains

Pink or scallop your plastic shower curtains instead of hemming them. Hems on shower curtains hold water and encourage mildew.

Silver Articles

Articles of silver on display such as photo frames, vases, etc., will not tarnish so quickly in damp or humid weather if after cleaning they are rubbed with a soft cloth on which has been sprinkled a few drops of household or machine oil.

Washing Hints

Don't use a detergent and a powder together in the washing machine, as they act against one another.

Detergent in warm water is best for nylon. Rinse once only and don't wring. They won't discolour either. If white nylon has gone yellow, wash in very hot water to bring it white again.

Add fabric softener to rinse water to stop synthetic clothes from clinging. (If you forget, rub hand cream on your hands, then rub hands over inside of dress).

On washing day, hang handkerchiefs by the side edge instead of the corner. Just as quick to hang, but they don't need pulling straight for ironing.

Wash woollens in detergent. It will even unmat a jumper.

Wash chamois gloves with soap, *not* detergent. Rinse in two clear waters, then a soapy one. Put 1 dessertspoon olive oil or glycerine in last rinsing water. Put some of the rinsing water in the fingers to inflate them when hanging out, so they won't stick together.

Pullovers which normally can't be spun dry , or wrung out by hand can easily be spun dried if they are rolled in towels with the ends well secured with rubber bands. Run a tacking thread around necks and cuffs before washing to prevent stretching.

If you put too much soap powder in your washing machine, drop in a spoonful or two of vinegar or a teaspoon of Epsom salts.

Put lemon juice in the machine (or peels in a muslin bag) to whiten your clothes. Turn corduroy garments inside out, before putting in washing machine.

To remove very dirty spots from clothing apply soap to the reverse side of the soiled area. Soap has a repelling or *"kicking"* action, and it is surprising how easy it is to wash the dirt out of, not into, the garment.

Before washing blankets or jumpers, pin a safety pin on the dirty spots, as, when they are wet, it is difficult to see a dirty mark.

To wash greasy overalls, put a cup of kerosene into the washing machine with the soap powder.

Fully automatic washing machines work just as well on cold water, saving considerably on hot water costs. Cold water results in fewer creases.

Add ½ cup white vineger to final rinse then fluff won't cling to dark colours.

Tie an old sock to the end of the hose on your washing machine, and as the machine empties, the fluff goes into the sock and not into the drain to clog it up.

Soap left in the machine could corrode the parts in time, so flush out excess soap once a month, by filling machine with clean water and ½ cup of water softener, or a packet of Epsom salts (or 2 tablespoons), or 2 cups white vinegar.

Try using half the usual amount of soap or detergent. You will be surprised to find your clothes just as clean and a lot easier to rinse.

A simple wire frame (an old coathanger will do the trick), some wool, a bit of patience and…ta-da! A poodle! *Instructions on page 216.*

13. A STITCH IN TIME

According to the *Guinness Book of Records* the fastest knitter in the world is Miriam Tegels of the Netherlands, who in 2006 clocked an impressive 118 stitches in one minute. However, when she met her chief rival—Scotland's Hazel Tindall—at the 2008 International World Speed Knitting Championships, Tegels's title was called into question. Tindall, in three minutes, racked up 255 stitches, while Tegels languished on 243.

If Tegels had been able to treble the result from her one-minute performance, she might have knitted 354 stitches in three minutes, but it seems that in knitting—as in running—what can be achieved in a sprint cannot be replicated over the longer haul. To put all of this in context, the average knitter knits between thirty and forty stitches a minute, and is a little slower when working in purl.

We will never know just how fast Marjorie knitted in her heyday, when she thought nothing of whipping up full-length dresses in Patons Totem, or patiently building a bedspread from seventy-eight eleven-inch squares. Perhaps Marjorie should be regarded as more of an endurance knitter, capable of pacing herself steadily over the distance, but also of pulling out one last speedy dash when the finish line is in sight.

Or, perhaps—given that knitters are not often crocheters, and crocheters rarely knitters—Marjorie is better regarded as a freakish pentathlete of the needlework world. Equally adept at knitting, crochet, cross-stitch, embroidery and machine sewing, Marjorie truly is a Renaissance woman.

—•—

DANIELLE WOOD, AUTHOR AND KNITTER

'Knitting is the way I relax, and it's also my favourite metaphor. It's proof that if you just keep going, stitch (word) at a time, you will eventually have a jumper (book).

Danielle Wood finds knitting for guinea pigs to be amazingly satisfying, and very quick. Here her daughter's crested agouti, Coco, models a rainbow jumper, for which Coco picked up a third prize at the Hobart Cavy Club Easter Show. Danielle intends to ask Marjorie how to do better next time…

'When you look closely at Marjorie's knitting, you can see that it is beautifully neat and perfectly tensioned. I like to think of Marjorie as a young girl knitting her own stockings by candlelight, and I'm in awe of the fact that she once knitted eighteen jumpers for the Campbell Town footy team.

'Even though I had the good fortune to learn from three very fine knitters—my mother and grandmothers—I find there are always more little tricks to learn. One of my worst knitting problems is that

I often find myself wondering if I'm going to have enough wool, either to make it to the end of one more row, or to complete my overall project. Marjorie's practical, tried-and-true knitting hints have saved me over and over again from the frustration of coming up short.'

If you are in doubt about not having enough wool to finish a jumper, knit the sleeves and back first, then put contrasting bands or Fair Isle on the front.

If you come close to the end of a ball of wool during knitting and wonder if you have enough for another row of knitting, measure the length across the garment. If it is four times that width, you will have enough yarn for one more row.

For an almost invisible join when adding a new ball at the middle of a row of knitting, knit one stitch from the new ball, then one from the old ball, for about 4–6 stitches and darn in the ends. Good for stocking or garter stitch.

—*M.B.*

Crochet Hook Case

Don't throw away the plastic case you bought your new tooth brush in, as it will hold nicely your crochet hooks.

"Everything in the world is good for something."

Crochet Work (stiffened)

Mix one tablespoon of gum arabic in a little boiling water, strain, than add the juice of a lemon. Take two tablespoons of the solution and mix well with four tablespoons of icing sugar. Dip article in this, then thoroughly squeeze and pull into shape, and let dry, frequently stretching to keep in shape. If it is a "dish" you have crocheted, put over a china dish to dry ; or,

Take 2 tablespoons of granulated white sugar and 1 tablespoon of boiling water. Place over low heat until sugar dissolves. Place the crochet in this until all is damp, then allow to dry. Especially good for crochet baskets or bowls for fruit.

A plain crochet doyley can be made into a dish, by drying it over a china fruit bowl.

Graph for knitting Australia, using one square as one stitch.

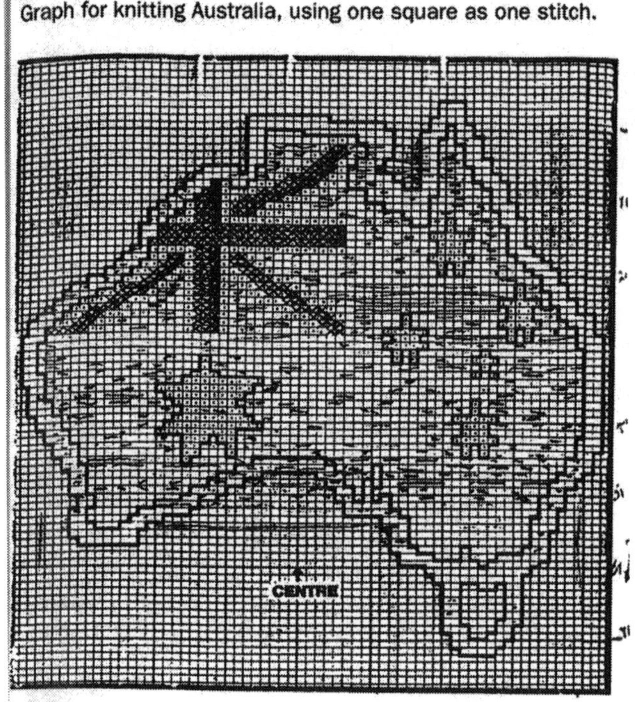

PUZZLE SLIPPERS

(Illustrated on Page 382)

Although these slippers only take 5 hours to knit with 8 ply wool and No. 8 knitting needles, once they were knitted it took me several days to try and work out how to assemble them. I will try to explain it at the end. A friend sent it to me from W. Aus. and the pattern pinned together in material, that I dare not unpin. Here goes. -

Cast on 16 sts.

Knit 30 rows, then 30 rows of stripes (using 2 colours, 2 rows, one colour, 2 rows another for the 30 rows), 30 rows of main colour, 30 rows of stripes, and 30 rows main colour.

Cast off.

Knit a second piece by casting on 16. K. 30 rows main colour, 30 rows stripes, 30 rows main colour.

Cast off.

*** This is how I managed to put them together. Imagine the drawing is the two lots of knitting (below).

First, sew the two together as shown. Then, fold over the long strip, sewing the 1st and 2nd squares to the 3rd and 4th squares. Now, lay the 5th square (of the long strip) over the 3rd square of the short strip (-the cast on edge - to the side of the 5th square, , on both sides of toe). Now, fold over the striped piece of the short strip and sew it to the remaining side of the 5th square which is the toe. Confused, well knit it, and see if you can put it together any easier. You can crochet around top if like.

This is how my friend said to assemble them:-

Place the 5 squares at right angles on top of the 3 squares and pin up. Stitch tog. plain 2 to stripe 3, plain 4 to stripe 2, plain 6 to stripe 5. The other side of plain 6, to plain 8, to other side of plain 8, to stripe 2, plain 1 to other side of stripe 5, and you'll have a slipper with triangle turned down cuffs.

(see also pattern before this one). Good luck.

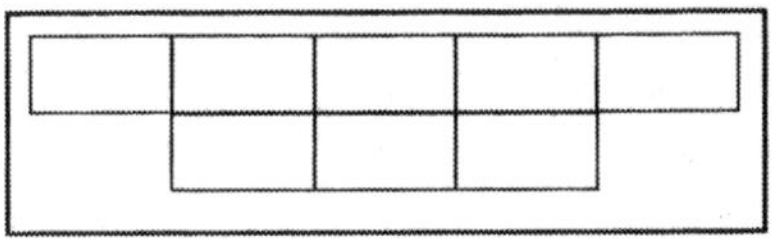

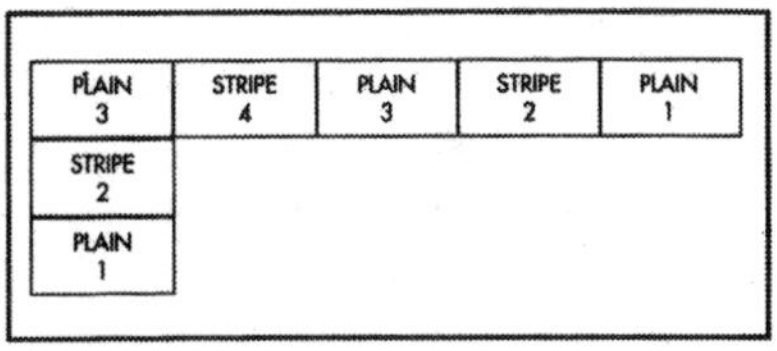

PLAIN 3	STRIPE 4	PLAIN 3	STRIPE 2	PLAIN 1
STRIPE 2				
PLAIN 1				

"Idealism increases in direct proportion to one's distance from the problem".

KNITTED SLIPPERS FROM TOPS OF PANTYHOSE

(Illustrated on Page 385)

It takes about 20 tops. Cut spirally about 2 cm (3/4 inch) wide. It doesn't matter about seam. In fact, it looks attractive when knitted up. The size of the needles will depend on what size the foot. I use 8 size for myself.

Cast on 35.

1st row - K.15, P.1, inc. in next st., K.1, inc. in next st., P.1, K.15.

2nd row - K.16, inc. in next st., K.3, inc. in next st., K.16. (I find it easier to take a loop from between sts. to make the st. instead of trying to knit 2 from one st.)

3rd row - K.15, P.1, inc. in next st., K.5, inc. in next st., P.1, K.15.

4th row - K.16, inc. in next st., K.7, inc. in next st. K.16.

Continue without more increases thus:-

5th row - K.15, P.1, K.11, P.1, K.15.

6th row - Knit.

Continue in garter st. until you have 52 rows or 26 ridges.

Right side facing, cast off 4, P.1, K.1, 6 times, K.11, K.1, P.1, 8 times.

Next row - Cast off 4, K.1, P.1, 6 times, K.11, P.1, K.1, 6 times.

Next row - P.1, K.1, 6 times, K.11, K.1, P.1, 6 times.

Repeat last row 25 times.

K.2 tog. across toe, K.1 row, K.2 tog. across toe, K.1 row.

Draw thread through remaining stitches and sew up front.

Sew up heel, and make a 2nd slipper.

"Better a little with righteousness than much gain with injustice." Proverbs 16:8.

KNITTED SLIPPERS

(Illustrated on Page 385)

Two skeins of base colour, 1 skein of secondary colour, 1 pair of No. 12 knitting needles (these are in maroon and blue).

Cast on 18 with maroon.

Row 1: Plain into back of stitch.

Row 2: Purl.

Row 3: Plain.

Row 4: Slip 2, take blue wool, K.2, slip 2, K.2, slip 2, K.2, blue slip 2, K.2, blue slip 2.

Row 5: slip 2, purl 2 blue, slip 2, purl 2 blue, slip 2, purl 2 blue, slip 2.

Row 6: same as row 4.

Row 7: same as row 5.

Row 8: knit plain with maroon.

Row 9: K 2, increase 1 stitch in each of the next 2 stitches within 4 stitches of each end, making 4 extra stitches on the needle.

Row 10: purl.

Row 11: plain.

Row 12: slip 2 maroon, K. 2 blue, and continue same as row 4,5,6,7,8,9,10 and 11 until you have increased to 42 stitches. There should be 6 coloured squares from the toe and 9 across. Cast off all but 18 stitches on the needle; continue making pattern until you have sufficient to fit around the sole to the ankle, and then join. Sew slipper to felt soles, using double linen thread only. Cast on 14 stitches and knit band required length for top of slipper. Make pom-poms and attach.

"If the shoe fits, wear it".

Buttonholes Knitted (Hints)

If the pattern says to cast on four (if you have cast off *four* in the previous row) *cast on five,* THEN, next row knit (or purl) two together on that spot (beginning) to make it four again.

For a neat knitted button hole, in the first row after the button hole has been made and using the right hand needle, pick up the loose thread which lies before the first cast on stitch, slip it on the left hand needle and work it together with the next stitch.

When working the row after buttonhole has been completed, with right-hand needle pick up purlways the loose thread, or threads, at base of buttonhole, slip it on to left-hand needle and work it together with the first stitch on left-hand needle, or,

When working the cast-on row of buttonhole, before slipping the last cast-on stitch on to the left-hand needle, pass the yarn from back to front between the needles, then slip the stitch on to the left-hand needle and complete row.

Knob Lost in Knitting

If you lose the knob off your knitting needle, glue the toothpaste cap onto the end of it.

Mohair

Make it go further by knitting each alternate row in ordinary matching two-ply wool.

COATHANGER COVER MADE FROM BREAD WRAPS

(Illustrated on Page 385)

3 plastic bread wrappers, 1 pair No. 8 knitting needles. Wooden coat hanger. Cut bottom off the wrapper, then cut spirally 1.25 cm. (1/2 inch) wide. Place all in a bowl and dust with talcum powder. Cast on 11 sts. Knit each row until work measures length of coat hanger, slightly stretched. Cast off. Leave length of plastic. Fold work in half over hanger, stitch together using remaining length of plastic.

"Thrift is a great revenue."

KNITTED WASHER
(with knitting cotton)

Cast on 26 stitches on No. 10 needles.

First row : Knit within 2 stitches of end. Turn, knit to end. Repeat, but each time leave 2 **more** on left hand needle until **all** are on that needle. At this stage you can join in another colour and repeat, or keep going with one colour until it makes a perfect round washer. Cast off. Sew together, (the cast on and cast off), and fasten off ends. I made one from string off the sewn up ends of a bag of sugar. It is lovely and soft and washes well.

KNITTED MITT DUSTER

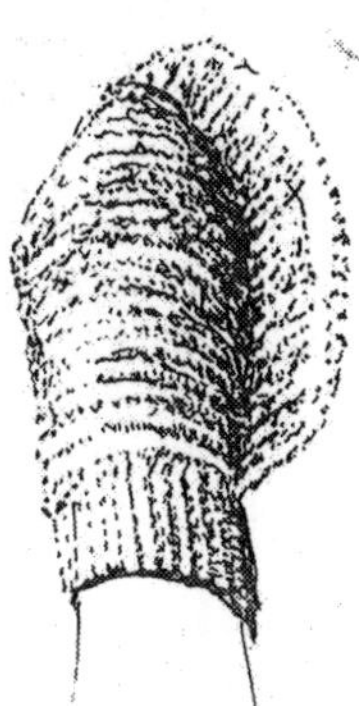

Excellent for cleaning, especially dusting the venetian blinds. Washes easily. Requirements : 2 skeins each of red and white candlewick cotton, No. 8 knitting needles.

With red wool, cast on 32 stitches. Work 10 rows in K.2, P.2, rib. Knit 3 rows, then Purl 1 row. Repeat these 4 rows 8 times.

Next row : (K.2 together, K.12, K.2 together) twice. K.1 row.

Next row (K.2 together, K.10, K.2 together) twice. P.1 row. Cast off.

Cut white into 4 inch lengths. Fold mitt in half and join side and top seam. With a crochet hook, knot 2 strands of white through every stitch in ridge rows on one side of the mitt.

Knitting Hints

If you have to store wool, push a mothball into the centre.

When knitting with black wool, use white needles, and vice versa.

Snap a press stud at the beginning of a row of knitting you want to mark, instead of the usual pin.

If you have to cast on a large number of stitches, knit a constrasting colour in with each 100th stitch, then count the coloured threads and multiply.

Do not knit into back of the stitch when casting on as this inevitably results in the cast-on breaking during the life of the garment.

If the cast on edge is breaking (because you forgot the above hint) unpick side seams to above the ribbing, draw a thread so as the pieces part, then unwind the band. Wash (to take out crimps) and re-knit by picking up the stitches again.

For a firmer seam, start *each* row by knitting into backs of *first* stitch.

Before slipping stitches on to a safety pin, thread a small button on the pin so the stitches won't tangle in the hinge.

If working two sleeves at once, use one ball and work from both ends of the ball, one end for each sleeve.

MATS I'VE MADE FROM WASTE MATERIAL

MAT FROM BREAD WRAPS

(Illustrated on Page 385)

47 bread wraps. Crochet hook.
Crochet 70 chain. Do 2 dc in first, then 1 dc in the next 68. Do 3 dc in last loop.

2nd row: Do 1 dc in each loop to end, then 4 dc across the end.

3rd row: 1 dc in each loop, and 6 dc across the end.

Keep the work flat by adding more each end, so it will end up an oval mat as illustrated.

The ends, next row, will have 8 dc in the 4 end loops, the next 10, and so on.

Repeat the dc around and around doing two into each dc at ends until it is 20 ins. (51 cm) wide.

P.S. Sometimes it is not necessary to do 2 dc into each stitch on the ends to keep it flat, other times, the increase is only necessary every 10th loop.

It takes 15 minutes to cut a bread bag spirally, and another 15 minutes to crochet it up. Cut the bread wrap 1/2 inch (12 mm) wide.

"Don't find fault, find a remedy."

MAT I MADE FROM 3 PAIR OF NOT-USED SLACKS

(Illustrated on Page 384)

First I undone the seams and pressed slacks. Then I cut them all into 5 cm. (2 inch) strips. Sew strips together. Plait them. Start from the centre and coil as you stitch the edges together, until it is a reasonable size. I backed mine with material. You can also make them from old stockings. If you want to dye the stockings a special colour, first colour-strip them.

"Thrift is a great revenue."

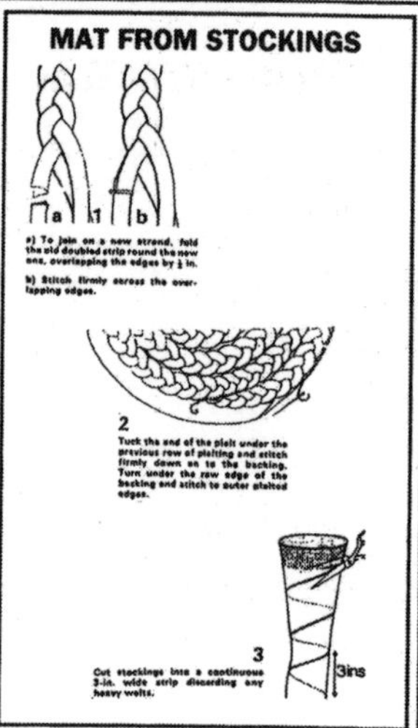

MAT FROM WOOL ODDMENTS (CIRCULAR)

You can make a pretty circular mat for the floor out of odd lengths of wool by crocheting long lengths of chain, then plait the chains. Start at centre of mat by stitching (on the back) neatly, round and round, easing it to keep it flat, and you will be very pleased with the finished article, as well as using up odd lengths of wool. It's better if it is 8 or 12 ply. A mat 94 cm. (37 ins) is a nice size.

Pins (in rhyme)

"Pins are most elusive things,
So very apt to stray.
Keep them near when cutting out,
This very simple way ;
Sew a little cushion to a firm elastic band,
Wear it like a bracelet,
And they'll always be on hand."

Buttonholes (stretched)

Sew them up before washing, then unpick when dry and they will be back into shape.

Buttons held Firmly

Sticky tape is good for holding buttons or press studs in place for sewing. Use it for attaching motifs or braid as well.

"I hear and I forget. I see and I remember. I do and I understand."

MESH SHOPPING BAG

Here is a cunningly contrived crochet bag that tucks into it's own case, and can be carried in your purse when it is not in use. I have given instructions for it to be made in Macrame Twine, but it could be made in a coarse cotton or silk equally as well.

MATERIALS: 1 ball of Macrame Twine No. 10 (or its equivalent in coarse cotton or silk which is sufficiently flexable to fold into a small space), 1 medium crochet hook.

ABBREVIATIONS: Ch, chain, dc, double crochet; sl.st, slip stitch; sts, stitches.

BASE: Begin at centre of circle. Work 6 ch. and join in a circle with a sl st.

1st round: 2 dc into each ch (12 dc), join with a sl st.

Now work into back of each dc in every round in following way:-

2nd round: * 1 dc into 1st dc, 2 dc into next dc, work from * to end; join with sl st.

3rd round: * 1 dc into each of 2 dc, 2 dc into next dc, work from * to end of round; join with a sl st.

Work on in this manner, working 6 equally spaced increases in alternate rounds until work measures 4 inches in diameter, or larger if desired **.

Begin mesh.

Next round: * Ch 10, then sl st into 4th dc of base, working through both threads, repeat from * to end of round, ending with a sl st into centre of 1st mesh.

Continue in this way slip stitching into centre of each of every mesh in previous round, until the bag measures 12 inches or desired length from base.

Fasten off securely.

TOP: Work same as base to **.

Fasten off.

TO MAKE UP

Press top and base on wrong side. Fold the chain mesh to wrong side of base. Place top over base, with right side on top, enclosing mesh. Slip stitch edges together for about two-thirds of the circumference, taking care to keep the mesh of the bag neatly enclosed inside. Strengthen the opening well with extra stitches. Fasten with a press stud. Crochet a chain about 20 inches. Slot chain through last round of mesh to form handles.

"Envy is a kind of praise."

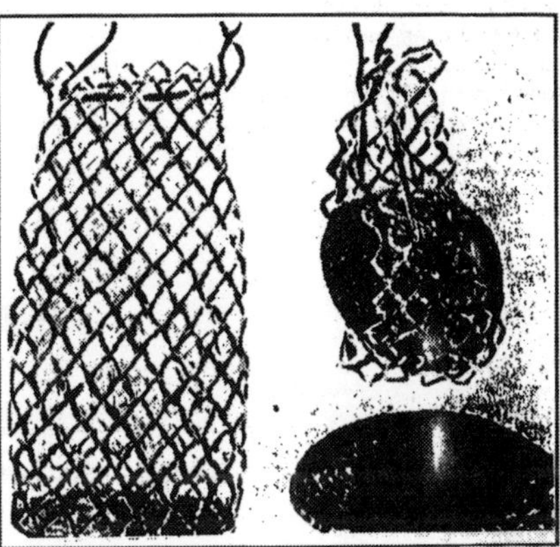

"Nothing can harm a good man either in life or death".

HANDY HINTS

DYE LOT IN WOOLS: If it is necessary to use a different dye lot, leave sufficient to work two rows, then work four rows – two with the new dye lot, two with the old – then continue with new dye lot and any difference in the dye lots will be less obvious.

KNITTING A BUTTONHOLE: When casting on for the top of the buttonhole, do so with the thumb method, then slip the first stitch to be worked, and work to the end of the row. On the next row, pick up the slipped stitch as if it had been dropped, and this will tighten the corner of the bottonhole.

KNITTING SOCKS: Heels last longer this way – on the flap, knit one stitch and slip the next. When your purl back next row your knitting will become double. Repeat till flap is completed.

SOCKS STORED: Hang them inside the wardrobe in a string bag.

SWEATER HINT: If the sleeves of your sweater are rough on your arms, line them with the legs of your old nylon stockings. It is warmer too.

WOOLIES DRIED: Use a baby bouncer (if you have one) to dry your woollen jumper on. The air circulates under and over.

WOOLLEN JUMPERS (peg marks): To remove peg marks from woollen jumpers simply hold the marked part over a steaming kettle; the marks will pull back into shape.

WOOL STORER: Use a bag made from unbleached calico to prevent moths and silverfish.

"Let sleeping dogs lie."

POODLE FROM A WIRE COAT HANGER AND YARN

Poodle from 2 (100g) balls of 14 ply yarn and a wire coat hanger, bent as on right. Illustrated on Page *388*
Cut a metre of wool, wind it around four of your fingers, tie it with another piece (around folded wool) then tie onto coat hanger. Keep doing this until the wire is covered, pushing them close together as you go. Make longer loops for the ears and tie ribbon on neck and sew on eyes, nose and mouth.

"If we had no faults, we would not take so much pleasure in noticing them in others".

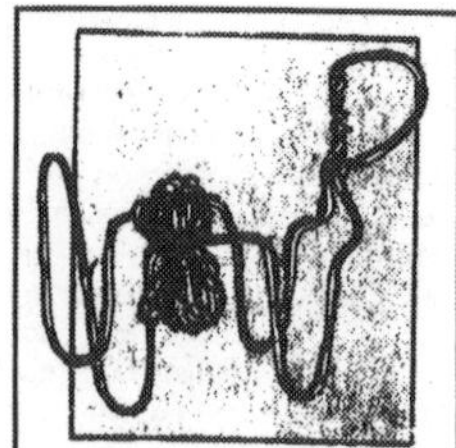

HANDY HINTS

MACHINE (oiled): After you have oiled your machine, run needle a few times through a blotter to absorb oil.
SCISSORS TIDY: An old glasses case makes an ideal holder for small scissors in your work basket.
SEWING HOLDERS: Save the containers that you buy flower plant annuals in, wash, then store your buttons, tape measure and pins in them in your sewing drawer.
SEWING SEAMS: Before letting out a seam, sew in the new, before ripping out the old. This eliminates pinning, and the amount of desired letout can easily be gauged from the old seam.
SEWING TIP ON COLLAR: Cut the under collar a little smaller, as the upper collar has to roll over it on the finished garment. Always insert the zipper before a collar is attached.
SHIRRING EASY: Use the zig-zag stitch on your machine and lay the elastic between the zig-zag on the wrong side of the fabric. Pull the elastic as you sew to get the tightness needed.
SHIRT (silk): Easier to iron if put in the refrigerator or freezer an hour before ironing.

HANDY HINTS

JEANS IRONED: Put in freezer five minutes before ironing. (Easier to iron).
JEANS LENGTHENED: To get rid of white hemline, apply ink and water mixed and applied with an old toothbrush, or, take a blue crayon and rub over line, then press.
JEANS "PRESS" DRY: Pull seams (inside and out) very hard before hanging on line, and pin back with three pegs on one line and front onto next line, and they rarely need to be pressed.
JEANS (snap fastener on): Put a drop of machine oil on the heavy snap fasteners on jeans to make them easier to snap.

Sewing Trolley

Use your tea trolley if you haven't a sewing room, then you can chase the sun when you want to do some sewing. If the trolley isn't in use, make a solid top for it, and use it as a permanent sewing table.

37

Sewing Hints and Ideas

- When baby grows out of his overalls or pyjamas, they can easily be lengthened by sewing the tops of an old pair of men's sox to the legs and arms. Stretch the cut off part of the sox to fit the leg as it is sewn in. The ribbed top will fit the ankle and wrist snugly.
- Always cut off selvedges on lined curtains, as this tends to draw curtains up on the sides and gives the drape a stiff appearance. Always use a flat seam with binding on the cross for lined curtains. Hand sew each one.
- Discipline cottons are crease-resisting.
  Combination means-wool and nylon, etc.
- Polished cottons are done by manufactures now, instead of by hand with beeswax as in olden days.
- **For the man on the Land :** When his riding breeches wear out, don't discard the leather piece that is on the inside of the legs. Sew with backstitch onto the sleeves lengthwise of hubby's coat, and he has a coat that will last him years longer, as generally the sleeves wear out in the elbows and there's no use for rest of coat.
- When sewing plastic material place a strip of paper underneath when machining. This prevents puckering and tearing and sews much easier. Tear paper away when finished. Have a bigger stitch on machine than with material.
- Make a young child's book by purchasing several nursery rhyme handkerchiefs, starch them stiffly, then stitch all together down one side.

SEWING IDEAS

Aprons . . .

Two pretty apron ideas can be made from old cotton head squares, or scarfs as we sometimes call them.

A. Cut off one corner to measurements shown. This piece is used for the pocket. Make a small hem on the pocket and thread it with a piece of elastic.

Press Stud Rhyme

"Press-stud pairs should always be
Matched with perfect symmetry.
Sew the knobs with even spacing,
Neatly to the upper facing.
Then, with tailor's chalk applied,
Press them to the underside.
Chalk marks now will clearly show
Where the matching half should go."

SOME HINTS FOR BETTER SEWING

Here are some dos and don'ts which will make your sewing easier, neater, and more professional - and more fun in the long run.

- Never fuss endlessly over your sewing, hand-stitching everything as if a sewing machine had never been invented. Remember that part of good sewing is to accomplish a detail simply and deftly.
- When making pale fabrics avoid marking up in coloured chalk. It is wiser to single-thread mark in a pale sewing cotton, and, of course, wash your hands frequently and dust with talcum.
- Never fidget or fiddle a sewing mistake. Either unpick it or completely ignore it. Fidgeting only makes a mistake worse.
- Always stay-stitch curve or bias edges to prevent stretching while sewing.
- Never use surface decoration that is badly sewn, as it will lose its decorative effect, detracting from, rather than improving, the look of your dress.
- Always allow yourself enough time to make a dress, or a particular detail, as too much attempted in too short a time only leads to mistakes which take time to rectify.
- Always pin a seam before tacking together and always tack before machining.
- Never use cheap or flashy trimmings; rather use fewer but better ones. However, always keep alive to trimming changes.
- Always avoid edge bulk by layer-trimming turnings to different widths.
- Always work with your garment flat on a table, never screwed up on your lap.
- Always press velvet on a special velvet board, or on a thick terry-towel.
- Always pin silk with thin steel needles, as this avoids ugly pin-holes.
- Always use as good a quality of a particular fabric as you can afford. It is better to use good quality cheap material than a poor quality of a more expensive type.
- Always use the correct length of zip. One that is too short will soon break.
- Always test a snippet of your fabric for pressing, stitching, shrinking, and general handling before making up.
- Never shirk making a particular detail correctly, for the correct way is generally the easiest way in the end.
- When making a difficult sewing process for the first time, always try it out on a separate piece of fabric before making it on your garment.
- Never use unshrunk interlining hoping that it will be all right; invariably it will shrink or twist during making or cleaning.
- Always make usable pockets on children's clothes, and always make their clothes for use.
- Never sew when you are tired or irritable; the few hours saved often lead to many more hours of unpicking mistakes.
- Never press on the right side of a seam if ironing on the wrong side will do. This will avoid shining and iron marks.
- Always steam away iron marks with steam from a kettle, never rubbing or laboring the mark, as this will make it worse.
- Always remove all tackings, pins, and lumps or bumps before the final press, for once they have left an imprint very little can be done to remove them.
- Never use trimming to disguise a badly made or a definitely out-of-fashion garment. By drawing attention to it, it will make it look even worse.
- Always use the correct needle size for both hand and machine sewing. The needle should pass through the fabric easily without breaking the fibres, yet be large enough to carry the sewing thread.
- Never fold up a half-made garment, squeezing it into a small box. Instead, hang it up, pinning vital seams together accurately. This will avoid many hours of unnecessary ironing.
- Always be adventurous with your sewing, doing that little bit more on each dress so that the excitement of achievement stimulates you to even more experiments.
- Always choose trimmings wisely, making sure you like a particular one before buying it, for, if you are doubtful at the beginning, you may hate it before the garment is finished.

"The popular concept that money is the root of all evil is wrong. It's not money, but the love of money that is a root of all kinds of evil."

"Whoever loves money never has money enough; whoever loves wealth is never satisfied with his income." Ecclesiasticus 5:10.

Stockings (old) Put to Good Use

Cut spirally, making one long piece when finished and use it for knitting slippers, shopping bags, bath mats, etc.

"Genius is one percent inspiration and ninety-nine percent perspiration."

"The last word of evolution is this — The race is not to the swift, nor to the strong, but to the wise."

Supper Cloth

Make a novel one, by getting your friends to autograph it, then embroider it all in bright colours. Mine has beautiful memories, and a lot of the folk have now passed on.

"People forget how fast you did a job — but they remember how well you did it."

There are cushions in the dining room
and also in the hall,
There are knitted toys and funny clowns
and pictures on the wall.
There are dresses in the wardrobe,
and evening bags in the drawer,
There are slippers galore that I'll never wear out,
and by the look of my patterns there'll be more.
There's shopping bags made from plastic bags,
and baskets made from cane,
Beautiful hats from stockings,
They send my friends insane.
Lace doilies grace the table tops,
My bedspreads are fantastic,
There are so many different home made mats,
and even ones I've crocheted in plastic.
There's home made vases and jewellery,
and trunks full of knitted ware,
There's patchwork rugs and curtains,
That makes visitors stand and stare.
Aprons, bedsocks, scarves and hankies,
Tablecloths, suppercloths and more,
You'll find them all in my home,
From the ceiling to the floor.
I have no tiresome worries,
of gifts for Christmas Day,
as I make all kinds of presents,
In my own particular way.
What is the secret of my skills
I am asked most every day,
I tell them perseverance and patience,
and the ability to pray,
as well as finish all you start,
Is one of my motto's too,
and if a thing's worth doing it's worth doing well,
Is applied to everything I do..

MAT FROM RAGS

The mat illustrated on Page *384* I made from pieces of rag on hessian. Take a piece of hessian, 100 cm. (39 1/2 ins) x 74 cm. (29 ins). With a biro, mark it from top to bottom into 4 cm. (1 1/2 inch) lines. It will take lots of 10 cm. (4 in.) squares of material to finish the job. A lady gave me mine, mostly thick material. She said she knew I would make something from them! I did, the same day.

What you do is take the square, fold it into three, lay the folded piece on the line you made with the biro and sew it with the machine. It takes about 32 each line. Start at the left side and make your way across the mat. It is better to bind the hessian first. I also put a row of black folded pieces on edges. It is admired by all who visit me. It only takes a few hours to stitch, once you have the squares cut out.

RUG FROM OLD SOCKS

The rug measures approximately 72 in. by 60 in. and is made up of 54 pieces of worn out tops of socks.

You cut the foot from the sock, then cut the top open and join each pair along the top edge. Continue to join the socks this way, blending the colors, until the rug is the size you want.

When the rug is finished sew on a backing made of any material you have. You can use old jumpers if you like.

"Misers may not be fun to live with, but make excellent ancestors."

ICE CREAM BUCKET COVERED IN BREAD WRAPS

Great for storing or carrying small cakes or scones.
Cover for a 5 litre icecream bucket and lid. Crocheted from bread wraps. Illustrated on page *385*
It requires 16 breadwraps for bucket and 4 for the lid. One bread wrap crochets about 3 rows on the upper part of the bucket. Cut 1/2 inch wide, dust with talcum powder.
Start with 6 chain. Join. Do 12 dc in the ring.
1st row: 2 dc in each dc.
2nd row: 1 dc in each dc. Repeat first two rows.
5th row: 1 dc in each dc. Repeat last row
7th row: 6 dc, 2 dc in next. Repeat all round.
8th row: 1 dc in each dc.
9th row: 5 dc, 2 dc in next. Repeat all round.
10th row: 4 dc, 2 dc in next. Repeat all round.
11th row: 1 dc in each dc.
12th row: 3 dc, 2 dc in next. Repeat all round.
13th row: 1 dc in each dc.
14th row: Repeat last row twice.
16th row: Dc 10, miss 1 dc. Repeat to end.
This should fit the bottom of the bucket. Now continue without increasing or decreasing until it fits over the bucket - about 33 rows.

LID

Do 6 chain. Join. Do 12 dc in the ring.
1st row: 2 dc in every dc.
2nd row: 1 dc in each dc.
3rd row: 1 dc, 2 dc in next. Repeat all round.
4th row: 5 dc, 2 dc in next. Repeat all round.
Repeat last round 3 more times.
8th row: 4 dc, 2 dc in next. Repeat all round.
Repeat last row twice more.
11th row: 1 dc in each dc.
Repeat last row 3 times.
15th row: 3 dc, 2 dc in next. Repeat all round.
16th row: 1 dc in each dc.
17th row: Repeat last round. This should now fit the top of the lid.
Punch holes around the top of the bucket and in the hollow of the lid (next to edge). Sew on covers with a length of the cut bread wrap, using a running or back stitch.

"I dread success. To have succeeded is to have finished one's business on earth. I like a state of continual becoming, with a goal in front and not behind."

COVER FOR A 1 KG. MARGARINE CONTAINER FROM BREAD WRAPS

(See illustration on Page 385)

First punch holes 12 mm. (1/2 inch) apart around the top of the container, then on the lid just inside the raised portion. You will need 7 bread wraps - 5 1/2 for the container, 1 1/2 for the lid. Cut the bottom off the wrap then the pleated piece, leaving one long sleeve. Now cut it in one long spiral piece, 12 mm. (1/2 inch) wide. Dust with talcum powder.
Crochet 6 chain. Join. Do 12 dc in this ring. Instead of joining the 12th to the 1st, I continue around and around until it is completed, as it is easier, but I mark each round by inserting a short piece of plastic, so I'll know where the round ends. Shift it every row.
Next row: 2 dc in every dc.
Next row: 1 dc in every dc. Repeat these 2 rows once.
Next row: 1 dc in every dc.
Next row: 3 dc, 2 dc in the next. Repeat all round.
Next row: 6 dc, 2 dc in next. Repeat all round.
Next row: 1 dc in each dc.
Next row: 8 dc, miss one dc. Repeat all round.
Continue without increasing or decreasing for 17 rows or until it fits your container. Sew onto container with a running stitch.

LID

Crochet 6 chain. Join. Work 12 dc in the ring.
Next row: 2 dc in each dc.
Next row: 1 dc in each dc. Repeat last 2 rows. Crochet 3 rows without increasing.
Next row: 6 dc, 2 dc in next. Repeat all round.
Fasten off. This should fit snugly inside the hollow of the lid. Sew onto lid. Without the lid it makes a useful holder for pot plants. With the lid it will hold from biscuits to cottons.

"Lazy hands make a man poor, but diligent hands bring wealth." Proverbs 10:4.

ARTICLES FROM STOCKINGS, BREAD WRAPS OR PLASTIC BAGS

Hats, crocheted from Bread wraps or stockings.

(Illustrated on Page 383)

About 16 required. Crochet hook No. 8 (or 4.00).

I cut the bag 1/2 inch wide in one long spiral length. Then I put it in a basin and sprinkle it with talc powder. You don't have to use talc when crocheting up supermarket bags as they are not sticky.

Make 5 chain. Join.

1st round: 8 dc into the ring. (I mark the end of each round, by inserting a length of plastic, about 6 inches long and 1/2 inch wide).

2nd round: 2 dc into each loop.

3rd round: * 2 dc into 1st loop, 1 dc into next loop, * repeat all round.

4th round: 1 dc into 1st loop, * 1 dc into next loop, 2 dc into the next, * repeat from * to *.

5th round: 1 dc into every loop.

6th round: * 2 dc into 1st loop, 1 dc into next 6 loops, * repeat from * to *.

7th, 8th, 9th, 10th, 11th and 12th rounds: Repeat last round.

13th round: 1 dc into every loop.

14th round: Repeat last round, then repeat until work measures about 6 1/2 inches.

Right side facing you do 1 dc into next 12 loops, miss 1 loop and repeat all round. Continue without decreasing for another 3 1/2 inches or length required.

BRIM

2 dc into first loop, 1 dc in next. Repeat all round.

2nd row: 1 dc into every loop. Repeat this row until width required. Trim as desired. Do the same with stockings using same pattern.

> *"The value of recycling*
> *Is great, that I can see;*
> *Which leads me to wonder,*
> *When they'll get around to me."*

VASE - USING BREAD WRAPS

(See it illustrated Page 385 on the right)

Find a bottle that's a little larger on the top than on the bottom, so that when the cover is completed, it doesn't slip down. Follow the same procedure as the pattern I've provided for covering a margarine container and thats it.

> *"If you aren't rich, you should always look useful."*

PEN OR KNITTING NEEDLE HOLDER

(See Page 385)

You can use the bottom half of plastic bottles, covered in crocheted plastic or stocking yarn to hold pens and pencils on your desk, or, on taller ones just cut off neck and use them for holding all your knitting needles. Follow the same pattern to cover as I have given for covering a margarine container.

> *"Waste not, want not."*

SHOPPING BAGS FROM STOCKINGS OR PLASTIC BAGS

(Illustrated on Page 385)

One way is to crochet one long piece sufficient for the two sides, cutting the stockings or plastic at least 1/2 inch in width, spirally. Make gussets of 4 inch strips and sew into the sides for added width. Make a hem on tops and insert a coathanger bended to fit. Cover with blanket stitch to hide the wire. Add a pocket inside for change or handkerchief.

Another one I crocheted I like best. I crocheted it from stockings, by using the crochet square on page , making 1 large square (14 ins.) for back, and another for front, the gussets at the side has 3 small squares of 4 ins square, and along the bottom I added 4 squares. You can line these with another 4 if you want it extra strong. I used the handles from 2 old buckets, covering them with blanket stitch after they had been inserted through the hem.

> *"Modesty is the only sure bait when you angle for praise."*

BELT KNITTED FROM STOCKINGS IN MOSS STITCH

(See Page 385)

Cut stocking 1/4 inch in width. With No. 11 needles, cast on 1. Increase each end of every row until there is 15 stitches, In moss stitch. Do 2 rows.

Next row: Knit 6, cast off 3, Knit 6.

Next row: Knit 6, cast on 3, knit 6.

Continue until belt is 27 ins. long, then decrease one stitch each end until there are none left. Cover a curtain ring with scallop stitch, then insert the end (without hole) through the ring and stitch down. Cover a button and place on the point where you stitched it. Cover another button and sew on the other end of belt about 3 1/2 ins. from the point. When wearing belt, push the other pointed end through the other half of ring and put button through the hole. I do not waste much in this household. It was drummed into me at an early age not to waste, to make do, or do without if you can't pay cash for it.

> *"Just as around your body,*
> *This little belt you wear,*
> *So may your life be circled*
> *By "heaps" of loving care."*

Zip Mending (when slide comes off one side)

Firstly, take down to bottom. On the side that is not catching, slash through canvas with a razor blade (just above the slide). Run slide up, feeding in teeth of zip above cut. They will lock at this point. With strong thread, sew over and over across zip where you slashed it to form a barrier when you pull zip down again.

"It's neat and ingenious, clever and slick,
And when in a hurry, it's terribly quick.
We call it a joy, a boon, and a blessing ;
The perfect adjunct to modern-day dressing.
But when it won't work, we give it a jerk,
We pull and we tear, and pray it will work.
For nothing can rile you or give you the pip,
Like that wonderful, horrible, maddening zip!

Zipper

The patent for a hookless fastener was first established by Mr. Whitcombe Judson and in 1913 a company was formed to manufacture it. Sometime later B. F. Goodrich Co. produced a ladies rubber rain shoe which he called the "Mystic Boot". When salesmen complained about the name saying that it was unattractive and unimaginitive, it was then suggested that the slide fastener be called a zipper.

Zips

Zips that won't work smoothly will work better after you run the point of a lead pencil up and down the fastener (the graphite does the trick), or with a wax candle ; or,

They will always run freely if you sprinkle talcum powder on them. It prevents them sticking too.

"Nothing is really work unless you would rather be doing something else.,"

ZIPPER HINTS: All zippers should be pre-shrunk before sewing in a garment. Lubricate a "cranky" zipper by rubbing with soap. When material around the zipper gets frayed, apply clean nail varnish to the region. It will dry and prevent zipper catching on the material when opening or shutting.

SOME HANDY HINTS

CANVAS STITCHING: Lubricate the underside of canvas with soap before stitching to prevent broken machine needles.

COATHANGER TRICK: Prevent frocks (especially ones with shoe string straps) from falling off coathangers by wrapping rubber bands around ends.

CROCHET D'OYLEYS INTO CUSHIONS: Make your unused lace d'oyleys into nice cushions. Take some colour material for the inside cushion and stuff. Have two d'oyleys the same size and sew to within 8 cm (3 in.) of d'oyley, leaving enough open to insert the cushion. Sew up opening. Makes a nice gift.

GATHERING: Fill the bobbin with shirring elastic and sew with a long stitch.

HANDICAPPED: If you have trouble doing up the laces in your shoes, thread hat elastic through the holes.

HEMS LET DOWN: Mix 2 tablespoons vinegar with 1 teaspoon borax and little hot water. Put on wrong side of material with old toothbrush. Let dry and then hem mark should be gone.

HEMS UNPICKED (thread from): If you want to use it again, press the curl out with hot iron.

IRON (cleaned on surface): Rub marks off with a damp cloth dipped in bicarb. soda. Or, soak a cloth in vinegar, and use elbow grease.

IRONING BOARD: Put aluminium foil over your ironing board, under the cover. Makes damp clothes easier to iron as the heat reflected by the foil helps dry them out. If making a new cover, cut material on the cross for a perfect fit.

IRONING BRAID: Iron the wrong side and braid will lie flat.

IRON TIP (Steam): Add a dessertspoon of ammonia to each cup of water and then you can use ordinary tap water in your steam iron without any buildup. Makes ironing smoother too.

KNITTING A COAT HANGER COVER: This is a very easy pattern with a lacy pointed edge. Use handicraft nylon or wool. I knitted one in white Ban-Lon, and it holds my dress beautifully without slipping. I used No. 8 needles. Cast on 15 stitches. **1st Row:** K11, yfwd, K2 tog, yfwd, K2. **2nd and alternate rows:** Knit. **3rd Row:** K12, yfwd, K2 tog, yfwd, K2. **5th Row:** K13, yfwd, K2 tog, yfwd, K2. **7th Row:** K14, yfwd, K2 tog, yfwd, K2. **8th Row:** Cast off 4 stitches, K to the end. Repeat these 8 rows until length required. Folding over cast-on edge to beginning of lacy peaks and stitch in place. Join ends. Wind wool round and round the hook to match. (yfwd means yarn forward).

KNITTING A ROUND ARTICLE: With this pattern you can knit a washer (with knitting cotton), a table mat, table centre or even a cushion cover. I have a centre on a pedestal I knitted in metallised goldfingering which looks most attractive especially as I have a large golden statuette on it. To knit a washer cast on 26 stitches with No. 10 needles. Next row knit to within 2 stitches, turn, slip the first stitch and knit to end of row. Next row knit to within 4 stitches, turn, slip first stitch and knit to end of row. Keep doing this by knitting to within 6, then 8, 10, etc., until you have gone right back to outside edge. Next row, knit one row right through. Next row, slip first stitch, knit to end of row. Repeat from beginning until it is a complete circle (about 12 repeats). The first section looks like a wedge when completed. Sew up the cast off to cast on edges. Takes about 4 hours to complete. For a cushion cover your will need more stitches, perhaps twice as many, all depending on size, and to make it colourful, use different colour for each section.

LACE TABLECLOTH: After washing, lay a sheet on the floor and lay cloth on it, then pull into shape. Let dry. Seldom needs ironing, and will look just a graceful on the table.

LAVENDER IN DRAWERS: Repels moths.

LAWN PETTICOAT RE-USED: Those very full frilly petticoats you have tucked away with deep embroidery bordering them, can be put to good use again, by unpicking and adding to the tops of your plain white sheets.

LINGERIE (black): To restore black colour, add strong tea or coffee to the rinsing water.

LIPSTICK CASE (for needles etc.): When you have used your lipstick, clean container, and use it for needles and thread to carry when travelling.

MATERNITY TOP: Use it for your daughter as a painting smock.

MILDEW ON RAINCOAT: Rub gently with steel wool and dry soap powder.

MOTH BAGS: Mix together 1/2 cup each of the dried, crumbled leaves of lemon verbena, tansy, southern wood and rosemary with a piece of cinnamon stick and a tablespoon of whole cloves. Sew flower pattered muslin bags and fill with the mixture; tie ribbons and loop around the neck of coat hangers.

NEEDLES (threaded): Cut thread on the slant if you have difficulty in threading a needle, or spray with hair oil.

NYLON (white): Wash alone, or with white clothes, as it picks up colours from towels, frocks etc. To prevent from turning yellow pre-soak in a baking powder solution.

PERSPIRATION FROM CLOTHES: Soak in salt water before washing, or use pre-wash laundry spray.
Or, put a paste of cream of tartar or bicarb. soda and vinegar on. Leave for 1/2 an hour. Rinse and wash.

PILLOW (herb): These are simple to make from remnants of fabric, lace, braid and ribbon. Cut 2 pieces to the size you want. On one piece sew braid or ribbon to decorate then sew three sides together making sure the decorative side is facing inwards. Make an inner bag the same size and stuff it with the following, mixed in order given – 4 tablespoons each dried thyme and rosemary needles, 8 tablespoons dried camomile flowers, 1 teaspoon rosemary oil, 1 tablespoon each orris root powder and powdered gum benzoin. Put into inner bag, sew up opening. Place into the decorated pillow case and stitch the opening. Use the fragrant pillow to induce sleep by putting it inside your pillow case. An ideal size is about 25cm (10in) square.
Or try this one – **mint and lemon** – 10 tablespoons dried mint, 5 tablespoons each dried lemon geranium leaves and dried lemon verbena, 1 tablespoon orris root powder, 1/2 teaspoon each peppermint oil and lemon grass oil.

PINS AND NEEDLES: Will slide more easily and will never rust if you store them in a bar of soap.

PLASTIC SEWING: Rub some talcum powder on the plastic, and the needle before sewing.

POMANDER: You won't smell of mothballs the first time you wear your fur at the beginning of winter if you hang one of these in your wardrobe instead. (You can use any citrus fruit.)
Take a small thin skinned orange and cover it entirely with whole cloves. If the skin is hard make holes with tooth picks. This takes time, but it is worth while. After you finish spiking it, roll in a mixture of orris root powder (chemists sell it) and cinnamon, equal parts. Wrap the pomander in tissue paper, put in closed box for a couple of weeks, shake and hang or put in your drawers. It will eventually dry hard, but the fragrance will last for years, and keep the moths at bay too. If you want to hang it, leave a space around the centre for a piece of ribbon or thread a piece of silk thread right through the fruit with a darning needle.

SAMPLER HINT: When doing cross stitch embroidery always have the bottom half of ALL crosses in one direction, and ALL top half that crosses them in the other direction.

SHOULDER BAG: Make a unique bag from stretch fabric, them sew on all your odd buttons. I don't think any home is without them. Plait some cords and sew on for a shoulder strap.

SHOWER CURTAIN: If no longer needed, sew up three sides and store blankets in it over summer.

SKIRT (better fit): Sew buttons on the waistband with elastic thread.

SKIRT (circular): Hang circular skirts on the line by the straight side seam. If you hang them by the waistline they might drop in the centre front and back.

SLIP (half): If you have no further use for a half slip, use it as a lining for a woollen skirt. Or, for putting over you head if someone is cutting your hair. Tighten elastic if use for this.

SLIPPERS (knitted – this is MY original pattern. K is knit, P is purl.):
Cast on 25 stitches on number 5mm (6) needles, using 3 strands of 8 ply yarn. Leave a length of yarn to use later when sewing up the back for heel.
1st Row: K12, increase twice in next stitch, K12 (27 stitches).
2nd Row: K4, P8, K1, increase twice in next stitch (purlwise), K1, P8, K4, (29 stitches)
3 Row: K12, P1, increase in next stitch, K1, increase in next stitch, P1, K12, (31 stitches).
4th Row: K4, P8, K1, increase in next stitch, P3, increase in next stitch, K1, P8, K4, (33 stitches).
5th Row: K12, P1, increase in next stitch, K5, increase in next stitch, P1, K12, (35 stitches).
6th Row: K4, P8, K1, P9, K1, P8, K4, (35 stitches).
7th Row: K12, P1, K9, P1, K12.
Repeat last 2 rows until there are 36 rows from the cast on row – 34 rows for a small foot, and 38 rows for a man. The plain side is now facing your.
Next Row: Cast off 3, K1, P1 (4 times), P1, K9, P1, K1, to end of row.
Next Row: Cast off 3, K1, P1 (4 times), K1, P9, K1, P1, to end of row.
Next Row: K1, P1 (5 times), slipping the first stitch instead of knitting it, K9, P1, K1, to end of row.
Next row: P1, K1 (5 times, slipping the first stitch purlwise instead of purling it, P9, K1, P1, to end of row.
Continue last two rows until you have 18 rows in rib etc. (19 rows for a man).
Toe: With right side facing slip 1, P2 tog. (5 times). K2 tog. (4 times), P2 tog. (5 times).
Next Row: K2 tog. (3 times). P2 tog., K2 tog. (3 times), K1. Cut yarn off, leaving 30 cm (12in.) to sew up with. Thread a bodkin with the yarn and take off remaining stitches. Fold in half – purlside inside – and sew up to the top of the 3 cast off stitches. Fasten off. Thread the yarn at the heel, and sew together the cast on stitches. Fasten off.

TABLECLOTH (heir-loom, I hope): Way back in 1950 I started to embroider a white linen tablecloth with names of my special relatives and friends. It is a cloth of many memories, as some have passed on, others have vanished and so on. In the centre I have Elizabeth R. and Phillip that I copied from a signed photo of Queen Elizabeth and Prince Phillip and family, that was presented to my Auntie Amy, the late Mrs Alf Martin of Ross, by the Queen at Government House on one of her visits. Aunt did sterling work at Government House upholstering suites etc. She did likewise at "Connorville" in Cressy before another of the Queen's visits. Another article that tells a tale in my home is my knitted bedspread, I knitted in 1967. It has 78 squares, and the majority of them I drafted. The squares range from favourite poetry, wedding dates, sentimental things, my pets, to even a map of Tasmania. It sure is a spread of memories.

THIMBLE HOLDER: Glue a small cork to the inside of your sewing drawer and use it as a resting place.

Even if flowers are expensive or out of season, there's no excuse for letting your house become colourless and drab. A varnished gourd or three can be the basis of an intriguing and inexpensive arrangement for your table or sideboard.

14. HOME BEAUTIFUL

It was Empire Day in 1955 when Marjorie Blackwell spent her first night in the dream home she had conjured in her imagination, designed on countless sheets of paper and doggedly supervised into existence. Though her marriage to Cliff Blackwell was already in strife by the time the building was completed, Marjorie nevertheless christened their home Climar, a romantic portmanteau. Famous for its apricot-bricked curves and a wrought-iron fence featuring musical notes, Climar is the achievement that Marjorie even today regards as her finest. Gone, now, are the sandblasted wading birds on the French doors that wrap around the front of the house, but still the structure is a well-known exemplar of 1950s taste, standing proudly on the main street of Campbell Town.

The Devonport home Marjorie bought with second husband Adrian, and where Marjorie still lives today, is Marian (first three letters of Marjorie, last three of Adrian), and its décor is a testament to its mistress's thrift and endeavour. A reporter for Hobart's *Mercury* once reported the experience of visiting Marian: 'You tip-toe dazedly past the big mirror wall in the hall, greenly enveloping you in reflections of ferns and potted plants. You go through the lounge, gazing in awe at the order, the signs of industry—clocks, eight vases on the mantelpiece, bric-a-brac, flower arrangements, homilies stitched authoritatively into cushions (Your home can be a castle if the one you love is there)…'

In Marjorie's aesthetic, crazy patchwork curtains and bedspreads are a perfect way to use up scraps of dress fabric; there is little that cannot be prettied up with a length of macramé twine and some dyed, crushed eggshell; a toilet roll implies a toilet-roll holder, and some scraps of lace, a celluloid doll and a posy of fabric flowers can be the ingredients of a spectacular one; handmade is better than shop bought; sentiment trumps colour scheme; and—most importantly—more is always more.

—•—

Marjorie and Eric in their museum.

MATTHEW EVANS, GOURMET FARMER AND FOOD WRITER

The presenter of the TV show *Gourmet Farmer* has made many discoveries in his new island home, and Marjorie Bligh is one of the most surprising and entertaining.

When gourmet farmer Matthew Evans next renovates his bathroom, he plans to take some sage advice from Marjorie Bligh. Photo courtesy of Random House Australia.

'She's full of wit and wisdom, much of it from an era that is not so long ago,' Matthew Evans says.

'My favourite of her tips is about making bathroom curtains from towelling as they will help absorb the steam. Her suggestion that you match them to your towel set reminds me of those lovely 1950s books for housewives, where they recommended dinner party tablecloths should match the hostess's frock (and that the vicar shouldn't sit next to the army lieutenant).'

A GLASS WATER SET

Needed : A wine bottle, 6 glasses, 2 balls macrame twine, clear lacquer, and a brush (old tooth brush is excellent), 2 tubes of liquid glue or "grip", but must be water tight.

Binding Method : Rest bottom of bottle on edge of table—the top in your lap. Holding bottle with left hand, squeeze 2 or 3 spots of grip on the the glass, smooth out until it is covered along strip you are going to work on. Wind macrame over gummed surface. Repeat the gumming and winding until bottle is covered. Push ends under neighbouring rows or taper and stick again. For the glasses : Copy the bottle, but only do one inch in macrame around bottoms. Lacquer when finished, which makes the covering tighter and gives a slight gloss. A waste paper basket can also be made with rope covering instead of macrame. An old tin could be used, and paint the inside to match.

" Marjorie Bligh's Homely Hints on Everything ". Sam wrote the story so fascinatingly that I would like to share some of it with you. Here is a portion – " You tip-toe dazedly past the big mirror wall in the hall, greenly enveloping you in reflections of ferns and potted plants. You go through the lounge, gazing in awe at the order, the signs of industry – clocks, eight vases on the mantlepiece, bric-a-brac, flower arrangements, homilies stitched authoritatively into cushions (Your home can be a castle if the one you love is there). Mrs. Marjorie Bligh is sitting at the kitchen table. In front of her are long strips of paper covered in tight curly writing. She has a pen in her hand and looks up, disturbed. I suppose you are wondering what I am doing she says severely ; while you are thinking of a reply your eye catches the bottles. They line the walls in serried rows. They snake around corners, reappearing briefly to dive into some shelved wall recess to mass glinting and spotless, layer upon layer, unmoving, unmoveable. I'm doing another book says Marjorie Bligh."

Then the story goes on to tell about my first book, contents, why I was writing the hint book, hobbies, how many copies of my first book I had sold and so on and so on. This story ends like this – " It is time to go. Mrs. Marjorie Alfreda Willis Bligh talks on and Eric hovers around, smiling, unobtrusive. She has not actually said so, but you feel Mrs. Bligh approves. She has given you a copy of her book (inscribed) for nothing ! And she has invited you back for a mash of her special vegetarian salad anytime. *'I'll eat raw vegetables and raw fruit too, It's better for you than Irish Stew'*. That's some of Marjorie Bligh's practical poetry and philosophy too. And as you leave she imparts the final great truth, that you feel has carried her through all troubles and tribulations. *'If you have a place for everything there is no need to worry'*, she says calmly."

Christmas Cards

Run a wide panel of coloured paper from the picture rail to the skirting board and fasten the cards to it ; or,

Choose a dried branch with plenty of twigs, paint it silver, then tie, or stick cards onto branches. Stand in a pot of sand.

Before sending Christmas cards to hospitals, etc., clean writing off with household bleach.

Christmas Decorations

Cover a coathanger with red paper, stick holly leaves on with glue and attach little bells, and a bow of ribbon at the centre. Other things of course, can be added. Hang on your front door or a wall.

Make artificial snow by adding a little water to a bowl full of soap powder and whip to a creamy consistency. Spread the *"snow"* where required and don't touch it for 12 hours.

Keep used camera flash bulbs, paint and hang on the Christmas tree branches for added colour. Dip in Epsom salts whilst paint is wet.

Christmas Decorations for the Table.

If you possess an old-fashioned cake stand, fill it with a pyramid of coloured balls (or baubles) and put short lengths of tinsel in between them, allowing some to trail over the edge of dish ; alternatively, make a cone from chicken wire, or stiff cardboard, then push paper doyleys through the wire (or through pre-made holes in card). Attach baubles and bows of ribbon to hairpins and push them through the centre of the doyleys.

Another delightful table decoration is to glue or nail a wooden pole onto a base. Fold some chicken wire to form a cone and place over pole. Make some organza roses from saucer-sized pieces, using three at a time, forming them into a rose shape and then push them into chicken wire with a pencil. Gather 4-6 sweets into a small posy and attach them to the wire frame. (Sweets should be the type with coloured wrapping, the paper tufted at each end.) To provide extra sparkle, intersperse silver tinsel among the roses.

Another table centre easy to make is — select a flat plate, stick 6 candles onto it with plasticine. Pinch white paper doyleys into small posies and place them round the edge of plate, secure them firmly, then fix into the middle of each, a coloured bauble ; or,

Christmas Tree (fire-proof)

To stop the needles falling, stand the tree in a bucket of hot water and an equal amount of crude glycerine (from the chemist). Stand the tree in the mixture for a couple of days before putting it into the tub of soil. To reduce fire danger, mix 120g (4oz.) of boric acid powder with 375g (12oz.) of borax, dissolve in 4.5 litres (1 gal.) of water. If the tree is small, dip the tree in the solution and let dry. If tree is tall, use a high pressure garden spray and spray tree outdoors with the solution.

Christmas Tree Strengthened

Spray with hair spray (if it is an imitation tree).

I was very embarrassed another evening when I had special visitors to supper, because Cliff – arriving home greasy and late – invited them out to the kitchen to see how his tea was laid out on paper. Before the visitors arrived I prepared the supper on my best embroidered white cloth, and on one end placed a sheet of brown paper with Cliff's knife and fork resting on it, hoping that when he had his tea he would remove it. He was always covered in grease because of his work, so the brown paper was there to prevent my cloth being ruined as he rested his arms on the table. He didn't mind when no one was there, eating off brown paper, as I always starch my tablecloths. He always enjoyed my cooking though, and ate as if he was starving, whereas Adrian ate as if the Queen was in attendance, and Eric " tidies up " after every mouthful which really " bugs " me, and you don't even have to " wash " his plate later. I guess it is not the beard that makes the philosopher.

Many years ago when I was living at Campbell Town I was the town's dressmaker. I also organised balls and dances for charities, so, naturally I created many dazzling evening gowns for myself for those special evenings. One was of white lace with a full circular shirt. When it showed signs of wear I cut it into strips about 4 inches wide and oversewed the edges on the machine and made a lovely nightgown case, similar to the above. In the centre I put a celluloid doll cut off at the waist. I made a frilly blouse of lace for it, and it graced my bed for many years. Its marvellous what you can do with left-overs and some deep thinking.

Furniture (white rings on polished)

Rub with a soft cloth dampened with spirits of camphor.

Windows (frosted)

Mix a tablespoon of Epsom salts in a 1/4 cup of lukewarm stale beer, until dissolved. Dab on with rag. Give a second coat when dry. Windows should be very clean first and do it to the inside of window.

The kitchen was "alive" with built-ins, even on the rounded walls. There were built-in flour and sugar bins and a two-way cupboard that opened into the dining room as well as the kitchen. There were floor to ceiling built-ins in the dining room as well ; these held a cocktail cabinet, china cabinet, as well as a large area to hold all my scrapbooks. But as the books started to go mouldy, I had an electric fire installed in the centre and in July 1961 block heaters were added throughout the house on the very day that I had a visit from the Warden, Mr. Reginal Taylor, and his wife.

The sewing room led off the kitchen and was on the west side of the home. The linen press occupied one wall, and the fireplace backed the one in the kitchen. A built-in chest of drawers held paper patterns, knitting books and needles, and there were compartments for cottons, scissors and so forth. On the top was a square fish tank with a walking fish therein, and the room also contained Mother's table, a stool, and a dressmaker's mirror.

All the things I've mentioned, plus linen, crockery and much, much more were stored in the first home together with the bath, basins, stove, etc., etc. so you can imagine how cluttered our first home was when "Climar" took so long to build. My nerves were very frayed, watching the house slowly grow, from my sunroom window, and more especially, when the workmen didn't turn up for days on end. I sat every night embroidering tablecloths, pillowslips, even 36 linen tea towels, made mats, stools, pictures, cushions, bedspreads and new lingerie, so the contents matched the home, and as it neared completion and I was taking the things down bit by bit and installing them in their new home, my cup was overflowing ; then the very night (a Tuesday) I was going to move in, I went down and lit the kitchen fire, turned every light on, sat in a chair and stared all around and was almost hysterical with joy. And I never had anyone to share that joy with me, as it was Empire Day (1955) and Cliff and the boys were too busy in the top paddock with their bonfire and crackers. *"Our efforts and others' encouragement play great parts in our lives."* (Empire Day, the 24th May, Queen Victoria's birthday, was always Bonfire night.)

The guest bedroom in Marjorie's Devonport home is a testament to her needlework skills. The top cushion is made from men's ties, the bottom cushion is knitted and the spread is crocheted. The room's curtains are a riot of crazy patchwork crafted from off-cuts from Marjorie's dancing gowns.

Handicraft Hints

FELT MAT

Cut old felt hats into 1 inch strips. Steam straight, then weave into a mat as you would darn a sock. Lasts for years and looks very effective.

A PASTE THAT KEEPS

Very handy for scrap books, or if you have children going to school.

Mix 1 tablespoon each of flour, sugar and starch. Add 1 teaspoon powdered alum. Mix to a cream with a little cold water. When free from lumps, pour on sufficient boiling water to make it transparent, but not too thick, as it gets thicker when it gets cold.

WASTE PAPER BASKET

Save used stamps and when you have enough, paste them onto a used ice cream carton (cleaned) and make an attractive waste paper basket for any room. Give a coat of clear varnish when finished. To get used stamps off envelopes, etc., soak them until they leave the envelopes, then put them face downwards until they dry, on a window sill or similar place.

SHELL ORNAMENTS

Buy a tin of putty and spread it over a cracked vase, flower pot, or just a marmite (large) jar will do. Make sure the putty is pliable. If it isn't add linseed oil until it is soft. Have the shells clean and dry and push the shells attractively into the putty until surface is covered. Paint them with a coat of colourless varnish. You can use pieces of pretty china instead of shells if you wish, and instead of putty, there are other foundations on the market, but they dry very quickly and putty does not.

ORNAMENTAL FLOWER POTS

Face cream jars make an excellent base for a small flower pot for the dressing table or corner shelf. Fill it with plaster of paris or sand will do, but you will have it fit a circle of cardboard on top of sand and push flower through afterwards. The artificial flowers are in all the shops now-a-days, and they can all be washed when dirty, or you might have an artificial posy that you still like, discarded, off an evening frock and so on. Hold it over a kettle full of steam and use that, or make some plastic foam or dyed stocking flowers. As you go on you get all sorts of ideas, even with feathers, or miniature ornaments.

EGG-SHELL DECORATION

Materials : egg shells, glue, and things to be decorated such as vases, book-covers, etc. Remove thin skin from egg. Break small, and glue onto object. When dry, paint in required shade.

FIRESIDE STOOL

Make a fireside stool, from treacle or golden syrup tins, and dyed sugar bag. You can make a small one with three tins, or a larger one with seven tins.

Cover each tin separately by cutting 2 circles ¾ of an inch larger than the top of tin. Measure around the tin next, and cut pieces of bag 12¾ inches x 4 inches (the size around a treacle tin). Sew up the short sides, sew one circle in, easing it slightly. Turn inside out. Put tin inside having the top of the tin at the opening.

Place some cotton wool or waste on the top of tin, place on the other circle and hand-sew it to bag casing around tin, first turning in the edges.

Flowers in Vases (tips on)

Gather flowers in early morning or late afternoon.

When cutting flowers, put them straight into a bucket of water. This keeps the cell tissues open and they keep fresh longer.

Strip the leaves from the stems before arranging in vase, as the leaves make water unpleassant, spoils the colour effect of arrangement, and, the flowers last longer without leaves. Also, cut the flowers on a slant, dip in salt and place in warm water in vase, except tulips as they need cold water. Thick, tough stems should be slit.

If you do not want to arrange flowers in a vase until the following day, wrap in newspaper and plunge them into tepid water for the night.

The spiral wire from an old note book, joined at ends, can be used as a flower holder, or even glad wrap or a plastic hair roller is effective in a small vase. If you have some sand, put that in the vase to hold the flowers upright. The water soon clears and flowers last longer.

For a mixed vase of flowers add a few drops of plant food to the water, or a piece of cut lemon, or, an aspirin or, a few drops of eucalyptus. You can also add 50g of sugar to one teaspoon of vinegar and one litre of water, or, 1 part tea to 4 parts of water. For long stemmed flowers add a teaspoon of household bleach.

Flowers from bulbs do not need a lot of water in the vase, provided you have plunged them into water before arranging them in the vase.

Wallflowers, sweet peas and lily of the valley do not mix in the one vase.

If flower stems are too short, push them into a drinking straw first.

Flowers with no stems will float in a bowl without being swamped, if you place them on a thin piece of cork or plastic foam.

If you want to lengthen a hollow stem flower, like a delphinium, push a stick in the hollow, but be sure the stem reaches the water.

Repair a bent stem of a heavy-headed bloom by pushing a toothpick through the centre and into the stem.

Candle wax at the base of the flower head, keeps bottom petals from falling off flowers, like chrysanthemums.

The bloom of some flowering shrubs has a tendency to wilt. Reduce problem by clipping off small shoots at the top.

Prolong the freshness of an arrangement by spraying with tepid water morning and night. If wanted for a special occasion, spray with hair spray, and completely cover with a plastic bag.

Virtually all flowers may be restored by the use of hot water. Place flowers in a jar of hot water, deep enough to cover ⅓ of the stems. Leave until cold. To banish odour, add a drop of mild disinfectant to the water. It also helps flowers to last out longer.

"Personality is to a man what perfume is to a flower."

ORNAMENTAL GOURDS
(when flowers are scarce)

An inexpensive and colourful decoration for your home can be had by growing ornamental Gourds. Sew the seeds in the Spring, like you would for pumpkins, etc. They like a very rich soil, heat and water, so put some manure into a hole, cover it with dirt, and plant the seed in the mound and keep them well watered. Provide stakes or grow them near a fence for preference. Allow the gourds to thoroughly ripen on the vines before picking, otherwise they will not keep and they do not attain their best colour until mature. Damaged ones will not keep either. Pick when the shell is hard and leave two or three inches of stem. To prepare for decorating, first wash in borax to remove all traces of soil. Then spread out in a cool, airy shed to thoroughly dry out, or take out all material from inside. Keep out of direct sunlight. When dry, give them a coat of clear enamel or liquid wax. There are some weird and wonderful shapes among them with warty skins. Some are like oranges or bananas, pears and so on. Pile on a dish on your buffet, they look like ornamental fruit. Sometimes they will only last a year, but other years, they will be still, as when first lacquered, when it is the time for planting seeds again. The term gourd is applied to the fruits of vines of several different species. As some of their names imply, they may be used as utensils. These include dipper, calabash and bottle gourds.

Hydrangea (preserving)

Stand the leafless stems in a mixture of one dessertspoon of alum to 5 cups of water in a warm, dark place, till they are ready, or,

cut blooms when the colour in the flowers have changed. Place in a vase filled to 1/3 with glycerine. Fill with water only as the level dimishes. It is not necessary to add more glycerine.

In another chapter you'll read a piece of poetry that Nancy Newman wrote in the book, as it is coupled with a gift she gave me. I also did the landscaping around the home. Because the house was on a slope, I had to build up the soil on the western and eastern sides with soil brought in to make the lawns level, and then the two levels were divided by rockeries and steps. I gathered all the rocks from the streets and wheeled them home in a barrow. Because my favourite song is the " Melody of Love ", I bought the music, sent it to my brother-in-law, Ted Gray, and he fashioned panels (for a fence) in wrought iron (by copying the music notes) and sent the panels up by rail. Eddie Lockett erected the fence in 1960, each line of song separated by a post, so, if you could read music you would see the first verse of " Melody of Love ". Ted also made two gates the shape of piano-accordions and Eddie added those too. I dug part of the western side for a vegetable patch, boxed out flower beds, filled them with plants, added shrubs and roses, and cherished " Silver Lining " as Mrs. Webster gave it to me, but the severing of that at ground level, and others, made me face the decision as to whether to stay in " Climar ", suffer until I was carried out, or leave and receive some happiness. In different parts of my scrapbooks I have such things as " He has been nice to me for four days,"

DRYING FLOWERS BY MICROWAVE

A microwave oven dries flowers and leaves quickly and easily, and preserves the colour and shape of the blooms much better than conventional drying methods do.

You will need:

* Several choice buds or flowers at the peak of their bloom; nicely shaped leaves.
* Silica gel (available at craft stores) or two parts cornmeal to one part borax.
* Plastic, glass, paper, or ceramic bowl or cup to contain the gel and a bloom.
* Fine-mesh sieve or strainer.
* Heat-resistant glass or ceramic container for water.
* Toothpicks
* Artist's brush
* 12-inch stem wire
* Floral tape

Microwave drying differs slightly from other drying methods, so follow the directions carefully.

1. Select flowers that are firm in shape. Cut stem to within one inch of blossom. Bright, light-coloured blooms can be preserved better than darker flowers, and thick-petaled blossoms are better than more delicate varieties.

2. Pour 1 1/2 inches of silica gel or cornmeal/borax mixture in a bowl. The container should be large enough to allow two inches between the top layer of gel and the bowl's top; this allows for the gel's expansion during heating.

3. Place the flower in the bowl stem first with the flower head facing up. Don't let the bloom touch the bowl's sides. With a sieve, gently lift the gel granules over the flower's top. Use a toothpick to spread gel under the petals, around and inside the centre so the bloom is completely coated.

4. Pour eight ounces of water into a glass or ceramic container. (A measuring cup is good.) Place this in one corner of the microwave oven. It remains there throughout the drying process.

5. Put the gel-covered flower in the oven. Do not cover the container. Dry one flower at a time to find proper timing. (Drying times vary depending on the number of flowers in the oven.)

6. Set your oven timer. The gel's colour changes from pink to blue as moisture is absorbed and the flower dries. Drying times range from several seconds to three minutes depending on the bloom's size and texture, whether you use gel or cornmeal/borax mixture, and your oven's heating capacity. Don't be afraid to experiment.

Use the chart overleaf as a timing guide for each bloom. For future reference, keep a record of drying time and size and type of flower.

7. When the timer stops, remove the flower container from the oven and set the bowl on newspaper. Don't touch the gel -allow it to cool for 30 minutes.

8. Pour off the top layer of gel. Gently lift out the flower, which will be limp, and place it on top of the remaining gel in the bowl. Let the flower "rest" until it is firm enough to handle (5 to 20 minutes). Save the remaining gel - once cool, it can be reused.

9. Gently remove the remaining gel granules from the flower with a brush; don't tear the petals. Place the bloom on top

TRAY FROM A PICTURE FRAME

Enamel or stain the frame after the backing and glass has been removed. When dry, replace glass, then lay a piece of pretty floral material, like polished cotton, or quilt a piece. I made one with satin, quilted, and it looks very elegant. Place a square of cardboard next, to act as a packing, then finally a sheet of 3-ply, and fix in place with brads. Glue a piece of felt on the 3-ply to prevent it from scratching the furniture and screw on two handles (one each end) and you'll have a tray that will be admired by all.

A PRACTICAL WALL HOLDER

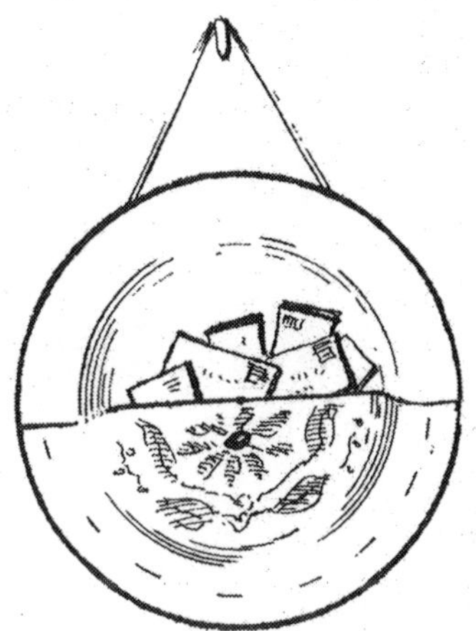

From two cardboard picnic plates, you can make [illegible] and wall holder for notes, unanswered letters, etc.

Cut one plate in half and secure by paper clips onto the other plate (left whole). You can also oversew it with plastic string, continuing all round until you reach top and leave two ends for joining and hanging on your wall. Paste a flower or motif on front from a used Xmas card. I coloured the half plate of the one I made with pink crayon before I attached it to the other plate, because the underside of a cardboard plate is white.

Picture Hints

- If you break the glass, replace it with plastic from the lid of a shirt box cut to size.
- Add alum to the paste before you paste on the brown paper at back. This keeps the silverfish at bay, or, mix a little ground cloves or a few drops of turpentine with the paste.
- Pictures will hang straight, if you tack a piece of foam on back. It will keep the wall clean too, and prevent scratches. Another hint is to hang pictures facing the wall, then turn them around to the front, crossing the wires as you do so.
- Before you hang a picture put adhesive tape on the wall where you are to knock in the hook, and the adhesive will help prevent chipped plaster and peeled paint.

Shell Decoration

Take an old picture frame, with a 3 ply backing. Cover with putty or Spakfilla, and push small shells into it. Add beads and, perhaps, a brooch in the centre. Cover with clear varnish when dry. It is best to work out a pattern first on paper, and have it beside you where you are working, as Spakfilla dries rather quickly or glue some onto a lid of a favourite box you might have in your treasures.

This elephant greeted Eric and I at the Cha-Am Beach Hotel in Thailand in March 1988. When I gave him money, he sat on the steps and played a mouth organ to us.

15. CARAVANNING & JETSETTING

Even the most committed housewife must leave her home occasionally, and with a few sensible precautions it will seem at her homecoming as if she had never been away. Marjorie has crafty methods to stop dripping taps leaving rusty marks on the bathroom porcelain in her absence, and to prevent musty smells developing in a shut-up house. She has several strategies for keeping her indoor plants watered, and if she's going away for too long to leave her porch light burning she'll still be able to illuminate her entrance in the event of arriving home in the dark.

During the glorious years when Marjorie was Mrs Cooper, most of her holidays were spent in a snug little caravan. Even her 1966 honeymoon took place in her home-away-from-home on wheels. But once she became Mrs Bligh she set her sights beyond the island state and began 'overseas gallivanting' in earnest.

As she trotted around the globe Marjorie collected not only an impressive arsenal of souvenir teaspoons, but also a new field of expertise. She can advise on how to make sure you've got sufficient suitcase room for all your overseas purchases, and on how to avoid jetlag with the help of a simple brown paper bag. She can tell you how to make your suitcase stand out from all the others on the carousel, and how to stop your wet soap getting all mucky in its travel case.

And she can tell you that though she's roamed far and wide, she'll always call Tasmania home. For its convenience, its fresh food and its lack of assault upon the bowels; for her friends, her home and her garden—the Apple Isle is Marjorie's Shangri-la made real.

—•—

"Without labour, nothing prospers."

For five months – 10th November 1952 until 30th April 1953 – I was very busy trying to win a trip to the Coronation of H.M. Queen Elizabeth II (which took place on the 2nd June 1953 in England). The prize was for two airfares to and from London, with first class accommodation, including meals, for two weeks ; also a car with chauffeur at the winner's command and two seats at some point on the route of the Coronation Procession were also included. I was approached to take part in the contest by a Wilkins Servis washing machine representative, Mr. Ian Burrows of Launceston, who was a friend of mine. To compete, I first had to own a Wilkins Servis washing machine, and secondly I had to submit names of people to Mr. Burrows, whom I could recommend to buy a Wilkins machine, and their names had to be on an official card. I worked hard trying to convince people that it was a good machine, but Ian worked harder, because through me, he sold 23 machines before the 30th April. I received a bonus of a new washing machine for selling the most in Australia before December 1952, and also £2 for every machine sold throughout the competition. Can you imagine how I felt when I received a letter on the 9th April (1953) to say I was still well up with the leaders, and the firm wished me success ! The morning of my birthday – 14th April – another letter came telling me that the competition was drawing to a close and that a Mrs. Young of Goulburn, N.S.W., a Mrs. Raymond of Queensland and a Mrs. Blackwell of Tasmania still led the field, and that there was not more than one credited sale difference between the three of them. I was so excited I couldn't work, eat or sleep, but the next morning I felt the bottom had fallen out of my world, as I received a telegram saying that Mrs. Young had won the trip. This was followed up by a letter explaining that she had five more sales than me, Mrs. Raymond two sales more, in second place, and I was third. If I had known that, of course, I would have bought six machines, and sold them later ! Nobody knows how disappointed and upset I was – so close and yet so far.

Hat (travelling)

Put the crown inside an empty ice-cream container, and pack clothes under the hat brim.

The tablecloth I am holding I crotcheted from old stockings. There are 280 squares all told and it has peaked edges. I won the Ethel Webster Silver Cup (pictured) in 1986 at the C.W.A. 50th Year State Exhibition for the best article made from waste with it. The hat and pullover I am wearing I also crocheted and knitted (pullover) from old stockings.

ODOURS IN SHUT HOME: Place lavender oil in a container in rooms in your home before you go on holiday, and it prevents that musty smell.

SECTION 4

Clothes, Hats, Shoes, etc.

"You're supposed to think like a man, dress like a queen, speak like a lady and work like a dog."

Beach Towel Pocket

A small pocket on a beach towel is handy for holding keys, money, or a handkerchief, so turn over a corner, stitch one side and put a zip in the other.

Pot Plants at Holiday Time

Punch a small hole in the centre of caps of several plastic bottles, and suspend one upside down over each hanging basket, so water will drip onto them. If you hang baskets directly over pot plants they in turn will get watered too, as the hanging baskets drip.

Or stand your pot plants on wet sponges on a saucer and the plant will suck up the water slowly.

Another way is to water them well then encase them (soil only) in aluminium foil, leaving plant exposed. Put in a cool, light place. The hardier ones can be buried in the garden, up to top of rims of pots in shady position ; or,

Cover them with plastic bags, then fasten with plant wire. The water that condenses inside the bag will suffice to conserve moisture for the plant while you're away.

If you are going away for a 3-week holiday, pop a plastic bag over your plant and secure with an elastic band around the pot. Then stand them on sheets of paper in the bath with the plug out.

Jet Lag

If you drink lots of water before, and after your long flights in a jet-liner you are less likely to get jet-lag, according to Dr. Nathan Smith, Professor at the University of Washington. "Sitting in an airliner is a little like sitting in the Sahara Desert," he said. "Not only is the air in the planes dry, but the rapid circulation of air in plane ventilation causes a substantial loss of body water."

Also I read once, that if you put your feet into brown paper bags, crumbled up first, then pull on your stockings and push your feet into old slippers for the long journey, it is a sure cure for jet lag. It helps the circulation, earths you and keeps your feet warm.

"Know the true value of time. Snatch, seize and enjoy every moment of it."

"Savour each hour, dwell not in the past,
Live each day fully, it may be your last." (I do).

Holiday Hints

Tie a coloured ribbon to your suitcase, so it is easily identified on the ramp.

Also, carry small plastic bags, for seeds, cuttings, etc., you might pick up.

A useful hold-all when travelling is a cushion cover — you can put your night clothes in it, and use it as a cushion during the day.

If you like to collect a souvenir when travelling but are not the spoon collecting type, buy cloth badges from each place and sew them to a travelling rug.

Place a thin layer of foam rubber on the bottom of the soap container to absorb moisture, and you won't have a messy container. Carry a tube of shaving cream. Only a small squeeze is needed to wash hands.

"Even a fool can make money – but it takes a wise man to spend it properly."

SUITCASES STORED: Rub petroleum jelly over the locks to help prevent them from rusting and put a cake of soap (uncovered) inside to keep away mildew and mustiness until the next holiday, then repeat.

"It's a happy home where the only scraps are those brushed off the dining room table."

Camping Hints

Take your ironing board along with you, when you next go caravanning. It comes in handy for an extra table for meals, writing, airing clothes, etc. Folds away for packing.

Keep flies at bay in the lavatory when out camping by putting ½ cup of kerosene and 1 cup of water into the tin first. The kerosene floats all the time until the tin is full, so forms a crust and prevents any odour. Also very good with people who have to use a commode.

Take some plastic garbage bags, and if it rains, you can soon convert them into a coverall for the children to hike around in.

"If distance were measured in terms of the heart,
good friends would be only a minute apart."

Caravan Clean of Sand

Leave an old clothes brush outside the door for the children to brush their feet with before entering. It isn't as messy as dipping feet in water.

A peerless scrapbooker, Marjorie has donated 191 of her volumes to the Tasmanian Archive and Heritage Office in Hobart, but keeps almost as many (and all the best ones) at home in Devonport.

16. WORDS & WISDOM

How to Make a Marj

Mix together the community of a small Tasmanian Midlands town, adding a dash of state school education and a generous helping of Sunday school. Take one small child, of precisely the same vintage as John F. Kennedy, Zsa Zsa Gabor and Vera Lynn, add to mixture and allow to marinate for fourteen years.

Remove young woman and transfer to workplace, stirring constantly while rapidly introducing many and varied domestic duties. Add one boyfriend and thoroughly agitate on the handlebars of a rickety old bicycle. Now swiftly splice in marriage one unexceptional Thursday, then decant to Campbell Town.

Keep warm until two boys appear in the mix, then percolate in curvaceous dream home for decades. When initial aromas of contentedness are overtaken by fumes of bitterness, moderate with a bouquet garni of success in show competition, then sweeten with the introduction of a second husband.

Drench in a syrup of love notes and breakfasts in bed, then swiftly remove and souse in a basin of grief. Steep in loneliness for a few years before splicing once again, this time to a silver-haired bus driver.

Infuse with comparisons to Dame Edna Everage and season, very liberally, with a heady mixture of book writing, gardening, needlework, newspaper columns, scrapbooks, toby jugs, souvenir teaspoons, Scrabble games, dancing gowns, poetry and organic compost.

Serve on a platter of frankness and garnish with a radish crocheted from preloved pantyhose.

To make a Marj takes many years
Pounds of laughs and gills of tears
You'll need tenacity, drive and grit
To learn to crochet, darn and knit
You'll need to garden, reap and sow
And be completely in the know
You'll need to call a spade a spade
And turn your hand to every trade
To tell the truth, it can't be done
When it comes to Marj, there's only one

—•—

BRIAN THOMSON, SCENIC DESIGNER

Brian Thomson became a Marjorie fan in 1970s London, when he, Barry Humphries and other homesick expats would read aloud from *At Home with Marjorie Cooper* as a restorative dose of Australiana.

In his youth, Thomson—whose lengthy credits include *The Rocky Horror Picture Show*, Edna Everage's *Housewife Superstar!* and *The*

Adventures of Priscilla, Queen of the Desert—was even known to pose as Edna's youngest and most beloved son, Kenny. Recently, he's been working with Barry Humphries again.

In London in the 1970s Brian Thomson would sometimes pose as Edna's son, Kenny. Photograph, from Thomson's personal collection, reproduced with the kind permission of Brian Thomson and Barry Humphries.

'I was asked to design something big for the reopening of Hamer Hall in Melbourne. Since the event coincided with Barry Humphries' final stage appearance in Melbourne, I came up with a big vase of gladdies. I looked to Marjorie's *A to Z of Gardening* for her thoughts on gladiolus and found a gem of a poem on the legend of the glad.'

GLADIOLUS, (*The Legend of the*)

Long years ago, traditions say two brothers hot with rage,
Were fighting for some land that lay within their heritage,
With grievous wounds both fell at last, but ere their breath was gone,
One cried, 'Why not forget the past, since brothers we were born?
A brother should be friend, not foe; and where our blood is spilt,
Into this ground my sword I'll throw, down to its very hilt.'
'And I will bury my sword, too,' the other brother said,
'Why not to ourselves be true, before we both are dead?'
With buried swords the quarrels cease and as the two divide
The land, they find at last where peace and happiness abide.

29

Some of my Favorite Poems etc., I have taken from the many scrap books I have made

What Love Means

This is the **Favourite** of all my favourites, and by some strange coincidence, as I, inquiring one day in a music store in Launceston, as to whether they had my favourite record called "The Melody of Love," the assistant said, "Yes, we have, but it has another 'something' on it as well, which is not sung, but read." I bought it and believe me or not, the following was also on the record. So I have this record which I cherish very much, with the story of "What Love Means," on it as well as the "Melody of Love." The wrought-iron fence around our home has the words of the Melody of Love set to music, and the gates are outlines of a piano-accordian designed by myself. Whatever else comes or goes, there will be nothing to take the place of that with its lovely words. Here is "What Love Means" :

I love you, not only for what you are, but for what I am when I am with you.

I love you, not only for what you have made of yourself, but for what you are making of me.

I love you for ignoring the possibilities of the fool in me and for laying firm hold of the possibilities of the good in me.

* * *

Music is the fourth great material want of our nature—first food, then raiment, then shelter, then music.

Time is the greatest gift there is. When time is gone, nothing else matters, so you must never waste it. You can't hoard it, like money — you can only spend it. But once its spent, you can't get it back. You must spend it wisely, the first time — for its the greatest gift you have.

HURT

When you have been hurt by something done or something said,
Try to put it from your mind and concentrate instead,
On the good points of the person who has injured you.
This is not by any means an easy thing to do,
Because you keep remembering the thing that grieved you so.
Better to remember all the nice things that you know!
Allow for human weaknesses; you have your share of them.
Perhaps you were too quick to take offence and to condemn.
Be generous and count the items on the credit side.
Resentment is a poison and its ill-effects spread wide,
Unless it's checked.
So pocket pride, resolving to forget;
Don't we all at times say things that later we regret.

* * *

'Half the world delights in slander and the other half in believing it'.

* * *

MISUNDERSTANDINGS

When you are misunderstood, in what you say or do—
Do not let the situation hurt or anger you.
Pray about it. Time will straighten out the tangled thread.
Say no word to worsen matters. Think kind thoughts instead.
If you know that you have always tried to do your best,
Do not be embittered or disgruntled. Let it rest.
If things done or said were done or said with good intent—
Leave it for the moment; things get worse with argument.
Oftentimes misunderstandings have a happy end—
And one we thought an enemy is turned into a friend.

JEALOUSY

Jealousy is poisonous, a cruel and deadly thing,
Causing much unhappiness and needless suffering,
It will warp your judgment, if it gets a hold on you,
And you'll lose the power to take a balanced point of view.
It will ruin friendships and divide a family,
It will wreck a business and bring catastrophe—
Breaking homes and marriages, it's something you must fight.
Whether you are in the wrong, or whether in the right.
Pray for strength to face the demon and to cast it out;
Turn your thoughts away—find something else to think about,
Put your mind on other things, in time the pain will go
And you'll wonder why you ever let it hurt you so.

* * *

No story is true until it is officially denied.

* * *

There is only one success—to be able to spend your life in your own way.

* * *

All problems become smaller if you don't dodge them but confront them. Touch a thistle timidly, and it pricks you; grasp it boldly, and its spines crumble.

I can go to my grave and say that I have never been idle ; I loathe it so always find something to do. Days are never long enough for all I want to do and I don't believe in the saying that *" Those who make the worst use of their time are the first to complain of its brevity."* My ultimate aim is to finalise all the endless projects that occupy my brain, or, even surpass them, and I ask God to give me work till my life shall end, and life till my work is done. On reading this book, one thing you will have to abide, is to remember that I am a novice at writing a book and only attended a State School, but because I call a spade a spade, I'll be as frank as I know how, in relating my good and bad experiences. I will try to tell you as much as I can without losing my dignity, as in one chapter I deal with divorce. That is ugly in anyone's eyes, but to remain sane, we sometimes have to partake in things we detest. *" He who cannot forgive others breaks the bridge over which he must pass himself."*

"I remember the cheese of my childhood
And the bread that we cut with a knife,
The children who helped with the housework
And the man who went to work, not the wife.
The cheese never needed an ice-chest,
The bread was crusty and hot,
The children always seemed happy,
And the wife was content with her lot.
I remember the milk from the billy
With the lovely rich cream on the top,
And the dinners straight from the oven
And not from the 'frige in the shop.
The kids were a lot more contented,
They didn't need money for kicks,
But a game with their mates in the paddock,
And sometimes the Saturday "Flicks".
I remember the shop on the corner
Where a penn'worth of lollies was sold ;
Do you think I'm a bit too nostalgic?
Or is it because I'm just getting old?"

RECIPE FOR SUCCESS

One I can thoroughly recommend, having the added virtue of keeping forever.

Mix equal amounts of :—

True love
Perfect Trust
Confidence
Cheerfulness
Kindness
Forgiveness

Add to the mixture a spark of interest in all your husband's doings. Top lavishly with patience. Serve ofen as it is always successful.

"A Swarm of B's

B hopeful, B happy, B cheerful, B kind,
B busy of body, B modest of mind,
B earnest, B truthful, B firm and B good,
B sure your B haviour B all that it should.

B sharp in the morning, and never B flat,
B ware most of all that you never B that,
B all of these things and whatever B fall,
B sure you'll B happy and B loved By us all!

CAMPBELL TOWN — by me

CAMPBELL Town, Campbell Town, the town of memories sweet,
AND green clad vales, and timbered hills, which every eye may greet,
MAY every one that lives here, enjoy the place like me ;
PLAINS filled with sheep and tall gum trees so beautiful to see.
BEAUTIFUL rivers to sit by, with picnic grounds galore,
ELEGANT churches, historic buildings, could you wish for anything more ?
LUXURIOUS cafes, recreation grounds and clubs for young and old.
LONELINESS is never heard of, or that's what I've been told.
THE Area School and all the shops and even the lovely Hall,
OR the popular swimming pool, and Gatty Memorial tall,
WILL take a lot of beating, I'm telling you, my dear,
NO place is any nicer, Is it because my home is here ?

* * *

'May you live as long as you want to, and never want as long as you live.
May you escape the terrors of hell, and safe in God's heaven dwell'.

* * *

TELL HER SO

Amid the cares of married life,
In spite of toil and business strife,
If you value your sweet wife,
Tell her so!

There was a time you thought it bliss
To get the flavour of a kiss;
A dozen now won't come amiss—
Tell her so!

Don't act as if she's passed her prime,
As though to please her were a crime—
If e'er you loved her, now's the time;
Tell her so!

You are hers and her's alone;
Well you know she's all your own;
Don't wait to carve it on the stone—
Tell her so!

Never let her heart grow cold,
Richer beauties will unfold.
She is worth her weight in gold;
Tell her so!

—Mrs. J. Whipple.

* * *

'As every thread of gold is valuable, so is every moment of time'.

* * *

Wear a smile and have friends; wear a scowl and have wrinkles.

* * *

Habit is a cable; we weave a thread of it each day, and at last we cannot break it.

MY DISLIKES

—by me

I don't like morning visitors who never want to leave,
Or the ones who come with gossip—they really make me heave.
People who break promises, of that, I'll say no more,
Or the ones who say nothing, but yet they take the floor.
I just detest a windy day, doors creaking now and then,
Flies dirtying up the windows are worse than untidy men.
I don't like thoughtless people who enjoy making rows,
Or washing up a separator, or milking jolly cows.
Dusting is an awful job, I'd rather weed the garden;
I don't like working in good clothes, for all those who do, please pardon.
People late for appointments are really on the nose,
So are sockettes with high heel shoes and brightly painted toes.
Of people who think they're better than those just up the street,
They're the ones with their minds not occupied and the ones I don't want to meet.
I've finished all my hates and likes, or most of them we'll say,
But whatever goes on before me, I'm always thankful at the end of the day.

POSSESSIONS

Do not be possessed by your possessions. Never be
Enslaved by things material, for this idolatry—
Squanders time that might be used in helping you to find
The riches of the spirit and the treasures of the mind.
Without them life lacks meaning and is just a vulgar race
For tawdry prizes. Things of charm and beauty have their place,
But in the background, not the foreground, of your reckonings.
Seek ye first the unseen kingdom. Do not worship things.
Seek what is eternal and affords the soul delight.
Put things in their proper order. Get your values right.

RECIPES WITH A DIFFERENCE

RECIPE FOR SERVICE:

Take 2 eyes, 2 ears, 2 hands, 2 feet, 1 large heart, 1 oz. of commonsense, and 1 good dash of willpower. Flour with humour and cheerfulness, and sprinkle with a good show of smiles. Blend all together with the milk of human kindness and the Love of God. Serve with liberality and sacrifice.

RECIPE FOR PRESERVING FRIENDS:

Select some sound hearts. Be very careful not to bruise them with unfeeling words. Take of milk of human kindness, one heartful, add to this plenty of tact, then warm the mixture with sympathy. Do not let it get too hot at first, lest it only ferment mischief. Knead with plenty of oil of unselfishness, to make all smooth. Beware of jars. The mixture should be kept in a warm corner of the heart. Years only serve to improve the flavour of friends thus preserved.

GRANNY'S BIBLE CAKE

Ingredients: (1) ¼ lb. Judges v. 25 (last clause); (2) ¼ lb. Jeremiah v. 1: 20; (3) ½ tablespoon 1 Samuel XIV v. 25; (4) 1 large Jeremiah XVII: 11; (5) ¼ lb. 1 Samuel XXX: 12 (second clause); (6) ¼ lb. Jeremiah XXIV: 1 (chopped); (7) 1 oz. Numbers XVII: 8 (blanched and chopped); (8) ½ lb. 1 Kings IV: 22 (first clause); (9) season to taste with 11 Chronicles IX: 9; (10) pinch of Leviticus 11: 13; (11) ½ teaspoon Amos IV: 5; (12) 1½ tablespoons Judges IV: 19 (last clause).

Method: Proverbs XXIII: 14 Nos. 1, 2, and 3, to a cream. Add No. 4, still Proverbs XXIII: 14. Add Nos. 5, 6 and 7 (Proverbs XXIII: 14 again). Add Nos. 8, 9, 10 and 11, having previously mixed them. Last, add No. 12 Leviticus XXVI: 26 in a slow oven for 1½ hours.

MY FAVOURITE CAKE RECIPE

4 lbs. of love, ½ lb. buttered youth, ½ lb. good looks, ½ lb. of sweet temper, ½ lb. of self-forgetfulness, ½ lb. powdered wits, ½ oz. dry humour, 2 tablespoons sweet argument, ½ pint rippling laughter, ½ cup commonsense.

Put the flour of love, good looks and sweet temper into a well-furnished house. Beat the butter of youth to a cream. Mix together blindness to faults, and self-forgetfulness, powdered wits, dry humour into sweet argument, then add them to the above. Pour in gently rippling laughter and commonsense. Work it together until all is well mixed. Then bake gently forever.

BASIC RECIPE: HOW TO BECOME A GOOD COOK

Take 2 oz. patience, 1 cup kindness, 4 oz. goodwill, pinch of hope, bunch of faith.

To these add two handfuls of industry, a packet of prudence, a little sympathy, a handful of humility. Add a jar of syrup of good humour, season the mixture with commonsense and simmer all together in a pan of daily content.

RECIPE FOR CONTENTMENT

Take a day at a time into life's golden bowl,
Add a little spice of laughter and a dash of self-control,
Sift in some kindly actions 'till the mixture is soft and light,
Add a prayer at eventide and your days will all be bright.

RECIPE FOR HAPPINESS

Combine one husband, one wife, and a number of children, assorted sizes. (These are optional, but add a delightful flavour). Using a strong unity, blend well together. Add a pinch of helpfulness, a sprig of loyalty, and a dash of patience. Mix a generous portion of smiles, and a few drops of tears. Fold into the mixture those ingredients. Stir well until it forms a light consistency. Sprinkle with a little kindness and garnish it with love. This delicacy, called Family Happiness, should not be taken with a grain of salt, but if completely digested, is good for heart nutrition. Regular servings provide minimum requirements for healthy, congenial living.

*   *   *

SCRIPTURE CAKE

4½ cups of I Kings 4, 22nd v., 1½ cups of Judges 5, 25th v., 2 cups of Jeremiah 6, 20th v., ½ cup of Judges 4, 19th v., 2 cups of I Samuel 30, 12th v., 1 cup of Numbers 17, 8th v., 2 cups Matthew 24, 32 v., 2 tablespoons of Psalms 19, 10 v., 6 tablespoons of Jeremiah 17, 11th v., pinch of Leviticus 2, 13th v., and season to taste of 2 Chronicles 9, 9th v.

Follow Solomon's directions for making a good boy, Proverbs 23, 14th v, and you will have a very good cake. Bake in moderate oven.

Translation :

4½ cups of flour, 1½ cups of butter, 2 cups sugar, ½ cup milk, 2 cups raisins, 1 cup almonds, 2 cups figs, 2 tablespoons honey, 6 tablespoons eggs, pinch salt, season to taste with spice. Beat well, and bake in moderate oven.

My mother had this in one of her cookery books. I have never made it, but added it because it is unusual. I should imagine it would take 3 to 4 hours to cook. Perhaps 1 tablespoon egg would be 1 egg.

RAISIN CAKE

First take a cup of butter,
All golden pure and sweet,
And two cups of white sugar
And these together beat ;
Two eggs all lightly foaming,
Of good sweet milk, one cup ;
Put in a little soda, to lightly raise it up
Then two teaspoons of cream of tartar,
And grate a lemon rind,
'Twill give a pleasant flavour
I'm sure that you will find.
Then add one cup of raisins
And just 4 cups of flour,
And put it in the oven
And bake it for one hour.
I'm sure 'twill be a nice one
If just right it bake,
I'm sure 'twill please your husband
When he shall taste the cake.

The ten commandments of success are –

1. Speak to people – there is nothing as nice as a cheerful greeting.
2. Smile – it takes 72 muscles to frown – only 14 to smile.
3. Call people by name – Everyone is pleased when you remember their name.
4. Be friendly and helpful – others will respond in like manners.
5. Speak and act as if everything you do was a genuine pleasure.
6. Be genuinely interested in people.
7. Be generous with praise – cautious with criticism.
8. Be considerate with the feelings of others – it will be appreciated.
9. Be thoughtful of the opinions of others – there are three sides to any controversy – yours, the other person's and the right one.
10. Be willing to give service – what counts most in life is what we do for others.

"There's always something to wreck your day, something obstructive to mar your way,
A thought to change blue skies to grey – if you let it.
There's always something to spoil your fun, disturb your mind when the day is done,
A cloud that threatens to hide the sun – if you let it.
Ignore what upsets you – the stones, the stings – find something good in whatever time brings.
Life will surround you with wonderful things – if you let it.

THINGS I LOVE

Composed by myself

I love the beautiful sunshine, the flowers and the dew,
But best of all in this wide world, I just love only you ;
I love all kinds of music, new songs that are born each day,
Spring time with all its glory, and clothes that are bright and gay.
I love any kind of hobby, from knitting down to plastic ;
I'm always making scrap books, I think they're so fantastic.
I love my roomy kitchen, with windows all around,
Where I can do my cooking with never ever a frown.
I love giving more than receiving—I hope you will agree,
And it's best to keep the golden rule and let your neighbours be.
I love the laughter of children ringing in my ears,
But few of us love the spoilt ones, they cause us too many tears.
I love both birds and animals, and of them I've quite a few ;
I never get sick of sewing, or trying on something new.
In these verses I have written some of the things I love best,
But in the verses to follow are my hates, even down to my guest.

WOMEN'S JOYFUL DAY

A great friend of mine gave me this, as, in her words, "it reminds me very much of you, and your day" :

Come what may, a woman's day is always filled with happy things.
Though trials intrude, no time to brood, a blackbird in the garden sings,
A dress to sew, a plant to grow, a special recipe to try.
Flowers to arrange and books to change, and there's a rainbow in the sky,
A child to dress, pet to caress, a local meeting to attend ;
Odd jobs to do, the shopping too, and write a letter to a friend.
It sounds so gay — a woman's day. And that's the easy way to take it :
Busy and blessed with interest, the way a happy heart can make it.

—Thanks, Dorothy

This is a quiz that Kian Way organized on my birthday for everyone to fill out.

Marjorie's 20 Question Quiz

1. In what year was Marjorie born? 1917 ✓
2. Where was Marjorie born? CAMPBELL TOWN
3. How many sisters did Marjorie have? 2 ✓
4. Which church at Ross did Marjorie attend as a youngster? CHURCH OF ENGLAND ✓
5. Marjorie's first job was at which well known property at Campbell Town? RICCARTON ✓
6. Marjorie is the mother of how many boys? 2 ✓

6a. What is remarkable about the boys' birthdays? BOTH ON SAME DAY ✓

7. Marjorie has outlived how many husbands? 3 ✓
8. Where was Marjorie's first iconic home? CAMPBELL TOWN ✓
9. What is the name of the home? CLIMAR ✓
10. What is the name of the tune on the fence of the home? ~~SONG~~ MELODY OF LOVE ✓
11. Who was the most successful exhibitor at the Campbell Town Show in the 1950's? MARJORIE BLACKWELL ✓
12. The name of Marjorie's first book that was released in 1965? MARJORIE BLACKWELL AT HOME ✓
13. What is the name of Marjorie's current home? MARIAN ✓
14. The replica of which well-known Tasmanian bridge is in Marjorie's back yard? BATMAN ✓
15. At what age was Marjorie when she was baptised at this church? 83 ✓
16. How many books has Marjorie authored? 6 ✓
17. Who is Marjorie's biggest fan? DAME EDNA EVERAGE ✓
18. What year was **Housewife Superstar** (the book) released and how old was Marjorie? 2011 94 years old ✓
19. How many hints has Marjorie created? Thousands ✓
20. What is Marjorie's best hint? LIFE IS FOR LIVING. ✓ DO UNTO OTHERS ✓

Bicarbonate of Soda

Bicarbonate of soda will clean your stainless steel sink, the refrigerator, plastic counters, tabletops and bathroom tiles ; also stains from china and enamel cookware.

BATHROOM TILES: Make a paste of bicarb. soda and bleach and scrub clean between the tiles with a nail brush. To finish off the tiles, polish with turtle wax for a super shine.

BATTERIES: Bicarb. soda mixed with water and scrubbed on battery terminals will leave a clean battery.

Batteries (for torches etc.) will keep for a long time if you store them in the freezer. They should be wrapped in foil and well sealed to keep out moisture.

----➧ **A teaspoon of carb. soda** to a cup of cold water acts as an effective underarm deoderant. Dry thoroughly, then dust with talc powder.

TOOTHPASTE: If you run out, use bicarb. soda, or remove the stains by soaking overnight in water and the juice of a lemon, brushing well next morning. To make a dentifrice, mix honey with finely powdered charcoal and brush teeth with that. To whiten teeth, rub with sage leaves.

Shoe Odour Removed

Shake small amounts of bicarbonate of soda into them and leave overnight. Shake out next day.

PICNICS: **Bicarb. soda cures almost any picnic hazards — bites, stings, itches, tired feet, scratches — and it will even clean cooking utensils.**

Duck Plucking

If you add a teaspoon of bicarbonate of soda, or same of washing powder or detergent to the boiling water that you scald your duck in, the feathers will come off more easily, as these help the water to penetrate better. Soak awhile, then plunge into cold water, or, wrap in a plastic bag to steam for several minutes.

*　　　　*　　　　*